FUNDAMENTALS OF BUY/SELL INVESTMENT TRADING PROGRAMS

BY SIR PATRICK BIJOU

License Notes

BOOK DESCRIPTION

At long last, it is here. This book will attempt to provide a concise understanding of **the Financial Market, Stock *Investment Algorithm,* and other basic economics of the Financial Market**. I discuss the various pros and cons of ***Buy/Sell Investment Trading*** and show you how you can put this knowledge in a self-help guide to trading. The stock market is a battlefield among traders with different beliefs, and it is the winner's belief that determines the destiny of the market. Therefore, my basic trading philosophy is to follow the winners. In this book, I concentrate on the type of traders who I believe are very likely to be winners: the big buyers and the big sellers, the institutional investors (pension funds, mutual funds, hedge funds, money managers, investment banks, etc.) who manage large sums of money and often buy or sell stock in large q uantity — I describe extensively the discoveries about the *Capital Markets and their hidden gems uncovering the know-how so that you can make vast fortunes, millions just like traders and investment bankers do. I reveal the secret strategy and formula that has taken me over 30 years to understand and discover. I am about to give away my secrets in just one book to make you a fortune and become a billionaire. Read this book; I promise you, it will be worth it, and you will not be disappointed!*

-Sir Patrick Bijou

As *you read this book, you'll discover:*

1. Instruments Traded in the Money Market
2. Value Investing and Growth Investing
3. Trading the Forex Market
4. Forex Players – Banks, Governments, Companies, and Traders.

5. ENTERING AND EXITING A MARKET
6. Adoption And Evolution Of FX Execution Algorithms
7. The Behavior Of Individual Investors
8. How to Read the Annual Report of a Company
9. Guide To Mutual Fund Investing
10. Fundamental And Technical Analysis.

Note: Once you have a clear understanding of ***Investment Algorithm,*** **Trading The Financial Market, Stock and Other Basic Economics of the Markets**, then your step into this world has only just begun.

Get your copy Now and Discover all about ***BUY/SELL INVESTMENT TRADING!***

ABOUT THE AUTHOR

I HAVE SOMETHING TO TELL

Sir Patrick was born in Georgetown, Guyana, South America, and resides in the UK. He is a UN Ambassador, Investment banker, philanthropist, and author. Sir Patrick is a renowned leading specialist in the debt capital markets, private placements, derivatives, and futures trading. As a distinguished trader on Wall Street, he has worked with multiple top banks such as Wells Fargo, Deutsche Bank, Credit Agricole CIB, Merrill Lynch, and others. He has established and managed Hedge Funds such as The Tiger Fund and became a notable Fund Manager at Blackstone. Sir Patrick was responsible for setting up the MTN & Private Placement Desk and dealer function at Lloyds Bank Plc. He was the first trader for Lloyd's treasury to increase self-led deals significantly from 4% to 32% in 2002.

His journey into content writing has allowed him to become an exceptionally motivated and enthusiastic author and professional communicator.

Sir Patrick is an avid lover of literature. He has published more than 35 books across several genres. How to Trade Derivatives and CFDs To Make Millions, Unlocking the Secrets of Bitcoin & Cryptocurrency Made Easy, Secret of Wealth Creation: Principal lessons on the secrets of building a long-lasting wealth, The future of Cryptocurrency. The Secrets of How to Make Six Figures (and More!), Blockchain And The World of Cryptocurrency, The Blueprint to Intelligent Investors, Intelligent Finance, Private Placement Programs, Beginners of Nowhere, Undying Lust, and Karmic Love are some of his famous works.

Sir Patrick excelled on his journey to become a highly educated and intellectual academic. Aside from being a notable investment banker, he is also currently a professional communicator, author, and philanthropist. His intelligence and educational achievements are evident in his role in multi-national organizations and financial institutions. These include investment banking and a Tier 1 Trader on Wall Street. He has left an impact everywhere he has graced, evident in feedback about him and his work.

Work History and Career

From his humble beginnings at Wells Fargo Bank on wall street, he has served as a private banker, fund manager, and an outstanding bond, futures, and derivatives trader on the trading floors. He established himself in his specialist field in the debt markets and private placement. His financial architecture and creative skills have seen him work with some of the best minds. He is an enigma in his field and founded the MTN & Private Placement Desk at Lloyds Bank PLC.

He has helped large corporations create new credit structures for international supply chains, SMEs for the public sector, private clients, and governments. His innovative and leadership skills have tailored funding and investments for various clients. One of his notable accomplishments was implementing over $1.3 billion in funding for social housing in the Bahamas, and he has gathered a wide range of expertise in venture capital and asset management portfolio. He has backed and advised several successful start-ups while running two significant Funds. His methods are sustainable, and he can boast one of the highest return ratios in the banking sector, assuring clients impressive profits and returns.

Sir Patrick helped create the economic phenomenon of Contract For Difference (CFD), a concept regarded as truly pioneering that today banks and trading institutions now adopt. Using clever leverage ratios, CFD has changed how trading is implemented across capital markets. He has written journals and books about CFD and how to become wealthy by executing his strategies and concepts in wealth creation. He is also a renowned and sought-after wealth manager, managing his trading platform in Private Placement through his desk at Credit Suisse Bank and DBS Bank. He has published several books on Private Placement Programs and Investment trading strategies, all of which have become notable best sellers.

Sir Patrick is a Global Ambassador for the International Rights and Welfare Association (IRAWA) and Ambassador of the Royal Diplomatic Club. In May 2021, he was appointed Ambassador by The Academy of Universal Global Peace USA as a governing board/trustees member and awarded The Human Excellency Award. He is also President of International Banking Relations of the Commonwealth Entrepreneurs Club. He sits as a Trustee and Governor on the board of NGOs and IGOs.

Beliefs

Sir Patrick believes that when people are learning, then they are growing. He is on a quest to make excellence a part of the people he meets. He considers every day as an opportunity to improve the world. He helps people to turn an idea into an opportunity. He teaches how to utilize creative thinking and innovative strategies to become an expert in wealth creation and a humanitarian. He believes no mountain is too high to climb if you have the right tools. Additionally, every obstacle has a solution, and the most challenging dream can be realized with imagination, creativity, and resilience.

TABLE OF CONTENTS

INTRODUCTION

In the real financial world, talking is cheap, and you must "show your muscle" through buying and selling. Therefore, a good theory should lead to profitable trading strategies. The stock market is a battlefield among traders with different beliefs, and it is the winner's belief that determines the destiny of the stock prices. Therefore, our basic trading philosophy is to follow the winners. But who are the winners? In this book we concentrate on the type of traders who we believe are very likely to be the winners: the big buyers and the big sellers. the institutional investors (pension funds, mutual funds, hedge funds, money managers, investment banks, etc.) who manage large sums of money and often buy or sell a stock in large quantity.

The internet and the evolution of technology have enabled many folks to become seriously successful traders. The whole process has become so simplified that most successful traders these days trade from the comfort of their own homes. As more people have leveraged this technology, the fat commissions paid by small investors to Brokerage Houses are almost forgotten. Online trading is by far the most convenient cost effective and accessible platform for anyone contemplating buying and selling shares.

The present-day move to ever higher degrees of automation on the trading floors of exchanges, banks and fund management companies is similar to the major shift to automated production and assembly that manufacturing engineering underwent in advanced economies during the 1980s and 1990s—this trend is likely to have a corresponding effect on the distribution of employment in the financial sector. Already, a very large proportion of transactions in the markets are computer generated and yet the characteristics and dynamics of markets populated by mixtures of human traders and machine traders are poorly understood. Moreover, the markets sometimes behave in unpredictable and undesirable ways. Few details are known of the connectivity network of interactions and dependencies in technology-enabled financial markets. There is recognition that the current global financial network needs to be mapped in order to gain an understanding of the current situation. Such a mapping exercise would enable the development of new tools and techniques for managing the financial network and exploring how it can be modified to reduce or prevent undesirable behaviour. New technology, new science, and engineering tools and techniques will be required to help map, manage and modify the market systems of the future.

CHAPTER 1

The Financial Market

Understanding Asset Classes

When you trade, you trade financial assets of one kind or another. There are different classes, or types, of assets such as fixed income investments - that are grouped based on having a similar financial structure and because they are typically traded in the same financial markets and subject to the same rules and regulations.

There's some argument about exactly how many different classes of assets there are, but many analysts commonly divide assets into the following five categories:

- Stocks, or equities - Equities are shares of ownership that are issued by publicly traded companies and traded on stock exchanges, such as the NYSE or Nasdaq. You can potentially profit from equities either through a rise in the share price or by receiving dividends.
- Bonds, or other fixed income investments (such as certificates of deposit – CDs) – Fixed-income investments are investments in securities that pay a fixed rate of return in the form of interest. While not all fixed income investments offer a specific guaranteed return, such investments are generally considered to be less risk than investing in equities or other asset classes.

- Cash or cash equivalents, such as money market funds – The primary advantage of cash or cash equivalent investments is their liquidity. Money held in the form of cash or cash equivalents can be quickly and easily accessed at any time.
- Real estate, or other tangible assets – Real estate or other tangible assets are considered as an asset class that offers protection against inflation. The tangible nature of such assets also leads to them being considered as more of a "real" asset, as compared to assets that exist only in the form of financial instruments.
- Futures and other financial derivatives – This category includes futures contracts, the forex market, options, and an expanding array of financial derivatives.

It isn't easy to classify some assets. For example, suppose you're investing in stock market future. Should those be classified with equities, since they're essentially an investment in the stock market, or with futures, since they're futures? Gold and silver are tangible assets, but are most frequently traded in the form of commodity futures or options, which are financial derivatives. If you invest in a real estate investment trust (REIT), should that be considered an investment in real estate or as an equity investment since REITs are exchange-traded securities?

Things are further complicated by the expansion in available investments. Exchange-traded funds (ETFs), for example, are traded like stocks on equity exchanges, but ETFs may be composed of investments from one or more of the five basic asset classes. An ETF that offers exposure to the gold market may be partly composed of investments in gold bullion and partly composed of stock shares of gold mining companies.

There are additional asset classes, such as artwork, various other collectibles, and peer to peer lending. Hedge funds and other sources of venture capital, along with markets that trade things such as Bitcoin and other alternative currencies, represent some other asset classes that are a bit more off the beaten path.

Generally speaking, the more an investment falls into the category of "alternative investment," the less liquid and the more risky it tends to be.

Good news! – You don't have to know for certain which asset class a specific investment falls under. You just need to understand the basic concept that there are broad, general categories of investments. That fact is primarily important because of the concept of diversification. Diversification is the idea that you can reduce the overall risk of your investment portfolio by investing in different types of investments, such as investments in different asset classes.

There is usually little correlation between the different asset classes. In other words, during periods of time when equities are performing well, bonds, real estate, and commodities may not be performing well for investors. However, during bear markets in stocks, other assets, such as real estate or bonds, may be showing investors above average returns. You can hedge your investments in one asset class, reducing your risk exposure by simultaneously holding investments in other asset classes. The practice of reducing investment portfolio risk by diversifying your investments across different asset classes is referred to as asset allocation.

The other reason to have a basic understanding of asset classes is just to help you recognize the nature of various investments that you may choose to trade. For example, you might choose to devote all, or nearly all, of your investment capital to trading futures or other financial derivatives, such as foreign currency exchange (forex). But if you do, you ought to at least be aware that you have chosen to trade a class of assets that is usually considered to carry significantly more risk than bonds or equities.

The extent to which you choose to employ asset allocation as a means of diversification is going to be an individual decision that is guided by your personal investment goals and your risk tolerance. If you're very risk averse have an extremely low risk tolerance then you may just want to invest only in the relatively safe asset class of fixed-income investments. Alternately, you may aim to further diversify within an asset class such as by holding a selection of large cap, mid cap, and small-cap stocks, or by investing in various industry sectors of the stock market.

On the other hand, if you're blessed with a high risk tolerance and/or having money to burn, you may care very little about diversification, being more focused on trying to correctly identify the asset class that currently offers the highest potential profits.

Types of Markets – Dealers, Brokers, and Exchanges

For the buying and selling of assets, there are several different types of markets that facilitate trade. Each market operates under different trading mechanisms.

The three main types of markets are:

1. Dealers (also known as the over-the-counter market)
2. Brokers
3. Exchanges

Dealer Markets

A dealer market operates with a dealer who acts as a counterparty for both buyers and sellers. The dealer sets bid and asks prices for the security in question, and will trade with any investor willing to accept those prices. Securities sold by dealers are sometimes referred to as being traded over-the-counter (OTC).

By acting as a counterparty for both buyers and sellers, the dealer provides liquidity in the market at the cost of a small premium that exists in the form of bid and ask spreads. In other words, dealers set bid prices slightly lower than the going market price and ask prices slightly higher than the market. The spread between this prices is the profit the dealer makes in return for assuming the counterparty risk.

Dealer markets are less common in stocks, more common in bonds and currency markets. Dealer markets are also appropriate for futures and options, or other standardized contracts and financial derivatives. Finally, the forex, or foreign exchange market is commonly operated through dealers, with banks and currency exchanges acting as the intermediary connecting dealers with buyers and sellers.

Of the three types of markets, the dealer market is usually the most liquid, because of the fact that the dealer's existence means that there will always be an available counterparty to traders wanting to buy or sell.

Broker Markets

A broker market operates by finding a counterparty for both buyers and sellers. When dealers act as the counterparty, the delay with brokers finding an appropriate counterparty results in less liquidity for brokered markets as compared to dealer markets.

Traditionally, stock markets were brokered. Stockbrokers would try to find an appropriate counterparty for their client on the trading floor of a stock exchange. This is the stereotypical image that Wall Street used to be known for, with men and women in suits yelling at each other. At the same time, holding pieces of paper representing their clients orders that they are seeking to fill.

Broker markets are used for all manner of securities, especially those with initial issues. A stock initial public offering (IPO), for example, will usually be launched through an investment bank which brokers the issue trying to find buyers. There is a similar procedure for new bond issues. Finally, brokered markets are also appropriate for tailored or custom financial products.

Exchanges

Of the three types of markets, the exchange is the most highly automated. However, if no buyers, and sellers are able to meet in terms of price, then no trades are executed. Because of the huge number of potential buyers and sellers trading through exchanges, such a situation is extremely unlikely and commonly only occurs in times of economic crisis. In practice, the large numbers of buyers and sellers make a stock exchange virtually just as liquid as a dealer market.

Although stockbrokers do still input orders for clients, the stock market is no longer truly a brokered market, having transitioned to operating as an automated exchange. Trades is executed based on order books that match buyers with sellers.

The advantage of an exchange is the provision of a central location for buyers and sellers to find counterparties. Exchanges are used for all manner of securities but are most appropriate for standardized securities such as stocks, bonds, futures contracts, and options. Exchanges typically specify the characteristics for securities that are traded on the exchange.

Exchange-Specified Characteristics

- Contract or Lot Size
- Contract Execution/Trading Months
- Tick Size

- Delivery Terms
- Quality

Delivery terms and quality are not commonly specified in stock exchange trading or bond trading. In a stock exchange transaction, all that is stated is the contract and tick size, as well as the execution, which is typically immediate.

Contract sizes for securities or financial instruments are typically set to a minimum amount. For example, a stock might only be available for purchase in lots of 100 on a certain exchange. Tick size is commonly the lowest denomination of a currency. On US stock exchanges, the lowest tick price is one cent. A minimum 100-lot contract size under such conditions might then have a minimum tick value of $1 ($0.01 x 100 shares per lot).

Delivery terms and quality are more appropriately used in reference to commodity trading and to derivatives involving commodity-like assets. Gold and diamonds, for example, have qualities and ratings. Additionally, there must be provisions for potential delivery of the physical asset to the buyer or contract holder. Such characteristics are specified by the exchange an asset or financial instrument is traded on.

The Fixed Income Market

Fixed income securities such as Treasury bonds are a type of debt instrument that provides returns in the form of regular, or fixed, payments and repayments of the principal when maturity is reached. These instruments are issued by governments, corporations, and other entities to finance their operations. They differ from equity, as they do not entail ownership in a company, but bonds usually have seniority of claim in cases of bankruptcy or default.

Fixed income securities are generally considered a safer investment than equities or other market investments, but do not usually offer investment returns as high as those that can be obtained through other investments.

The term fixed income refers to interest payments that an investor receives, which are based on the creditworthiness of the borrower and current market rates. Generally speaking, fixed income securities such as bonds pay a higher rate of interest - known as the coupon - the longer their maturities are. At the end of the term or maturity, the borrower returns the borrowed money, known as the principal, or par value, amount.

The primary risks associated with fixed income securities concern the borrower's vulnerability to defaulting on its debt. In turn, this risk is incorporated in the interest or coupon that the security pays the investor. Additional risks involving the exchange rate for international bonds can be of concern, as well as the risk that changes in interest rates may increase (or decrease) the market value of a bond currently held. This is known as interest rate risk.

Credit/default risk arises if the issuer of a security is unable to pay interest and/or principal in a timely fashion. The probability of credit/default risk occurring depends on the issuer's ability to meet their financial obligations and on their credit worthiness. There is a negative correlation between credit rating and yield – the lower a bond issuer's credit rating, the higher the yield that will be offered to compensate for higher risk. A change in the issuer's credit rating affects the value of their outstanding fixed income securities.

There is a purchasing power risk associated with fixed income securities because the real rate of return on fixed income investments equals the rate of return minus the rate of inflation. During periods of high inflation, the real rate of return on fixed income investments may become negative.

Bond Pricing

The price of a bond depends on several characteristics that apply to every bond issued. These characteristics are as follows:

- Coupon, or lack thereof - A bond may or may not come with attached coupons. A coupon is stated as a nominal percentage on the par value of the bond. Each coupon is redeemable per period for that percentage. A bond may also come with no coupon. In this case, the bond is known as a zero-coupon bond. Zero-coupon bonds are typically priced lower than bonds with coupons.
- Principal/par value - Every bond comes with a par value – the principal amount that is repaid at maturity. Without the principal value, a bond would have no use. The principal value is to be repaid to the lender (the bond purchaser) by the borrower (the bond issuer). A zero-coupon bond pays no coupons but guarantees the principal amount at maturity. The interest paid on a zero-coupon bond is delivered in the form of the bond price being less than the principal amount that will be paid at maturity. For example, a zero-coupon bond with a par value of $1,000 might be available for purchase for $900. When the purchaser of the bond receives the $1,000 par value on the bond's maturity date, they have, in effect, received approximately 10% interest on the bond.
- Yield to maturity - Bonds is priced to yield a certain return to investors. A bond that sells at a premium (where price is above par value) will have a yield to maturity that is lower than the coupon rate. Alternatively, the causality of the relationship between yield to maturity and price may be reversed. A bond could be sold at a higher price if the intended yield (market interest rate) is lower than the coupon rate. This is because the bondholder will receive coupon payments that are higher than the market interest rate, and will therefore pay a premium for the difference.

- Coupon Periods to Maturity – Bonds vary in the number of coupon payments that occur until the bond matures. More frequent coupon (interest) payments are considered more desirable and typically increase the price of a bond.

All else being equal, the following statements about bond pricing are true:

- A bond with a higher coupon rate will be priced higher. A bond with a higher par value will be priced higher.
- A bond with a higher number of periods to maturity will be priced higher.
- A bond with a higher yield to maturity or market rates will be priced lower.

An easier way to remember this is that bonds are priced higher for all characteristics except for yield to maturity—a higher yield to maturity results in lower bond pricing.

The Money Market

The money market is an organized exchange market where participants can lend and borrow short-term, high-quality debt securities for one year or less. The market allows governments, companies, or banks and other financial institutions to obtain short-term securities to fund their short-term cash flow needs. It also allows individual investors to invest small amounts of money in a low-risk market. Some of the instruments traded in this market include Treasury bills, certificates of deposit, commercial paper, bills of exchange, and short-term mortgage-backed or asset-backed securities.

Large corporations with short-term cash flow needs can borrow from the money market directly through a dealer while small companies with excess cash can lend money through money market mutual funds. Individuals traders who want to profit from the money market can invest through a money market bank account or money market mutual fund. A money market mutual fund is a professionally managed fund that buys money market securities on behalf of individual investors.

Functions of the Money Market

The money market contributes to a smooth-running economy of a country by providing short-term liquidity to governments, banks, and other large organizations. Investors with excess money that they do not immediately need can invest it in the money market and earn interest.

Here is the main functions of the money market:

#1 Financing Trade

The money market provides financing to local and international traders who are in an urgent need of short-term funds. It provides a facility to discount bills of exchange, and this provides buyers of goods with immediate financing to pay for such goods. The money market also makes funds available for other units of the economy, such as agriculture and small-scale industries.

#2 Central Bank Policies

The central bank is responsible for guiding the monetary policy of a country and taking measures to ensure a healthy financial system. Through the money market, the central bank can perform part of its policy-making function efficiently. For example, the short-term interest rates in the money market represent the prevailing conditions in the banking industry and can guide the central bank in developing an appropriate future interest rate policy. Also, by adjusting the interest rates at which government-issued debt, such as Treasury bills and bonds, are offered, the central bank can influence interest rates for all types of fixed-income financial instruments.

#3 Growth of Industries

The money market provides an easy avenue for companies to obtain short-term loans to finance their working capital or other cash flow needs. Due to the large volumes of transactions, companies may experience cash shortages in regard to buying raw materials, paying employees, or meeting other short-term expenses. Through commercial paper or similar financing, they can borrow and obtain funds almost immediately for a relatively short loan duration. Although the money market does not provide long- term loans, it influences the overall capital market and can help companies obtain long-term financing. The capital market benchmarks its interest rates based on the prevailing interest rate in the money market.

#4 Commercial Banks Self-Sufficiency

The money market provides commercial banks with a ready market where they can invest their excess reserves and earn interest while maintaining liquidity. The short-term investments such as bills of exchange can easily be converted to cash to support customer withdrawals. Also, when faced with liquidity problems, they can borrow from the money market on a short-term basis as an alternative to borrowing from the central bank.

Instruments Traded in the Money Market

Several financial instruments are created for short-term lending and borrowing in the money market, such as the following:

#1 Treasury Bills

Treasury bills are considered the safest money market instruments because they are issued with a full guarantee by the United States government. They are regularly issued by the U.S. Treasury to refinance Treasury bills reaching maturity and to finance government deficits. T-bills have a maturity of one, three, six, or twelve months. They are sold at a discount to their face value, and the difference between the discounted purchases price and face value represents the interest rate paid to investors. They are commonly purchased by banks, broker-dealers, individual investors, pension funds, insurance companies, and other large institutions.

#2 Certificates of Deposit

A certificate of deposit (CD) is issued directly by a commercial bank, but it can also be purchased through brokerage firms. It has a maturity date ranging from three months to five years and can be issued in any denomination. Most CDs have a fixed maturity date and interest rate, and they extract a penalty for cashing in the CD prior to the time of maturity. Any time after the expiry of the CD's maturity date, the principal amount and interest earned is available for withdrawal. CDs are insured by the Federal Deposit Insurance Corporation (FDIC).

#3 Commercial Paper

Commercial paper is an unsecured loan issued by large institutional buyers to finance short-term financial needs such as inventory and accounts receivables. It is issued at a discount, with the difference between the price and face value of the commercial paper being the profit in interest paid to the investor. Typically, only large institutions with a high credit rating can issue commercial paper, and it is, therefore, considered a very safe investment.

Commercial paper is issued in denominations of $100,000 and above. Individual investors can invest in commercial paper indirectly through money market funds. Commercial paper usually has a maturity date of less than one year from the date of issue.

#4 Banker's Acceptance Notes

A banker's acceptance note is a short-term debt instrument issued by a non-financial institution but guaranteed by a commercial bank. It is created by a drawer, providing the bearer the right to the monetary amount indicated on its face at a specified date. It is often used in international trade because of the benefits to both the drawer (issuer) and bearer (holder). The holder of the acceptance note may decide to sell it on a secondary market. The date of maturity for banker's acceptance notes usually ranges between one month and six months from the date of issue.

#5 Repurchase Agreements

A repurchase agreement, commonly known as a "repo" is a short-term form of borrowing that involves selling a security with an agreement to repurchase it at a higher price at a later date. It is commonly used by dealers in government securities who sell Treasury bills to a lender and agree to repurchase them at an agreed upon price at a later date. The Federal Reserve buys repurchase agreements as a way of regulating the money supply and bank reserves. Repo dates of maturity range from overnight to 30 days or more.

Money market exists to facilitate short-term cash flow needs. The fact that most money market instruments are issued by either government entities or large financial institutions, and also mature within a short period of time, they are considered among the safest of fixed income investments—However, short- term maturities and low risk translate to lower profit potential for investors. For example, while a 10-year bond issued by a private corporation might offer investors a 5% interest rate, a three-month Treasury bill might only offer an interest rate return of just 1%.

The Stock Market

The stock market refers to public markets that exist for issuing, buying, and selling of stocks that trade on a stock exchange or over-the-counter. Stocks, also known as equities, represent fractional ownership in a company, asset, or security, and so the stock market is a place where investor can buy and sell ownership of such investable assets. An efficiently functioning stock market is critical to economic development, as it gives companies the ability to quickly access capital from the public.

Purposes of the Stock Market –

Capital and Investment Income

The stock market serves two very important purposes. The first is to provide capital to companies that they can use to fund and expand their businesses. If a company issues one million shares of stock that initially sell for $10 a share, then that provides the company with $10 million of capital that it can use to grow its business (minus whatever fees the company pays for an investment bank to manage the stock offering). By offering stock shares instead of borrowing the capital needed for expansion, the company avoids incurring debt and paying interest charges on that debt.

The secondary purpose that the stock market serves is to give investors – those who purchase stocks – the opportunity to share in the profits of publicly-traded companies. Investors can profit from stock buying in one of two ways. Some stocks pay regular dividends (a given amount of money per share of stock someone owns). The other way investors can profit from buying stocks is by selling their stock for a profit if the stock price increases from their purchase price. For example, if an investor buys shares of a company's stock at $10 a share and the price of the stock subsequently rises to $15 a share, the investor can then realize a 50% profit on their investment by selling their shares.

History of Stock Trading

Although stock trading dates back as far as the mid-1500s in Antwerp, modern stock trading is generally recognized as starting with the trading of shares in the East India Company in London.

Throughout the 1600s, British, French, and Dutch governments provided charters to a number of companies that included East India in the name. All goods brought back from the east were transported by sea, involving risky trips often threatened by severe storms and pirates. To mitigate these risks, ship owners regularly sought out investors to proffer financing collateral for a voyage. In return, investors received a portion of the monetary returns realized if the ship made it back successfully, loaded with goods for sale. These are the earliest examples of limited liability companies (LLCs), and many held together only long enough for one voyage.

The formation of the East India Company in London eventually led to a new investment model, with importing companies offering stocks that essentially represented a fractional ownership interest in these companies, and that offered investors dividends on all proceeds from all the voyages a company funded, instead of just a single trip. The new business model made it possible for the companies to ask for larger investments per share, enabling them to easily increase the size of their shipping fleets. Investing in such companies, they are often protected from competition by royally-issued charters, which became very popular due to the fact that investors could potentially realize massive profits on their investments.

The First Shares and the First Exchange

Company shares were issued on paper, enabling investors to trade shares back and forth with other investors, but regulated exchanges did not exist until the formation of the London Stock Exchange (LSE) in 1773. Although a significant amount of financial turmoil followed the immediate establishment of the LSE, exchange trading overall managed to survive and grow throughout the 1800s.

The Beginnings of the New York Stock Exchange

Enter the New York Stock Exchange (NYSE), established in 1792. Though not the first on U.S. soil – that honor goes to the Philadelphia Stock Exchange (PSE) – the NYSE rapidly grew to become the dominant stock market in the United States and eventually in the world. The NYSE occupied a physically strategic position, located among some of the country's largest banks and companies, not to mention being situated in a major shipping port. The exchange established listing requirements for shares, and rather hefty fees initially, enabling it to quickly become a wealthy institution itself.

Modern Stock Trading – The Changing Face of Global Exchanges

Domestically, the NYSE saw meager competition for more than two centuries, and its growth was primarily fueled by an ever-growing American economy. The LSE continued to dominate the European market for stock trading, but the NYSE became home to a continually expanding number of large companies. Other major countries, such as France and Germany, eventually developed their own stock exchanges, though these were often viewed primarily as stepping stones for companies on their way to listing with the LSE or NYSE.

The late 20th century saw the expansion of stock trading into many other exchanges, including the NASDAQ, which became a favorite home of burgeoning technology companies, which gained increased importance during the technology sector boom of the 1980s and 1990s. The NASDAQ emerged as the first exchange operating between a web of computers that electronically executed trades. Electronic trading made the entire process of trading more time and cost-efficient. In addition to the rise of the NASDAQ, the NYSE faced increasing competition from stock exchanges in Australia and Hong Kong, the financial center of Asia.

The NYSE eventually merged with Euronext, which formed in 2000 through the merger of the Brussels, Amsterdam, and Paris exchanges. The NYSE/Euronext merger in 2007 established the first trans-Atlantic exchange.

How Stocks are Traded – Exchanges and OTC

Most stocks are traded on exchanges such as the New York Stock Exchange (NYSE) or the NASDAQ. Stock exchanges essentially provide the marketplace to facilitate the buying and selling of stocks among investors. Stock exchanges are regulated by government agencies, such as the Securities and Exchange Commission (SEC) in the United States, that oversee the market in order to protect investors from financial fraud and to keep the exchange market functioning smoothly.

Although, the vast majority of stocks, are traded on exchanges, some stocks are traded over the counter (OTC), where buyers and sellers of stocks commonly trade through a dealer, or "market maker," who specifically deals with the stock. OTC stocks are stocks that do not meet the minimum price or other requirements for being listed on exchanges.

OTC stocks are not subject to the same public reporting regulations as stocks listed on exchanges, so it is not as easy for investors to obtain reliable information on the companies issuing such stocks. Stocks in the OTC market are typically much more thinly traded than exchange-traded stocks, which means that investors often must deal with large spreads between bid and ask prices for an OTC stock. In contrast, exchange-traded stocks are much more liquid, with relatively small bid-ask spreads.

Stock Market Players – Investment Banks, Stockbrokers, and Investors

There are a number of regular participants in stock market trading.

Investment banks handle the initial public offering – IPO - of stock that occurs when a company first decides to become a publicly- traded company by offering stock shares.

Here's an example of how an IPO works. A company that wishes to go public and offer stock shares approaches an investment bank to act as the "underwriter" of the company's initial stock offering. The investment bank, after researching the company's total value and taking into consideration what percentage of ownership the company wishes to relinquish in the form of stock shares, handles the initial issuing of shares in the market in return for a fee, while guaranteeing the company a determined minimum price per share. It is therefore in the best interests of the investment bank to see that all the shares offered are sold, and at the highest possible price.

Shares offered in IPOs are most commonly purchased by large institutional investors such as pension funds or mutual fund companies.

The IPO market is known as the primary or initial market. Once a stock has been issued in the primary market, all trading in the stock thereafter occurs through the stock exchanges in what is known as the secondary market. The term "secondary market" is a bit misleading, since this is the market where the overwhelming majority of stock trading occurs day to day.

Stockbrokers, who may or may not also be acting as financial advisors, buy and sell stocks for their clients, who may be either institutional investors or individual retail investors.

Equity research analysts may be employed by stock brokerage firms, mutual fund companies, hedge funds, or investment banks. These are individuals who research publicly-traded companies and attempt to forecast whether a company's stock is likely to rise or fall in price.

Fund managers or portfolio managers, which include hedge fund managers, mutual fund managers, and exchange-traded. Fund managers are important stock market participants because they buy and sell large quantities of stocks. If a popular mutual fund decides to invest heavily in a particular stock, that demand for the stock alone is often significant enough to drive the stock's price noticeably higher.

Stock Market Indexes

The overall performance of the stock markets is usually tracked and reflected in the performance of various stock market indexes. Stock indexes are composed of a selection of stocks that is designed to reflect how stocks are performing overall. Stock market indexes themselves are traded in the form of options and futures contracts which are also traded on regulated exchanges.

Among the key stock market indexes are the Dow Jones Industrial Average (DJIA), Standard & Poor's 500 Index (S&P 500), the Financial Times Stock Exchange 100 Index (FTSE 100), the Nikkei 225 Index, the NASDAQ Composite Index, and the Hang Seng Index.

Bull and Bear Markets, and Short Selling

Two of the basic concepts of stock market trading are "bull" and "bear" markets. The term bull market is used to refer to a stock market in which the price of stocks is generally rising. This is the type of market most investors prosper in, as the majority of stock investors are buyers, rather than sellers, of stocks. A bear market exists when stock prices are overall declining in price.

Investors can still profit even in bear markets through short selling. Short selling is the practice of borrowing stock that the investor does not hold from a brokerage firm which does own shares of the stock. The investor then sells the borrowed stock shares in the secondary market and receives the money from that sale of stock. If the stock price declines as the investor hopes, then the investor, can realize a profit by purchasing a sufficient number of shares to return to the broker the number of shares they borrowed.

For example, if an investor believes that the stock of company "A" is likely to decline from its current price of $20 a share, the investor can put down what is known as a margin deposit in order to borrow 100 shares from his broker. He then sells those shares for $20 each, the current price, which gives him $2,000. If the stock then falls to $10 a share, the investor can then buy 100 shares to return to his broker for only $1,000, leaving him with a $1,000 profit.

Analyzing Stocks – Market Cap, EPS, and Financial Ratios

Stock market analysts and investors may look at a variety of factors to indicate a stock's probable future direction, up or down in price.

Here's a rundown on some of the most commonly viewed variables for stock analysis.

A stock's market capitalization, or market cap, is the total value of all the outstanding shares of the stock. A higher market capitalization usually indicates a company that is more well-established and financially sound.

Publicly traded companies are required by exchange regulatory bodies to regularly provide earnings reports. These reports, issued quarterly and annually, are carefully watched by market analysts as a good indicator of how well a company's business is doing. Among the key factors analyzed from earnings reports are the company's earnings per share (EPS), which reflects the company's profits as divided among all of its outstanding shares of stock.

Analysts and investors also frequently examine any of a number of financial ratios that are intended to indicate the financial stability, profitability, and growth potential of a publicly traded company.

Following is a few of the key financial ratios that investors and analysts consider:

***Price to Earnings (P/E) Ratio*:** The ratio of a company's stock price in relation to its EPS. A higher P/E ratio indicates that investors are willing to pay higher prices per share for the company's stock because they expect the company to grow and the stock price to rise.

***Debt to Equity Ratio*:** This is a fundamental metric of a company's financial stability, as it shows what percentage of company's operations are being funded by debt as compared to what percentage are being funded by equity investors. A lower debt to equity ratio, indicating primary funding from investors, is preferable.

***Return on Equity (ROE) Ratio*:** The return on equity (ROE) ratio is considered a good indicator of a company's growth potential, as it shows the company's net income relative to the total equity investment in the company.

Profit Margin: There are several profit margin ratios that investors may consider, including operating profit margin and net profit margin. The advantage of looking at profit margin over just an absolute dollar profit figure is that it shows what a company's percentage profitability is. For example, a company may show a profit of $2 million, but if that only translates to a 5% profit margin, then any significant decline in revenues may threaten the company's profitability.

Other commonly used financial ratios include return on assets (ROA), dividend yield, price to book (P/B) ratio, current ratio and the inventory turnover ratio.

Two Basic Approaches to Stock Market Investing –

Value Investing and Growth Investing

There are countless methods of stock picking that analysts and investors employ. Still, virtually all of them is one form or another of the two basic stock buying strategies of value investing or growth investing.

Value investors typically invest in well-established companies that have shown steady profitability over a long period of time, and that may offer regular dividend income. Value investing is more focused on avoiding risk than growth investing is.

Growth investors seek out companies with exceptionally high growth potential, hoping to realize maximum appreciation in share price. They are usually less concerned with dividend income and are more willing to risk investing in relatively young companies.

Technology stocks, because of their high growth potential, are often favored by growth investors.

Exchange-Traded Funds

An exchange-traded fund (ETF) is an investment fund that holds assets such as stocks, commodities, bonds, and foreign currency. An ETF is traded like a stock, throughout the trading day, at fluctuating prices. They often track indexes such as the NASDAQ, S&P 500, Dow Jones, and Russell 2000. Investors in ETFs do not directly own the underlying investments but instead have an indirect claim and are entitled to a portion of the profits and residual value in case of fund liquidation. Their ownership shares or interest can be readily bought and sold in the secondary market.

ETFs have begun to eclipse mutual funds as a favored investment vehicle because they offer investments beyond just stocks, and because of the fact that ETFs often have lower transaction costs than the average mutual fund.

Different Types of ETFs

There are many types of ETFs, including the following:

Stock ETFs – These hold a particular set of equities or stocks and are similar to an index. Stock ETFs commonly holds a selection of stocks in a given market sector.

Index ETFs – These ETFs has portfolios that are designed to mimic the performance of a specific stock index, such as the S&P 500 Index. They only make portfolio changes when changes happen in the underlying index.

Bond ETFs – These are specifically invested in bonds or other fixed-income securities.

Commodity ETFs – These ETFs hold physical commodities, such as agricultural goods, natural resources, and precious metals.

Currency ETFs – These are invested in a single currency or a basket of various currencies, and are widely used by investors who wish to gain exposure to the foreign exchange market without using futures or trading the forex market directly. They usually track the most popular international currencies, such as the U.S. dollar, the euro, the British pound, or the Japanese yen.

Inverse ETFs – These are funds built by using various derivatives to gain profits through short selling when there is a decline in the value of broad market indexes.

Leveraged ETFs – These funds mostly consist of financial derivatives that are used to amplify percentage returns. It's important to note that while leveraged ETFs increase profit potential, they also likewise increase risk.

Real Estate ETFs – These funds invest in real estate investment trusts (REITs), real estate service firms, and real estate development companies.

Advantages of Investing in ETFs

There are many advantages to investing in an exchange-traded fund, including:

Cost benefits: ETFs usually offer a significantly lower expense ratio than the average mutual fund. This is in part because of their exchange-traded nature, which places typical costs on the brokers or the exchange, in comparison with a mutual fund which must bear the cost in aggregate.

Accessibility to markets: ETFs offer exposure to asset classes that were previously hard for individual investors to access, and provide investors with the possibility to own assets such as emerging markets bonds, gold bullion, or crypto-currencies. Because ETFs can be sold short and used to apply other more sophisticated investment strategies, they represent a broader range of opportunities for investors.

Transparency: Hedge funds and even mutual funds operate in a not-so-transparent manner as compared to ETFs. Hedge funds and mutual funds usually report their holdings only on a quarterly basis. In contrast, ETFs clearly disclose their daily portfolio holdings.

Liquidity: Because they can be bought or sold in secondary markets throughout the day, ETFs are extremely liquid. This is in contrast to mutual funds which can only be bought or sold at their end-of-day closing price.

Tax Efficiency: Generally, ETFs pose a major tax advantage over mutual funds for two main reasons. First, ETFs reduces portfolio turnover and offer the ability to avoid short-term capital gains that incur a higher tax rate.

Second, ETFs can overcome rules that prohibit selling and claiming a loss on a security if a very similar security is bought within a 30-day window.

Potential Drawbacks of ETFs

Despite the abovementioned benefits, ETFs encounter some challenges as well. For instance, they provide higher exposure to previously unattended asset classes that could bear risks that equity investors might not be familiar with. Some sophisticated examples such as leveraged ETFs involve complex or unfamiliar portfolio structures, tax treatments, or counterparty risks, which require clear understanding of the underlying assets.

Additionally, ETFs carry transaction costs that should be carefully considered in the process of portfolio creations, such as Bid/Ask spreads and commissions.

Who are the biggest ETF management companies?

As of 2017, there are thousands of ETFs in existence. If you want to know who the largest ETF management companies are, here is a list of the top ten fund companies ranked by assets under management.

1. BlackRock
2. Vanguard
3. State Street Global Advisors
4. Invesco PowerShares
5. Charles Schwab
6. First Trust
7. WisdomTree
8. Guggenheim
9. VanEck
10. ProShares

Commodity Futures Trading

Commodity futures trading is an often-overlooked investment arena. There are a number of reasons for this. First of all, it's simply not an investment that's publicly touted as widely as stock trading and other more common investments. Commodity futures trading is different from stock trading, so it does require traders to learn how to handle investments in a different type of market. Also, many investors have been scared away from commodity trading by horror stories from investors who lost huge sums in the commodity markets. The truth is that while commodity trading is a higher risk venture than conservative fixed-income investments or traditional stock trading, it is nonetheless a market in which it is possible to generate high returns that more than justify the additional risk.

Understanding Futures Contracts

Commodity futures are traded in the form of contracts of a standardized size (for example, 5,000 bushels of wheat) that expire in different months. This is obviously different from stock shares that have no expiration date and can be held indefinitely. Futures for a given commodity can usually be traded as far ahead in time as two to three years, however, the vast majority of trading nearly always occurs in the contract with the closest expiration date, known as the "front month."

Futures prices are more subject to sudden, volatile price changes than stocks typically are. A stock that has a long history of steady price appreciation or dividend payouts is likely to continue that trend. But with commodity futures, a downtrend in price can change to an uptrend literally overnight due to factors such as an unexpected freeze or drought during growing season.

Futures contracts are divided into five main categories: Agricultural futures, such as corn, wheat, orange juice, and cocoa Livestock futures, such as lean hogs and live cattle Energy futures, such as oil, heating oil, and natural gas Metals futures, such as gold, silver, and copper Financial futures, such as Treasury bonds, stock indexes, and currencies.

Fundamental and Technical Analysis in Commodity Trading

Fundamental forces of supply and demand are what ultimately move commodity prices. Therefore, there is a high percentage of commodity traders who use fundamental analysis to attempt to predict futures prices. Commodity traders glean information on the commodity markets from sources such as financial newspapers, research information from brokers, and government reports.

Advisory services that traders can subscribe to are an important source of information. Some advisory services feature their own expert meteorologists offering weather forecasts for important crop-growing regions, and send their investigators out to make personal estimates of eventual expected crop sizes.

Despite the fact that genuine supply and demand factors are what drive commodity prices, technical trading is still enormously popular among commodity traders. In fact, many of the most well-known technical indicators that are applied across many other investing markets, such as stocks and forex, were first developed by commodity traders.

Advantages of Commodity Trading

Unlike stock trading or investing in mutual funds or ETFs, commodity trading offers tremendous leverage. In trading commodity futures, you typically only have to put up about 10% of the total futures contract value. This enables you to make much higher percentage gains with your trading capital. For example, you could hold one S&P 500 Index futures contract with a margin deposit of just over $20,000, while it would take several hundred thousand dollars to buy each of the actual stocks contained in the index. A 20% rise in the Index would return you a more than 100% profit from buying a futures contract – you'd realize approximately the same absolute dollar amount in profit as from buying the stocks in the index. Still, you would have made that profit with a much smaller investment.

Commodity futures trading may also offer lower commissions and trading costs, although, with all the discount stock brokerages that exist now, that's not as much an issue as it was 20 years ago.

Commodity trading holds an advantage over illiquid investments such as real estate since any money in your account that is not being used to margin market positions that you're holding is readily available to you at any time.

One really key advantage – a double advantage, actually – that commodity trading offers is diversification within simplicity. There are commodity futures available to trade that cover virtually every sector of the economy – agriculture, energy, precious metals, foreign exchange, and stock indexes. However, unlike the stock market where there are thousands of stocks to choose from – often hundreds within any given industry – there are only a few dozen commodity futures contracts to choose from. So, for example, if cotton prices rise, then you can profit handsomely by being invested in cotton futures contracts, whereas if you were trading stocks, there are hundreds of companies to choose from whose fortunes might be affected by the price of cotton but that would also be affected by other market factors. You might end up buying stock in a company whose share price falls due to other market factors, despite a favorable change for the company in terms of cotton prices.

Finally, in commodity trading, it is just as easy to profit selling short as buying long. There are no restrictions on short selling as there are in the stock markets. Having the potential to profit just as easily from falling prices as from rising prices is a major advantage for traders.

Commodity Trading Secrets – Find Your Market

Here is a little-known secret about consistently successful commodity traders: They almost always specialize in trading either a single market, such as cotton, or a small market segment, such as precious metals or grain futures.

No one has yet offered a completely satisfactory reason for this fact, but it remains a fact that very few traders seem capable of trading all commodity markets equally well. There was a fairly well- known trader back in the 1980s who had a nearly flawless trading record in the cotton market. Copying his cotton trades back then would have been about the closest thing to just printing piles of money for yourself. Year in and year out, he called market highs and lows and trend changes almost as if he'd traveled into the future and already seen them all unfold.

However, this uncannily brilliant cotton trader had one fatal flaw: He also loved trading the silver market. Unfortunately for him, he was just as outrageously bad at trading silver as he was outrageously good at trading cotton. His weakness was compounded by the fact that while he typically traded long-term trends in the cotton market, he day traded the silver market, which provided him with fresh opportunities to lose money every trading day of the week.

How did this all play out for him? Well, in one year when he made over a million dollars trading cotton futures, he ended up filing a net loss in trading for the year. That's right – his horrifically bad silver trading had more than wiped out every bit of his huge profits from trading cotton.

(Fortunately, this story does have a happy ending. After two or three years of stubbornly losing money trading the silver market, the gentleman did finally accept the fact that, "I just can't trade silver," and very wisely stopped doing so. He continued piling up a fortune trading cotton over the next several years, and finally retired from trading with the very concise proclamation that, "I've made enough money and I've had enough fun.")

And so we say: Find your market. It may take some time – and some losing trades – to do this, but it isn't really all that difficult to determine, over a reasonable period of time, what you seem to have a knack for trading – and what you don't have a knack for trading. A simple review of your trades over, say, a six-month period should pretty clearly show you what markets you're frequently doing well in and what markets you aren't having success with. As you trade, you'll probably also develop a feel for which markets you feel most confident in trading. Trust your instincts on that score. If profitably trading oil futures comes easily to you, then just stick with that and don't go trying to complicate your life by trying to master trading some market that's obviously more difficult for you. Why make your trading life more difficult than it need be? You'll likely fare much better by gradually adding trades in related markets such as natural gas or heating oil.

Large institutional traders such as banks have learned this basic truth about trading well. At the trading desks in a bank, you'll rarely, if ever, find the same person assigned to trading both the gold market and the soybean market. The common arrangement is to have commodity trading very specialized, usually with one trader or one team of traders and analysts assigned to trading just one segment of the futures markets, such as energy futures or precious metals futures.

Commodity Trading Secrets – Prices Tend to Trend

The supply and demand quotient for basic raw materials is usually much less subject to ongoing volatility than is the case with stocks. Certainly, there are some very volatile trading days, such as those occur at the end of major bull or bear trends when there are long-term market reversals or following a crop report that comes out unexpectedly good or bad. But generally speaking, there tend to be sustained periods of time when high demand or short supply controls a market, driving prices higher, or when oversupply or lack of demand drives prices lower.

To confirm this, one need look no further than the past several years in oil prices. After experiencing a multi-year bull market that drove oil prices over $100 a barrel, from 2014 onward, oil prices entered a sustained downtrend, eventually carrying the price back below $40 a barrel.

Similar action occurred in a protracted bull market that drove grain prices to record high in first decade of this century, followed by a general decline in prices that has generally been sustained since 2009. Again, while there are occasional sharp and volatile movements in commodity prices, commodities typically experience overall bull or bear trends that last several years.

Therefore, trend-following trading strategies especially as applied to long-term time frames such as daily, weekly, or monthly charts tend to work well in commodity trading. To demonstrate the wisdom of trading with the trend, one noted technical analyst devised a very simple trading strategy and then fine-tuned it by matching it to the long-term trend according to the daily chart. The basic trading strategy he devised was as follows: Buy a new 10-day high and sell short a new 10-day low. It doesn't get much simpler than that.

That basic strategy worked well enough. It wasn't a huge moneymaker, but it was at least profitable overall. However, when adjusted according to the overall trend as indicated by the daily chart, the strategy performed markedly better. The adjustment he made was to only take trading signals that were in the same direction as the overall long-term trend. In other words, if the daily chart showed an overall bullish trend, then he would only follow the trading signals to "buy a new 10-day high," while ignoring the trading signals to "sell a new 10-day low". Conversely, in an overall bear market, he would only take the sell signals, while ignoring buy signals.

He tested his strategy refinement by trading both strategies – the basic and version adjusted to only take trades in the same direction as the existing trend – using separate trading accounts, over the same one-year period of time. The fine-tuning of the trading strategy yielded an impressive improvement in profitability. The fine-tuned version of the strategy, the one which only traded with the existing trend, generated approximately 180% more in profits than did the basic strategy that took both to buy and sell signals regardless of the existing long-term trend.

There's another good reason to employ a solid, long-term, trend trading strategy when investing in commodities. While commodities do tend to enjoy long-term trends, on a daily trading basis they tend to be just the opposite – excessively volatile. Day trading commodity futures – because of the leverage available which makes even small price fluctuations significant as far as potential profits or losses on any given day – does indeed offer tremendous opportunities for profits. However, it's extremely risky. Any commodity trader who's been at the game for a while can tell you stories of days when the price of a given commodity has gone from limit up (the maximum daily price advance allowed by the exchange) to limit down (the maximum daily price decline allowed), and then back to limit up again, sometimes within just a three or four hour period. The odds of being able to successfully navigate your way through price runs like that are slim and none.

Commodity Trading Secrets – Take Advantage of the Nature of the Market

Wise commodity traders know to pay attention to a factor that is almost unique to commodities as opposed to other investment vehicles and which tends to significantly drive prices – seasonality. Nearly all major commodity markets usually tend to follow established seasonal price patterns. A simple example is heating oil and natural gas futures. Both of these commodities tend to, year in and year out, rise into the winter months when demand is highest and decline into summer as demand falls off.

Certainly, there may be specific economic conditions that disrupt this general pattern from time to time. Still, over any 10-year period, one can reasonably expect such general season price trends to run true at least seven or eight years out of 10.

There are specific seasonal patterns that traders can watch for, and take advantage of, in commodity trading. Years ago, famed futures trader, Jake Bernstein, put together a book on seasonal trends detailing dozens of seasonal patterns that occur throughout the year in the various commodity markets, along with the historical record of what percentage of the time the markets stayed true to each seasonal pattern. More recently, seasonal trading software that incorporates such data has been created and is available for traders to use.

Trading seasonal patterns is not a guaranteed win nothing in trading ever is but it definitely offers traders an extra edge. Seasonal patterns can be used as confirming indicators of an existing trend, or as cautionary contrary indicators that may make a trader wisely watchful for an upcoming trend change.

If nothing else, proper awareness of seasonal tendencies in various commodity markets can at least help you avoid suffering huge losses. For example, only the bravest of traders ever holds a large short sell position in orange juice futures heading into winter when just one overnight freeze can send the price of orange juice futures prices suddenly soaring.

Recent Developments in Commodity Futures Trading

The commodity futures markets have has been hurt in recent years by both regulation and failures of regulation. Government attempts to regulate commodity trading have, unfortunately, resulted in misguided legislation that has negatively impacted the markets while failing to provide much in the way of real protection for independent traders. For example, the infamous Dodd-Frank Act in the U.S., enacted in 2014, effectively prohibited banks from conducting short-term trading of their own accounts in the futures markets, leading to a huge decline in liquidity in some markets as many banks exited the commodity trading business.

Not only has legislation resulted in direct negative impacts on the commodity trading markets, it has failed to effectively address real issues such as price manipulation. There have been several cases in recent years of large-scale traders manipulating commodity prices. Still, government regulators have either failed to respond, or in some cases even completely ignored this problem.

Commodity trading has also suffered from the loss of several major brokerage firms and commodity trading companies. Ironically, many of these companies went out of business as a result of losing millions trading their own accounts. Accusations of accounting fraud have led to the demise of once well-known commodity brokerage firms such as Refco.

Learning about commodity trading offers traders significant advantages, such as high amounts of leverage and the opportunity to ride sustained bull or bear trends. However, commodity trading is not a charitable organization that hands out suitcases full of money to anyone who wants some. Just as is the case with any other investing arena, it takes discipline and practice to become a highly-skilled and successful commodity trader. One of the major challenges is learning how to take advantage of the leverage offered without exposing yourself to excessively high risks and potentially disastrous losses.

If you enter the business of commodity trading with proper caution – realizing that you need to learn how to successfully navigate a completely different trading arena than that of stocks, forex, or other investments – then there's no reason that you can't reap the rewards of highly profitable investments, all earned with the use of a minimum amount of trading capital.

CHAPTER 2

Trading the Forex Market

Whether you're an individual trader or a financial or investment professional, the foreign exchange (forex) market, also known as the currency or foreign currency market, is where the money is literally. Forex trading amounts to approximately $5 trillion (yes, trillion, not billion) per day. By comparison, the approximately $700 billion a day bond market and $200 billion a day in stock trading worldwide appear relatively small in size. The total daily value of all the stock trading in the world equals just about one hour's worth of trading in the forex market every day.

Forex Players – Banks, Governments, Companies, and Traders.

There are several distinct groups of participants in the forex market. The largest group of forex traders, in terms of the total dollar value of trading that they account for, is comprised of commercial and investment banks. Banks conduct a large amount of currency trading on behalf of their customers who are involved in international operations. They also serve as market makers in forex trading and trade heavily in their own accounts. (If a banker ever cautions you against forex trading, you might want to ask them why, if forex is such a bad investment, their bank invests such huge sums in the forex market. Just a thought.)

Governments, through their central banks, are also major players in the forex market. The central bank of a nation will often adopt large positions of buying or selling its currency in an attempt to control the currency's relative value in order to combat inflation or to improve the country's balance of trade. Central bank interventions in the forex market are similar to policy-driven interventions in the bond market.

Large companies that operate internationally are also substantially involved in forex trading, trading up to hundreds of billions of dollars annually. Corporations use the forex market to hedge their primary business operations in foreign countries. For example, if a U.S.-based company is doing a significant amount of business in Singapore, requiring it to conduct large business transactions in Singapore dollars. It might hedge against a decline in the relative value of the Singapore dollar by selling the currency pair Sgd/Usd (Singapore dollar vs. US dollar).

Last, but certainly not least, are individual forex traders, speculators who trade the forex market seeking trading profits. This group includes a disparate cast of characters, from professional investment fund managers to individual small investors, who come to the market with widely varying levels of skill, knowledge, and resources.

Learning Forex Trading – Currency Pairs

The forex market trades fluctuations in the exchange rate between currency pairs, such as the euro and the US dollar, which is stated as Eur/Usd. In the quoting of exchange rates, the first currency in the quotation is known as the base currency and the second currency is the quote currency. The exchange rate for a currency pair appears as a number like 1.1235. If the pair Eur/Usd is quoted as 1.1235, that means that it takes $1.12 (and 35/100th) in US dollars to equal one euro.

The most widely traded currency pairs are, naturally enough, those involving the currencies that are most widely used worldwide – the US dollar (Usd), the euro (Eur), and the British pound (GBP).

Learning Forex Trading – Pips

Generally, the smallest fluctuation in an exchange rate is called a "pip." With most currency pairs, which are quoted to four decimal places, a pip equals 0.0001. The primary exception is Japanese yen currency pairs that are only quoted to two decimal places so that a pip equals 0.01. Many brokers now quote to five decimal places, with the last number signifying a fractional 1/10th of a pip.

The value of a pip depends on both the currency pair being traded and what lot size is traded. For one standard lot, a pip commonly equals $10 (US); trading mini-lots, a pip equals $1; and trading micro-lots, a pip equals ten cents. The value of a pip varies slightly depending on the currency pair being traded, but those figures are roughly accurate for all pairs.

Advantages of Forex Trading – Leverage, Liquidity, and Volatility

One of the major attractions of forex trading is the unparalleled leverage that is available to forex traders. Leverage is the ability to hold a market position with only a fractional amount of the market value of the instrument being traded. This fractional amount is known as "margin." Leverage is expressed as a ratio that shows the amount of margin required by a broker to hold a position in the market. For example, 50:1 leverage means that a trader only needs to put up 2% of a trade's total value to initiate a trade. Some brokers offer up to 1000:1 leverage.

High amounts of leverage mean that forex traders can utilize a very small amount of investment capital to realize sizeable gains. For example, by putting only around $10 in margin money, trading micro-lots with 500:1 leverage, a trader can realize a profit of approximately $20 (double his investment) on just a 20-pip change in the exchange rate. Given that many currencies pairs often have a daily trading range of 100 pips or more, it's easy to see how traders can realize substantial gains from very small market movements, using minimal amounts of trading capital, thanks to leverage.

However, traders have to keep in mind that just as leverage magnifies profits, it also magnifies losses. So, a trader, might only commit $10 of his total trading capital to initiate a trade but end up realizing a loss substantially greater than $10.

Liquidity

The extremely high volume of trading that occurs in the forex market each trading day makes for correspondingly high levels of liquidity. High liquidity makes for low bid-ask spreads and allows traders to easily enter and exit trades throughout the trading day. The bid-ask spread on major currency pairs, such as Gbp/Usd, are typically much lower than the bid-ask spread on many stocks, which minimizes transaction costs for traders.

For large institutional traders, such as banks, high liquidity enables them to trade large positions without causing large fluctuations in price that typically occur in markets with low liquidity. Again that makes for lower total trading costs and thus larger net profits or smaller net losses.

Higher liquidity is also considered by many traders to make markets more likely to trade in long-term trends that can more easily be analyzed with the use of charting and technical analysis.

Volatility

As previously noted, many of the most widely traded currency pairs often have a daily trading range of up to 100 pips or more.

Combined with high leverage, this daily volatility makes for significant opportunities to realize profits within the range of price fluctuations that occur within a normal trading day.

The advantage of volatility is enhanced by the fact in forex trading, it is just as easy to sell short as it is to buy long. There are no restrictions on short selling such as those that exist in stock markets. A wide daily trading range, with equal opportunities to profit from both buying and selling, makes the forex market very attractive to speculators.

Forex Trading Strategies – Fundamental Analysis

As with other investment markets, there are two basic strategic approaches to forex trading – fundamental and technical.

Fundamental analysis trading is generally more favored by long-term traders, those who buy (or sell) and hold a currency pair for an extended period of time—fundamental analysis is based on economic conditions, both within specific countries and globally.

Throughout most trading days, various economic reports from the different countries in the world are released. The indications, positive or negative, coming from such reports are the main drivers of major changes in exchange rates between currency pairs. Suppose, for example, several positive reports on the United Kingdom's economy are issued within a three-month time frame. In that case, that is likely to increase the value of Gbp against other currencies such as Eur and Usd.

Among the most significant economic reports issued, those most likely to impact the currency markets, are gross domestic product (GDP), the consumer price index (CPI), the producer price index (PPI), various employment and consumer confidence reports, and the policy decisions of central banks.

Fundamental analysis may also be based on global economic trends. For example, if the usage of cotton is rising worldwide, then countries that are major cotton producers can be expected to benefit, and the relative value of their currency may be expected to increase.

Interest rates, which are set by a country's central bank, are a major factor in determining the relative value of a currency. If investors can realize significantly higher gains from money held in interest-bearing accounts in the United States than from interest-bearing accounts in other countries, then that makes the US dollar more attractive, and therefore likely to increase in value relative to other currencies.

Forex Trading Strategies – Technical Analysis

Many forex traders favor technical analysis in determining the trading positions they adopt. Technical analysis based on charts of price movements in a market, with the aid of various technical indicators – is generally favored by speculators and short-term or intraday traders, although long-term traders may also utilize technical analysis.

Technical analysis is analysis that is based on past price movement and market behavior (such as volume or volatility), Technical indicators include trend indicators such as moving averages and market strength, and momentum indicators such as the relative strength indicator (RSI).

A basic technical trading strategy might be something as simple as buying a currency pair when the price/exchange rate is above a 50-period moving average, and selling the pair when it is below the 50-period moving average. Some technical traders utilize a single technical indicator for trades, while others apply multiple technical indicators as trade indicators. For example, the simple technical trading strategy just outlined, using a moving average, might be combined with a momentum indicator such as the MACD, with trades only being initiated when certain price levels and momentum levels exist.

Technical traders analyze charts of varying time frames based on the trader's individual trading time frame preference. Traders who make very quick, in-and-out of the market trades, may concentrate their analysis on a 5-minute, or even 1-minute time frame chart.

Traders with a longer term trading time frame are more likely to apply technical analysis to hourly, 4-hour, or daily charts.

The Forex Market – The Profit Opportunity Market

Forex trading has exploded in popularity since retail trading by individual small investors became more readily available around the turn of the century. The ability to open a trading account with amounts as small as $50-$100, and the possibility of then turning such a small amount into millions within just the space of a few years, is an almost irresistible draw.

However, the lure of "easy money" from forex trading can be deceptive. The fact is that only a small percentage of traders are consistent winners in the currency trading market. The keys to success in forex trading include not just a good, sound trading strategy, but exceptional trading discipline, patience, and risk management. Many super-successful forex traders have summed up the secret to their success as something like, "Just avoid taking big losses until you stumble into a huge winner. Most traders fail because they gamble away all their trading capital and don't have any money left to trade with when a 'million dollar' trading opportunity finally comes around".

Basic Economics Of Financial Market

Economics is the study of resource allocation and decision making. With any type of investing, economics have a fundamental role. Two economic principles that are advantageous to understand before investing are supply and demand and business cycles.

Supply and Demand

The main principle behind the supply and demand of an asset is that as supply increases, demand decreases, and as demand increases, supply decreases. As a result of the relationship between supply and demand, pricing is affected. When demand is high and supply are low, the buyer of the asset is willing to pay a higher price due to the asset's current rarity. Using the same logic, when supply is high and demand is low, the price the buyer is willing to pay for asset at hand decreases due its abundancy. When, the amount of supply, meets the amount of demand for an asset, the price is said to be at equilibrium. The figure below illustrates these principles:

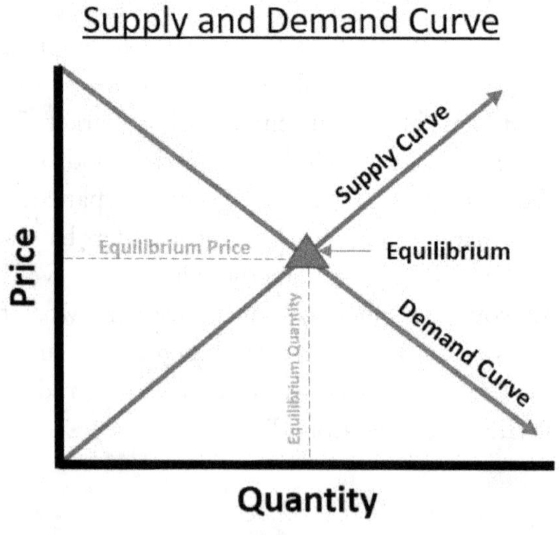

Business Cycles

A business cycle is an explanation of economic activity and movement. Business cycles are applicable on a small scale to companies and on a larger scale to countries. Business cycles are marked by four distinctive periods: peaks, contractions, troughs, and expansions. The peak of a business cycle is the height of economy activity. The peak is followed by the contraction period. The contraction period is a time of decreasing economic activity, generally marked by decreasing employment and decreasing sales. Following the contraction period, the trough is the lowest point and bottom of economic activity. The trough is followed by the expansion period in the business cycle. The expansion period is a time of increased economic activity, generally marked by lower unemployment rates, increased sales, and high growth.

INVESTABLE MARKETS

When looking to either invest or trade, it is imperative to understand what the market is and how the market operates. There are four possible markets one can invest or trade on the equity market, the currency market, the options market, and the futures market.

Equity Market

The equity market, also commonly known as the stock market, is a means for companies to raise capital. Companies raise capital through issuing stock. A stock is a share of a company representing part ownership and a claim to the company's assets and earnings. Furthermore, there are two types of stock: common stock and preferred stock. A common stock generally entitles the owner to a claim to voting rights and dividends. A dividend is a periodic payout of earnings from a company to its shareholders. A preferred stock generally does not grant voting rights but does receive dividends and claim of assets and earnings before common stock. An owner of stock, preferred or common, is known as a stockholder. The amount of claim a stockholder has within a company is proportional to the amount of shares owned compared to the total amount of shares on the market. Therefore, the price of a stock is representative of a proportion of the market valuation of the worth of a company. The market valuation of the worth of a company is found by multiplying the total number of shares of a company by the price per share of the stock and is known as the market cap.

The sizes of a company's market cap correlates to the size of the company and categorizes companies on the stock market. Companies generally with less than two billion in market cap are known as small cap stocks. While companies generally with more than ten billion in market caps are known as large cap stocks. Although the exact market cap values may vary by definition, the definition of small cap and large cap stocks themselves does not. Large cap stocks refer to large, stable companies like Alphabet Inc. or General Electric whose size mitigates volatility through its liquidity and solvency. Small cap stocks refer to smaller, less stable companies who are less likely to be able to absorb or sustain significant losses. As a result, small cap stocks are generally seen as more volatile than large cap stocks. Furthermore, small cap stocks are seen to have more potential for growth than large cap stocks because a small cap stock may become a large cap stock in the future.

In addition to looking at the cap size of a company, it is important to identify the sector the company is in. A sector is a group of companies that produce the same type of goods or services in an economy. There are many possible sectors a company can identify with but some of the most common in stock trading are: technology, healthcare, energy, financials, materials, and utilities.

Understanding sectors is important in investing and trading equities because different sectors have different risk profiles. A risk profile describes the potential for losses or gains as a result of expected volatility. For example, comparing the risk profile of the utilities sector to the healthcare sector, the utilities sector is generally less volatile. With this knowledge, if an investor wanted less volatile, steady growth, he or she may invest in an electricity company in the utilities sector. If an investor wanted to take on more risk for hopes of a higher return over time, he or she may invest in a pharmaceutical company in the healthcare sector.

While one can invest in a company within a sector, it is also possible to invest in a sector itself through the use of an exchange traded fund or ETF for short. Exchange traded funds are funds that own underlying assets and divide the ownership of the assets through shares. The price per share of an ETF is determined by the total price of all underlying assets added together divided by the number of shares on the market. ETFs can be bought and sold the same way as common stock on the stock market. Furthermore, ETFs make it possible to invest in sectors when the underlying assets of the ETF are the stocks of the companies in a particular sector. That being said, it critical to look at the underlying assets an ETF is comprised of before purchase to really know what is in the ETF. Furthermore, when looking to invest in a particular stock, it may be useful to track an ETF representing the sector the stock is a part of. By following the sector and the stock, a stockholder can compare returns to the sector as a whole and get a sense of the stock's volatility compared to the other stocks of the same sector.

Along with stocks and ETFs, there is another type of asset traded on the equity market called mutual funds. A mutual fund is an entity that invests and manages a pool of money from and for investors. Mutual funds allow the opportunity for investors with small amounts of capital to have their money invested and managed professionally without hiring a personal financier. Mutual funds are able to use the pooled money to invest in the equity market in places where a small time investor may not be able to. With that being said, each investor owns a portion of the fund's holdings proportional to the amount of shares of the fund he or she owns. The price per share of a mutual fund is based on the mutual fund's net asset value. The net asset value of a mutual fund is the fund's assets minus any outstanding liabilities divided by the total number of shares on the market. Just as with ETFs, before buying into a mutual fund it is pertinent to understand the underlying information of the fund. The prospectus of a mutual fund details the fund's investment types, past performance, risk tolerance, goals, and associated fees. With mutual funds there are generally three fees that may apply: front end load fees, back end load fees, and yearly fees. A front end load fee is a percentage of the original investment or flat fee that is taken out when at the time of entering a mutual fund. For example, if someone invests 500 dollars in a mutual fund with a five percent front end load fee the mutual fund takes 25 dollars with the fee and the investor is left with 475 dollars invested: $500 - (500 \times 0.05) = 475$. A back end load fee works the opposite way as a front end load fee and the fee is collected when an investor withdraws his or her capital from the mutual fund. For example, if an investor puts 1000 dollars in a mutual fund with a six percent back end load fee and after a year the investor withdraws his or hers accumulated money, now at a value of 1200 dollars, the investor would receive 1128 dollars after the fee is applied: $1200 - (1200 \times 0.06) = 1128$. Some mutual funds may also have a yearly fees outlined in the prospectus which go towards pay for the costs of running the fund and managing the money invested in the fund. A mutual fund without commission, a front end load fee, or a back end load fee is known as a no load fund.

While front end load and back end load fees may apply to mutual funds, there are other commissions associated with buying and selling stocks and ETFs. The commissions associated with trading on the equity market come from the coordination of how stocks, ETFs, and mutual funds are traded. Stocks, ETFs, and mutual funds are traded on a stock exchange. A stock exchange is a hub for trading; it matches sellers with buyers and executes transactions as efficiently as possible.

The largest stock exchange in the world is the New York Stock Exchange (NYSE) and it is open from 9:30 AM to 4:00 PM EST

Monday through Friday. In America, 9:30 AM to 4:00 PM EST Monday through Friday are the standard trading hours for the equity market. The everyday person does not have access to openly trade on an exchange. However, the everyday person does have access to a broker. A broker, which is generally a firm, facilitates trades received from investors to the stock exchange for the investors. Most brokers do not provide these services for free and charge a commission for executing a trade for an investor. Furthermore, commissions are paid on per trade basis. It is important to keep track of commission costs while trading the equity market to keep track of true profits and losses. For example, if someone buys one share of a 100 dollar stock and there is a seven dollar commission, then buying the stock costs seven dollars in commission and selling the stock costs another seven dollars; owning one share of this stock would not become profitable unless the price per share of the stock increased to above 114 dollars. The amount of increase per share to cover the costs of commissions could be diluted by buying more than one share; as the cost of commission does not change, owning more shares would require less of an increase in price per share to be profitable.

At this point, it has been shown that stocks, ETFs, and mutual funds can be invested in on the stock market with associated fees. The next question at hand is: how does one choose a stock and determine a good investment from a bad investment? There are two types of analysis that investors commonly use to evaluate potential stock investments with: fundamental analysis and technical analysis.

Fundamental analysis is assessing the price of a company's stock by looking at the intrinsic value associated with its earnings, revenues, expenses, market capture, growth prospects, competition, and any other relevant business or financial data. On a basic level, fundamental analysis generally starts with looking at earnings reports. An earnings report is a report released once per quarter of the year publicly announcing a company's quarterly financial performance and outlook on the future. Earnings reports include quarterly sales, revenues, and profits/losses. With fundamental analysis, a company's profitability is a very important factor for growth and valuation of a company's stock price. An unexpected drop in sales and revenues of a company in an earnings report more often than not will follow with a drop in the company's stock price as the company appears less profitable. At the same rate, a company whose earnings report beats expectations can be expected to see a stock price increase as it appears to be a strong, more profitable company. Fundamental analysis of a company does not have to be done at a quarterly rate and for long-term investing it may be more useful to look at all of a company's historical reports to capture a better image of a company's market and financial standings. Furthermore, fundamental analysis of a company's competitors and sector can give a lot more information about a company from a broader, more comparative point of view. The sales and revenues of a company may be increasing over time, but if a company is increasing in sales and revenues at a pace slower than other the companies in the same sector there may be a better investment available.

There are also some related short-hand terms that an investor may use to fundamentally analyze a stock. The price to earnings ratio or P/E ratio is the price per share divided by the earnings per share. A low P/E ratio can either mean a company is doing very well or it is currently undervalued. A high P/E ratio can be interpreted to have higher expected earnings in the future compared to companies with lower P/E ratios. Comparing P/E ratios within a sector is a good fundamental analysis practice in analyzing a stock. Another common term used in stock trading, and sometimes perceived as the most important, is earnings per share. Earnings per share or EPS is the net income of a company divided by the total number of shares on the market. EPS is used to measure the profitability of a company on a per share basis.

The other type of analysis, technical analysis, assesses investment opportunities by looking at historical prices and trading volumes to identify patterns and predict future price behavior.

Historical prices of securities can be analyzed on many different time intervals; minute prices, hourly prices, daily prices, weekly prices, and full history prices. The historic prices per interval are commonly summarized by candlesticks. A candlestick, also known as a bar, is a box and whisker plot that shows a security's open, close, high, and low over a given length of time. The open of a security is the price of the security at the beginning of the interval. The close is the price of the security at the end of the interval. The open and close constitute the box of the plot. The high of a security is the greatest recorded price and the low of a security is the lowest price during the time interval; the high and the low constitute the whiskers of the box. The volume of a stock is the amount of shares traded on the stock market. The amount of shares traded can then be grouped by price movement: the amount of shares that were bought over a period of time when the price increased and the amount of shares over a period of time that were bought (or sold) when the price decreased. Technical analysis of a stock may show that it statistically probable that after three days of high amounts of volume traded and price decreases that the fourth day may see a price increase.

This is just an example, but for an investor using technical analysis, it may be a scenario with enough information to warrant buying the stock on the fourth day. Whether using fundamental analysis, technical analysis, or a bit both for investment decision making, there is another useful tool for analyzing a stock called a beta value. The beta value of a stock is found through regression analysis and is a measure of volatility in price changes of a stock compared to movements in the market—the market is measured through the use of indexes. An index is a measurement of a section of the market through adding the stock prices of the market section. Indexes are not a tradable security but can be traded through ETFs comprised of the same stocks the index follows. The most common indexes are the Standard & Poor's 500 and the Dow Jone's Industrial Average. The Standard & Poor's 500 or S&P 500 is generally accepted as the best capture of the market as it follows 500 of some of the largest stocks from all sectors and accounts for about 75 percent of the total stock market. The Dow Jone's Industrial Average or DJIA follows the 30 largest, richest, and most traded stocks on the stock exchange. Due to the amount of companies and broad range of the companies it follows, the S&P 500 is perceived as the general market indicator for the direction of the market. Thus, the beta value of a company is generally calculated using the S&P 500 as a measure of the market. As mentioned before, beta values, through regression analysis, measure the change in price of a stock in comparison to a change in the market. A stock with a beta value of one means that the stock can be expected to move in the same direction as the market; if the market increases, the stock should increase by a relatively close percentage. A beta value below one means the stock should be expected to move in the same direction of the market less; if the market decreases, the stock should decrease by a smaller percentage. Lastly, a beta value above 1 means that the stock should move in the same direction of the market but at a faster rate; if the market increases, the stock should increase by a greater percentage. A negative beta value would work in similar regards but in the opposite direction of the market.

Beta values help measure the effects of market volatility and the price change of any given stock in comparison, but then it is also important to measure volatility. The Volatility Index or VIX, also known as the "fear index," measures the market's 30-day volatility expectation. The 30- day expected volatility is made from the implied volatilities from the S&P 500. The VIX can be followed just like an index and not a tradable asset, but the implied information from the VIX may be helpful in making trades. VIX values greater than 30 are perceived as there being a period of high volatility and uncertainty in the future. VIX values below 20 are generally perceived as times of normal volatility without extenuating circumstances.

Finally, there is one more market circumstance that investors should be aware of with the equity market: the introduction of new stocks to the market. An initial public offering or IPO is when a company becomes publicly available on the market. A private company may want to go public, i.e. issue shares on an exchange, to raise capital. The IPO is the first time anyone outside the company will be able to openly invest in the company. The price per share at an IPO is calculated through fundamental analysis of the company, comparison to similar companies, and is a base valuation of the company's worth. Following the IPO, the stock price may have a period of increased volatility associated with the stock as it does not have a price history. Without technical analysis as an option, investing in IPOs requires in depth fundamental analysis.

Currency Market

Money is made and lost on the currency market through exchange rates and trading currencies. Currencies are traded on the Foreign Exchange and the currency market is often referred to as the Forex. Currency trading on the Forex is done by trading currency pairs. A currency pair is the relationship between the values of two currencies. Currency pair ticker symbols are six letters long and comprised of both abbreviated currencies. The first currency listed in the ticker symbol of the pairing is known as the base currency and is the currency being bought. The second currency listed in the ticker symbol of the pairing is known as the quote currency and is the currency being sold—an example of a currency pair that is commonly traded is the EURUSD. In this example, the euro (symbol: EUR) is the base currency and the United States dollar (symbol: USD) is the quote currency. When trading the EURUSD currency pair, United States dollars are being sold to buy euros. The amount of United States dollars it takes to buy the euro is known as an exchange rate if the EURUSD ticker was trading at a value of

1.1400, then it would take 1.1400 United States dollars to buy 1.0000 euro.

Profits or losses can be achieved in trading the Forex as exchange rates change. Changes in exchange rates are measured in pips. A pip is one ten-thousandth of a dollar or 0.0001 in decimal form. Thus, if the EURUSD currency pair was bought at a value of 1.1400 and sold at 1.1401. The profit would be one pip or one ten-thousandth of a United States dollar.

One ten-thousandth of a dollar is not a lot of money. This is why currencies are traded on a lot system. A standard lot is 100,000 units of base currency. Purchasing a standard lot of EURUSD results in the value of a change in one pip to be worth 10 United States dollars: 100,000 × 0.0001 = 10.

The complete lot system is as follows:

Lot Name Size 1 Pip Dollar Change per Pip

- Standard 100,000 × 0.0001 10
- Mini 10,000 × 0.0001 1
- Micro 1,000 × 0.0001 0.1000
- Nano 100 × 0.0001 0.0100

From the table above, it is apparent that the more base currency one can purchase, the more a one pip change in a currency pair value is worth. To make or lose 10 dollars per pip with the EURUSD currency pair, one would have to trade a standard lot. Following the example from before, where the EURUSD is valued at 1.1400, purchasing a standard lot would cost 114,000 United States dollars. This is a decently large amount of capital that many small-time traders may not have on hand. This issue is combatted through buying on margin. Buying on margin or leveraging is borrowing more money than one has to seek higher profits and using one's own money as collateral. In the United States, the largest one is allowed leverage his or her money with a broker is 50:1. Buying a standard lot of EURUSD at a value of 1.1400 on a margin of 50:1 would only requires a capital investment of 2,280 United States dollars: 114,000 ÷ 50 = 2,280. Buying on margin allows for greater possible profits but there is also an associated higher level of risk. If the leveraged losses equal the amount of money in an account the broker will exit the trade to protect itself from losses. For example, if a trader purchased a standard lot of EURUSD at the value of 1.1400 on margin for 2,280 dollars and the value dropped 230 pips to 1.1170, the losses would be 10 dollars a pip for a total loss of 2,300; 20 dollars more than the account value and the trader would owe the broker 20 dollars in addition to losing his or her whole account. A 230 pip change would be an extreme, but not impossible, event and it is important to understand the risks associated with leveraging.

Volatility in exchange rates help classify currencies into categories. In currency trading, the less volatile currencies are the currencies of the world's larger, more stable countries; predominantly the United States dollar, the Euro-zone euro, the Great Britain pound (symbol: GBP), the Australian dollar (symbol: AUD), the Canadian dollar (symbol: CAD), the New Zealand dollar (symbol: NZD), the Japanese yen (symbol: JPY), the Swiss franc (symbol: CHF). The EURUSD, USDJPY, GBPUSD, USDCHF, USDCAD, AUDUSD, and NZDUSD currency pairs are known as the majors. The majors are known for containing the USD, being the most liquid currency pairs, and being the most frequently traded currency pairs. There is also a subcategory called the minors, which consists of currency pairs of the same currencies but without the USD. Furthermore, the minors are not as liquid as the majors. Some examples of minor currencies pairs that could be traded is the EURCAD and the GBPJPY. In addition, currency pairs that consist of the USD and currencies from emerging, less stable countries are known as exotic pairs. Exotic pairs tend to be more volatile and may consist of currency pairs such as USDZAR, for example; comparing the United States dollar to the South African rand.

Volatility in currency pairs and exchange rates comes from comparing economies. The value of a currency is representative of a country's economic situation. Thus, changes in economic status have an effect on the value of a currency and exchange rates. Relative to other economies, the weaker an economy, the less value its currency has and the stronger an economy, the more value its currency has. For example, if the United States economy is getting stronger, the United States dollar is becoming more valuable and the EURUSD value may fall as it takes fewer dollars to buy euros.

Today, it is very easy to follow a country's economic situation by following the news and economic indicators. Furthermore, economic calendars exist to help identify important economic news releases. Important economic news that has a macroeconomic impact in a country may be jobless claims, changes in interest rate, unemployment rates, changes in gross domestic product of a country, and changes in the consumer price index. It is important to understand how such macroeconomic factors impact currency pairs to get a sense of the direction currencies are heading in.

The currency market is open twenty-four hours a day, five days a week. The currency market's round the clock accessibility is a result of differing time zones and hours of operation of different exchanges. The major exchanges are open during the following times (EST):

- Exchange Open Close
- Frankfurt, Germany 2:00AM 10:00AM
- London, Great Britain 3:00 AM 11:00 AM
- New York, United States 8:00 AM 4:00 PM
- Sydney, Australia 6:00 PM 2:00 AM
- Tokyo, Japan 7:00PM 3:00AM

As new markets open each day there is increased volatility in the currency market. The increased volatility is a reflection of new investors reacting to news that was released earlier in the day. Knowing when markets open and close can help explain market volatility when there is not new news being released and should be taken into consideration when deciding what times during the day to trade.

Furthermore, it is important to note that the currency market is a commission-free market. Instead of a commission there is a pip spread. A pip spread is the difference between values one can buy and sell a currency pair at. It generally costs one to three more pips to buy a currency pair than it does to sell the same currency pair. If the EURUSD was valued at 1.1400 buy price and the pip spread was two pips, then the sell price would be 1.1398. Thus, buying two standard lots of EURUSD and selling them immediately would result in a loss of 20 dollars. The pip spread has to be overcome before any profits can be achieved but it is a small-percentage, one-time cost to pay for a trade.

Options Market

The options market is one of the more lucrative markets to invest in. An option is a contract ensuring the right, but not the obligation, to either buy or sell an asset at a certain price at an expiration date. Options are a derivative security, meaning the price of an options contract is derived from an underlying asset. The writer of an options contract is the seller of the contract. The buyer or holder of an options contract has the right to buy or sell the underlying asset. The price the underlying asset is to be bought or sold at is called the strike price. The strike price and the price to buy an option contract are not the same and should not be confused with one another. The price to buy an options contract is generally much lower than the price of the underlying asset which helps distinguish between the two. The price of an options contract is determined through supply and demand of the underlying asset, the relation of the strike price and the current price of the underlying asset, the amount of expected volatility of the underlying asset, and the length of the contract.

An option is said to be in the money if exercising the right to buy or sell the underlying asset at the strike price is profitable to the holder. An option is said to be at the money if by exercising the right to buy or sell the underlying asset at the strike price the holder profits enough to break even with the cost of purchasing the option. Lastly, an option is out of the money if the holder would incur a loss by exercising the right to buy or sell the underlying asset at the strike price.

The right, but not the obligation, to buy an asset at a certain strike price is called a call option. The holder of a call option is in the money if the price of the underlying asset is higher than the strike price because the holder has the right to buy the underlying asset from the writer for less than it is worth. If the price of the underlying asset is lower than the strike price, the holder of the call option would not opt to exercise the option because the holder could buy the underlying asset on the market for less. In this scenario, the holder would incur the loss of the price it took to purchase the option. The writer of a call option thinks the price of the underlying asset will decrease below the strike price over the term of the contract.

The right, but not the obligation, to sell an asset at a certain strike price is called a put option. The holder of a put option is in money if the price of the underlying asset is lower than the strike price, because the holder has the right to sell the underlying asset to the writer of the put option for more than it is worth. Suppose the price of the underlying asset is higher than the strike price, the holder of the buy option would not opt to exercise the option because the holder could sell the underlying asset for more on the market. In the case of put options, the writer of the put option thinks the price of the underlying asset will increase above the strike price over the term of the contract.

To gain a better understanding of options and the profit schemes for holders and writers here is an example:

Suppose the price per share of a stock is currently 80 dollars a share. A writer believes that the stock price won't change very much in the next three months and sells a three-month, 80 dollar strike price call option on the stock and a three-month, 80 dollar strike prices put option—the writer prices both options at five dollars each. Buyer A believes that the stock price is going to increase over the next three months so Buyer A purchases the call option from the writer. Buyer B believes the opposite and thinks the stock price is going to decrease over the next three months so Buyer B purchases the put option from the writer. Buyer A's and Buyer B's profit schemes depending on the stock price compared to their respective options are as follows:

Buyer A's and Buyer B's profit schemes at the same strike price and purchase price are mirrors of each other; the shape of the profit scheme in these graphs is the same shape for any buyer of a call option or put option. The writer of the options has a flipped profit scheme.

He is combining the profit schemes from selling both a call option and a put option. Along with the two types of options there are also two styles of these options. A European style option is an option that can only be exercised at the expiration of the option. A mnemonic device to help remember that European style options are only exercisable at expiration is that both words starter with "e" and thinking expiration when one hears European. The other style of option is the America style where the option may be exercised at any time before the expiration. The American style option is more flexible because if the strike price on the underlying asset is ever in the money the holder can profit at that time if he or she wants.

Options are also closely associated with the equity market and can play an important role in hedging. Hedging is the process of mitigating potential losses. For example, a stock owner may buy a six-month put option on the same underlying stock at a strike price equal to the current price of the stock. As a result, the stock owner is ensured that he or she will not suffer losses for any drop in stock price over the next six months. The options market and the equity market are often very much intertwined because many options contracts are written with stocks as the underlying asset.

From the writing side of options, maximum profits are achieved through sale of contracts that are out of the money. When options contracts are out of the money, the underlying asset is never exchanged between the writer and the holder. An out of the money put option will not require the writer to buy the underlying asset; and an out of the money call option will not require the writer to sell the underlying asset. In either case, the underlying asset never exchanges hands and the writer makes a full profit from the sale price of the contract. Furthermore, since the underlying asset never exchanged hands from the writer to the holder in the case of an out of the money call option, the writer never had to have purchased the underlying asset. Writing options contracts without owning the underlying is known as naked writing. Naked writing is a legal practice but if a call option contract was in the money and exercised, the writer has an obligation to sell the underlying asset and therefore must purchase and sell it.

Futures Market

The futures market is another one of the more risky, more complex, and more lucrative markets. The futures market is a means to buy and sell futures contracts and commodities. A futures contract is a derivative security wherein two parties agree to transact some amount of an asset at a future date for a particular price. A commodity, often the asset of a futures contract, is a basic good used in commerce. Some examples of commodities that are commonly traded in futures contracts include: grains, beef, and barrels of oil.

Futures contracts are created to help suppliers of an asset avoid the volatility of the market. On a basic level, take a farmer for example. A farmer may plant his corn when the price per bushel of corn is four dollars. Subsequently, the farmer plans his expenses and expected profits based off the projection that the price per bushel of corn will still be four dollars a bushel when he harvests. Due to the market volatility of the price per bushel of corn, it is possible that the price per bushel of corn may differ from four dollars at the time of harvest. At the time of harvest, if the price per bushel of corn is greater than four dollars the farmer would make a greater profit when he sells his corn, but if the price per bushel of corn is less than four dollars the farmer may not have profited enough to sustain his farm during the next crop. The farmer avoids the risk of the price per bushel dropping below four dollars by the time he harvests by entering into a futures contract. When the farmer plants seeds, he enters into a four dollar per bushel futures contract with a company that buys raw corn. In this manner, the farmer is assured to sell his corn for four dollars a bushel when he harvests it. If the price per bushel of corn is greater than four dollars at the time of transaction between the farmer and the company buying, the company buying the corn profits from buying the corn below the market price. If the price per bushel of corn is less than four dollars at the time of the transaction, the farmer is more profitable as he is getting a better price for his corn than the market is currently offering.

As seen with the example of the farmer, changes in the price of the underlying asset of a futures contract can make the contract more or less profitable to each party. The value of a future contract comes from the difference in current market price of the underlying asset and sale price associated with the contract. The greater the current market price of the underlying asset increases above the price in the contract, the more valuable the contract is to the buyer of the asset.

Similarly, lower the current market price of the underlying asset decreases below the price in the contract, the more valuable the contract is to the seller of the asset. The value of futures contracts are settled on a daily basis.

The price of a futures contract is directly associated with the value of the contract. The price and value of a futures contract is most often affected by supply and demand. There are many factors that can affect the supply and demand of an underlying asset of a contract. The prices of agriculturally based futures contracts can be affected by the weather. A dry season may lower the supply of a type of produce and as a result buyers of the produce would be willing to pay more; ultimately, increasing the current market price until the supply can meet the demand. The prices of futures contracts based off of meat prices could be affected by diseases or infections amongst livestock. A disease amongst livestock could reduce the amount of animals available to butcher in the future and an infection amongst livestock could make the meat unsellable. Depending on the nature of the underlying asset, it is important to understand what factors will ultimately affect the price of a contract and how.

Furthermore, most investors in the futures market are speculators because investors tend to not want to end up buying or selling thousands of bushels of corn, drums of oil, or any other physical asset from buying or selling futures contracts. As, a speculator, in the futures market, an investor is not responsible for the delivery or purchase of any underlying assets. Instead of trading cash for a physical asset, transactions amongst speculators are settled in cash alone.

ENTERING AND EXITING A MARKET

One can enter a market one of two ways: a long position or a short position.

Long Positions

Long positions are situations where one profits from a price increase of an asset. In a long position, one generally buys an asset and sells the asset at a later time if the price of the asset at the time of sale is higher than the price it was purchased at then the investor makes a profit. If the price of the asset at the time of sale is lower than the price it was purchased then the investor incurs a loss.

Example: Suppose the price of Apple stock is 100 dollars per share today and you think the price will be greater than 100 dollars tomorrow. Because you think the price per share is going to increase tomorrow you take a long position and buy one share of Apple stock today; costing you 100 dollars. You now own one share of Apple. Let's say you were right in your original assumption that the price of Apple stock would increase and the price per share of Apple stock tomorrow is 110 dollars. You can sell the share for 110 dollars and profit ten dollars on your original investment of 100 dollars. There is always the possibility that your original assumption is wrong and the price decreases the next day. If the price per share of Apple stock dropped to 90 dollars per share and you sold your share your profit would be -10 dollars; or a ten dollar loss.

Short Positions

Short positions work in opposition to long positions as one profit from a decrease in the price of an asset. A short position works by borrowing the asset one wishes to short from someone else. Upon borrowing the asset, one sells it immediately. At a later time, one buys the asset back and returns the asset to its original owner; this process is known as buying to cover as one buys the asset to cover one's obligation to return the borrowed asset. If the price decreases, the borrower, the owner of the short position, profits the difference between the price the asset was sold at and the price the asset was bought back at upon being returned. If the price increases, the owner of the short position incurs a loss when buying back the asset to return to the original owner because the borrower is buying back at a higher price than, he or she sold it for.

Example: Say you are looking at Apple's stock again at a price of 100 dollars, but this time you think that the price tomorrow will be lower than it is today. Because you think the price per share is going to decrease to decide to short one share of Apple today. Through a broker, you borrow a share of Apple stock and sell it immediately for 100 dollars. You now own that 100 dollars, but you also own the obligation to return the one share of Apple stock you borrowed. Let's say you were right in your original assumption that the price per share of Apple stock was going to decrease and tomorrow the price per share is 90 dollars. You can buy to cover one share of Apple for 90 dollars. In this situation your profit is 10 dollars; the original 100 you received selling the borrowed share minus the 90 dollars you paid the next day to buy and return the Apple share you borrowed the day before. If your original assumption was wrong and the price per share of Apple increased the next day to 110 dollars, you would incur a 10 dollar loss; buying to cover a share of Apple stock the next day at 110 dollars would require the 100 dollars you received when you sold the share the day before and 10 dollars of your own capital.

Relationship between Long and Short Positions

The relationship in profit between long and short positions is an inverse relationship. That is to say, when a long and short are entered at the same time and same price, if the price increases the short will produce a loss and the long will produce a profit; if the price decreases, the short will produce a profit and the long will produce a loss.

Positions in the Options Market

The inverse relationship between long and short positions is helpful in understanding the type of position the writer and the buyer of an options contract are in. With a call option, the writer maximizes profits when the price of the underlying asset decreases below the strike price of the contract. Therefore, the writer has a short position. The buyer of a call option has a long position because the holder profits most from price increases above the strike price. With a put option, the writer maximizes profit when price of the underlying asset increases above the strike price of the contract. In this case, the writer has a long position. The buyer of the put option has a short position because the holder benefits most when the price of the asset is below the strike price of the put option.

Positions in the Futures Market

In the futures market, the buyer of a future contract has a long position. The buyer's long position is a result from the fact that a price increase of the underlying asset above the price in the contract is increasingly profitable for the buyer. In contrast, the seller of a futures contract profits the more the price of the underlying asset decreases below the price in the contract. Therefore, the seller of a futures contract has a short position.

Entry Order Types

- Market: Entering a long position, a market order is an entry that buys into a market at lowest, most immediate price available. Entering a short position, the market order will sell a security at highest, most immediate price available.
- Limit: A limit order executes an order at a specific price or better. A limit order to buy long will execute when the market price is equal to or lower than the limit price. A limit order to sell short when the market price is equal to or greater than the limit price.
- Stop: A stop order to buy long is to buy at market above the current market price if the order price is reached. A stop order to sell short is to sell at market below the current market price if the order price is reached.

- GTD & GTC: GTD and GTC stand for good till date and good till canceled, respectively. With a GTD order, an end date can be associated with an entry order and if the order is not executed or filled by the specified date, the order will be terminated. A GTC entry order will stay on the market as long it took the order to be executed and filled or cancelled manually.

Exit Order Types

- Market: A market exit will sell or buy to cover at the most current prices on the market.
- Stop Loss: A stop loss is an order that will exit the market at a specific amount of losses incurred compared to the purchase price.
- Limit: A limit order as an exit will sell a long position at the limit price or higher and buy to cover a short position at the limit price or lower.
- Trailing Stop Loss: A trailing stop loss is a stop loss that takes profits into consideration. The specific amount of losses an investor is willing to incur, stays constant but the price of execution changes. For example, a stock may be purchased at 100 dollars with a 10 dollar trailing stop loss. Without an increase in price, the trailing stop loss acts like a regular stop loss and will exit the position at a price of 90 dollars. Although, if the price of the stock increases to 105 dollars before decreasing, the trailing stop loss would then exit the position if the stock price were at 95 dollars instead of 90.
- Take Profit: A take profit order will exit the market at market price only if a specific profit level is reached.
- GTD & GTC: GTD and GTC work the same way for exit orders as they do for entry orders.

MARKET MOVEMENT

Markets tend to move in one of three directions: upward, downward, or sideways. When a market is moving upwards consistently with higher highs and higher lows it is called an uptrend. Uptrends are associated with the expansion period of the business cycle and may differ between sectors by start, volatility, and duration. With increasing prices, long positions are more profitable than short positions during uptrends. When a market is moving downwards consistently, with lower highs and lows it is said to be in a downtrend. Downtrends are associated with the contraction period of the business cycle, and also may differ by sector. Downtrends are more profitable for short positions than long positions as prices are decreasing. Due to volatility in the markets trends do not move smoothly on a lineup or down. Instead, trends oscillate upwards or downwards. When a market isn't oscillating upwards or downwards the market is known to have a sideways trend. A sideways trend is a horizontal price movement. Sideways trends are generally associated with the peaks and troughs of the business cycle and demonstrate a time price direction uncertainty. It may be difficult to identify what type of trend a market is moving in and subsequently what type of position to take, if any, but that is what creating a strategy is for.

CHAPTER 3

FX Execution Algorithms

Execution Algorithms In The FX Market: Taking Stock

Background to FX execution algorithms

For the purposes of this report, FX execution algorithms are defined as automated trading programs designed to buy or sell a predefined amount of FX according to a set of parameters and instructions, with the objective of filling the order. At their most basic level, EAs automate the process of splitting a larger order (eg USD 100 million), hereafter known as the "parent order," into multiple smaller orders (eg 100 transactions of USD 1 million each), known as "child orders," and executing them over a period of time separately rather than all together. EAs seek to assist the user in entering into or closing a predefined position by either buying or selling a particular currency pair in one direction. In this way, they are distinct from other common types of algorithms used in the FX market which involve both buying and selling currencies. Examples of the latter include market-making algorithms, which typically seek to restore the liquidity provider's net aggregate position to a neutral or close-to-neutral value, and opportunistic algorithms, which are commonly used by principal trading firms and hedge funds to generate profit.

FX EAs allow users to navigate the fragmented FX market by aggregating liquidity and facilitating access to the various types of liquidity pools and trading venues, which would be difficult, if not impossible, manually. A significant implication is that they give market participants more direct control over how their transactions are executed. Prior to the emergence of FX EAs, this had been the domain of the market- makers, hedge funds and other sophisticated financial institutions.

At the same time, in using FX EAs, market participants carry market risk until completion of the trade which they need to manage. In this way, FX EAs differ from other methods of trading such as "risk transfer" where market risk is swiftly shifted from end users (e.g. funds, corporates and small banks) to liquidity providers. When market participants execute a "risk transfer," they request a price from their liquidity provider (a request-for-quote (RFQ) or a request-for-stream (RFS)) and trade the full size of the ticket at the price received from their counterpart.1 The direct cost of this immediate risk transfer, the bid-ask spread, is the compensation paid to the liquidity provider for taking on the market risk.2 In this sense, the risk transfer price constitutes an almost instantaneous "all-in" price that typically depends on the transaction size, the prevailing liquidity conditions and market volatility. In contrast, when market participants execute via EAs, it is up to users to decide in what way and how fast to reduce market risk through the choice and parametrisation of algorithms – the result of which will be a trade-weighted average price known only at the end of execution plus an associated fee that EA providers typically charge for the usage of their EAs.

Adoption And Evolution Of FX Execution Algorithms

Drivers of FX execution algorithm adoption

EAs started to emerge in the FX market in the early-2000s, after having been first available in the equity market for several years. Based on information collected in the context of this report, usage of FX EAs has increased significantly in the past two decades, and is now estimated to account for 10–20% of daily spot FX volume in major currencies. According to the latest figures from the Bank for International Settlements (BIS) Triennial Central Bank Survey of Foreign Exchange and Over-the- counter Derivatives Markets, this equates to approximately $200–400 billion worth of FX spot traded via EAs each day globally.

Growing adoption of FX EAs has been driven in part by the rising electronification of the FX market. In spot FX, end users can now access liquidity via a range of electronic platforms. BIS FX Triennial Survey data suggests that electronic execution of spot FX has increased from about 55% of total spot FX turnover globally in 2010 to about 70% in 2019. The commoditised nature of FX spot trading has lent itself particularly well to rapid and widespread adoption of EAs in contrast to other markets such as corporate bonds or even FX options, which are much more diverse in terms of the products that are traded. Crucially, electronification has been supported by an exponential increase in computing power, lower data storage costs and the ability to transfer data almost instantly. These technological advancements have enabled a dramatic increase in both the frequency of trading activity and the speed of information flow in the FX market and have driven growing adoption of algorithms in FX, as they have in other financial markets.

FX EA adoption has been both a response and a contributor to continued and growing fragmentation across a wide array of electronic trading venues (Moore et al (2016)). This fragmentation has been driven by increasing competition among trading platforms and different market players especially by liquidity providers and new trading venues seeking to gain market share by offering innovative ways to access liquidity, match counterparties or provide trade data. Whereas in the past FX trading predominantly took place at just a few electronic trading venues currently known as the primary trading venues the market today comprises a large number of trading venues, each with its own unique set of trading rules and idiosyncrasies. FX EAs provide users with a means to monitor, navigate and execute in the fragmented FX market.

Regulatory changes have also contributed to increased EA adoption raising both the demand from end users for EA services and the supply of such services by liquidity providers. Many users use FX EAs to demonstrate compliance with so-called "best execution" requirements. This concept has gained significant traction among market participants following the implementation of the European MiFID II regulation in equities and other markets. While FX spot trading is typically not subject to the same regulatory requirements,4 the practices have likewise become commonplace even in the FX market. This rise in demand on the end user side for more automated and traceable execution has coincided with a notable reduction in risk appetite and principal risk warehousing on the liquidity providers' side, as bank balance sheets have become more constrained and costly to deploy in the aftermath of the global financial crisis (Debelle (2018)). This has further facilitated the proliferation of EAs, as they rely less on liquidity providers' capacity to absorb risk.

Finally, it should be noted that significant increases in the adoption of FX EAs have taken place over the last decade, which has been a period of historically subdued volatility in the FX market. One view is that this low volatility environment may have been supportive of user adoption, as the cost to users of taking on market risk during such periods is generally lower. That said, the sharp increase in FX EA usage in March 2020, when FX market volatility reached multi-year highs due to the Covid-19 pandemic, suggests that EAs remain a useful tool for users even during periods of increased volatility.

Evolution of FX execution algorithms

FX EAs have evolved in sophistication since their initial development. For instance, order slicing techniques have evolved from very simplistic approaches (based on time or number of slices) to more sophisticated approaches, with the latest generation able to dynamically adapt to market conditions. Broadly, there are three generations of algorithms:

- First-generation algorithms: The pioneering EAs generally had simple mechanical rules and were modelled after early algorithms in the equity market. The earliest FX EAs sought mainly to automate traders' practice of splitting parent orders into child orders, and followed strictly predetermined execution schedules. Their lack of sophistication generated distinct trading patterns that were easy for other market participants to detect.
- Second-generation algorithms: In subsequent iterations of FX EAs, providers strove to develop EAs that reduce market impact and avoid leaving distinct trading patterns by introducing some randomization in the size and timing of child orders. Nevertheless, these algorithms remained essentially on statically defined schedules, and continued to be susceptible to detection through the use of more sophisticated forecasting and pattern recognition techniques.
- Third-generation algorithms: By the mid-2010s, FX EAs started to use complex statistical models to drive algorithmic decisions and react more dynamically to changes in market conditions, with the aim of further reducing market impact and signalling. These EAs leveraged the increasing availability of real-time market data and computing power to assess market conditions in near- real time, and to inform subsequent execution decisions.

Prevalence Of FX Execution Algorithms

To gain insight into the usage and provision of FX EAs, the study group conducted a survey of large buy-side and sell-side market participants and a series of interviews with sophisticated market participants on preferences, offerings, motivations and challenges related to EA usage and provision. Among these large global institutions, roughly half were already using FX EAs, which is relatively high compared with other metrics on EAs' FX market share, but similar to results from a survey conducted by the GFXC, where 40% of respondents indicated that they use algorithms in their trading. Meanwhile, 55% of the potential providers (i.e banks and principal trading firms) in this group of large institutions were already offering FX EAs to their clients, and half of the remaining 45% noted they were considering offering these tools.

The survey also found that respondents were predominantly using EAs to trade FX spot, while EA usage for FX derivatives such as non-deliverable forwards (NDFs) where electronification did, not gain traction until 2008 was nascent. EA usage was most prevalent in liquid advanced economy currencies and used less for emerging market economy (EME) currencies. Users' average ticket sizes for advanced economy currencies were also about 50–100% larger than in EME currencies.

Users And Usage Of FX Execution Algorithms

Rationales for using FX execution algorithms

Survey respondents indicated that they use EAs primarily to reduce trading costs or market impact. Others may use EAs to ensure execution within some allocated period of time, or to trade close to or better than particular benchmarks. Finally, EAs are often used by market participants for greater operational efficiencies related to trade entry, trade monitoring and trade settlement. EAs automate what is otherwise a manual process. EA transactions are generally settled as one single ticket regardless of the number of individual child orders, significantly reducing operational costs.

Customer Groups Of FX Execution Algorithms

The study group's survey and interviews with EA providers suggest that institutional investors, such as asset managers and hedge funds, are among the more common users of EAs. These market participants have the ability to accept some market risk in order to reduce execution costs by minimising the bid-ask spread paid, and reducing the market impact of their trades, especially for large-sized orders.

Banks – typically small to mid-size regional banks that do not offer EAs – were also found to be users of EAs. Yet penetration rates and volumes transacted were smaller than those of the buy side. These entities generally used EAs alongside other modes of execution, and mainly targeted swift execution. Many provider banks also allow EA access inside their own organisation by desks that need to transact FX so-called in-house users. Notably, feedback from providers suggests that in-house users typically have access to the same suite of EAs as are offered to clients, suggesting that tools for strictly proprietary use do not seem widespread among providers.

Non-financial corporations represented the smallest segment of EA users among FX market participants, in line with their generally smaller FX footprint. Some corporations deliberately stay away from EAs, which requires relatively deep market expertise and understanding of technical aspects of FX transactions. These institutions prefer traditional execution styles such as voice trading for risk transfer or use of fixing orders. Others, however, find they have the required level of sophistication in their organization. These included several large multinational corporations for which EAs accounted for about 20–25% of their FX transaction volumes.

Finally, the survey also covered central banks' use of EAs, particularly 15 central banks from Asia-Pacific, Europe, North America and South America. Several central banks use EAs for

some activities such as reserve portfolio rebalancing, but such usage is relatively limited. Two central banks indicated possible future use of EAs, while more than half of those surveyed noted that EAs are not necessary for their trading activities, which is likely to be due to their relatively low frequency of trades. A few central banks suggested that they were not able to use EAs because of internal restrictions.

Preparing, Monitoring And Assessing The Use Of FX Execution Algorithms.

Most users apply EAs alongside other methods of execution. According to the survey results, EAs accounted for about 32% of their overall FX transaction volumes. And when determining whether to use an EA as opposed to other available means of execution, factors such as the size, currency pair, urgency and timing of the trade, and current liquidity conditions were typically considered.

Following a decision to use FX EAs, users also have to consider the choice of EA provider(s), the type of EA, the types of liquidity pool(s) /trading venues to execute in, and the parameterisation of the EA, all of which can affect the quality of execution. Notably, 64% of survey respondents who were using EAs had access to five to ten EA providers for their execution, implying a broad range of diverse EA offerings and specifications they had to choose from.

EA users also have to actively manage the trade-offs inherent in FX execution, e.g balancing market impact, market risk and opportunity cost. For instance, a more passive style of execution (involving waiting longer to finalise a trade) can lower the average price of execution in comparison with an aggressive trade (aimed at executing a trade quickly and/or involving crossing the bid-ask spread). Moreover, with the trade execution being distributed over a longer period of time and the individual child orders being smaller, market impact is also expected to be diminished. However, the more time a trade takes to be executed, the longer a market participant is exposed to market risk, which leads to higher disparity of actual outcomes.

Central Bank Usage Of FX Execution Algorithms

Among the 15 central banks that were surveyed, five central banks reported using EAs, with the extent of usage varying widely. One central bank indicated that it used EAs for almost 90% of overall volumes, two used EAs for about 25–30% of overall volumes, and the other two central banks used EAs for less than 10% of their overall FX volumes. Central banks' use of EAs for FX trading was concentrated in developed market currencies. More than half of them used time sliced algorithms for more than 70% of their transaction volume. Most central banks indicated that they have three or more FX EA providers.

Ten of the 15 central banks reported that they were not currently using EAs. Of these, two are currently considering the future use of EAs. Six highlighted that they did not consider the use of EAs necessary due to the relatively low volumes of their activities in the FX market, while two highlighted internal restrictions on the use of such systems. Overall, central banks were relatively cautious when using EAs and would not use them outside their main trading hours. When using EAs, all of them had people overseeing the execution. Most of the users attached limits to the orders, mainly limit price controls.

For central banks that have adopted EAs, the main motivations were to reduce trading costs, improve desk productivity, and access multiple liquidity pools in order to reduce market impact or footprint. Some central banks also cited improving execution consistency, transaction cost analysis and confidentiality as reasons for using EAs. None of the central banks highlighted pre-trade analytics or best execution requirements as key motivations for their

use of EAs trade-offs need to be addressed explicitly. Unsurprisingly, the recent GFXC survey found that lack of experience and understanding were common reasons why users choose not to make use of EAs at all.

Finally, when using EAs, users also highlighted the need to closely monitor market conditions, as well as to invest in people skills and technology to assess the performance of an execution ideally before, during and after a trade. For this, some rely on built-in execution analytics on EA platforms to monitor each trade throughout its life cycle. Pre-trade analytics give users' information on the prevailing market conditions and can be used in the selection of the specific execution algorithm and its appropriate parameters (eg over which time frame an order should be conducted). Real-time statistics may inform traders on the percentage of their order filled and whether execution is proceeding as scheduled, and help determine if a change in trading strategy or parameter is required. Finally, post-trade analytics such as transaction cost analysis (TCA) are used to assess the difference between the average cost of execution and a relevant benchmark (Box B). TCAs can help users better assess the extent to which they are adequately compensated for carrying the market risk of the execution.

Transaction Cost Analysis

Transaction cost analysis (TCA) is aimed at evaluating the quality of trade execution by comparing the final traded price of the execution against a benchmark. TCA can take many forms and will depend on largely on the type, size and frequency of FX activity being undertaken. For an active market participant, TCA typically forms part of the broader process of proving and documenting best execution, which has become a common practice in recent years. In particular, regulations such as MiFID II have placed increased demands on traders to demonstrate that they have taken "sufficient" steps to obtain the best execution possible on a trade. Even though spot FX is not within the scope of these regulations,

some participants apply similar best execution criteria across all products. Best execution regulatory requirements have subsequently encouraged the adoption of electronic trading more broadly and algorithmic trading more specifically, since electronic execution provides increased transparency around pricing and execution. TCA also helps the buy side manage relationships with their counterparties more effectively by allowing the discussion of execution quality to be based on quantitative metrics.

TCA depends on a number of key metrics. Detailed TCA requires accurate time stamps throughout the trade life cycle. These can then be measured against granular, high-frequency price data, and further analysis of price slippage, market impact and the ratio of rejected trades. Other metrics can include comparisons against the market at different times, such as when the order arrives at the trading desk, during the time of the execution and after the end of the execution.

TCA can be processed by liquidity providers, trading platforms, third-party TCA providers or the end user. Even though the calculations themselves are typically not too complicated, accessing and processing the required data as well as choosing an adequate benchmark can be a challenge in the absence of a complete consolidated tape in the FX market.

Providers Of Execution Algorithms

Institutions Providing FX Execution Algorithms And Their Offerings

The main providers of EAs tend to be large international banks, many of which initially built the algorithmic technology for their own trading activity. In response to end- user demand, they then adapted their technology to offer their clients a suite of EAs.

A small number of non-bank liquidity providers and specialised independent firms also provide client-facing FX EAs. Non-bank

liquidity providers chiefly refers to principal trading firms (PTFs) which developed highly sophisticated algorithms for their own trading activities. While, the provision of client-facing FX EAs by PTFs, is still nascent, it is expected to grow in the coming quarters. Finally, there is also a number of independent providers. These are technology firms that operate only as vendors (not as broker or dealer), providing clients with software and technical support to execute trades algorithmically.

A few small to mid-size banks, which generally lack the resources to independently develop EAs, offer their clients "white-labelled" EAs acquired from other providers, particularly technology firms. This approach allows these smaller banks to provide a much-demanded EA offering to their existing client base, while limiting their own development costs.

Distribution Channels And Tailoring Of FX Execution Algorithms

Providers make their algorithms available through multiple channels. Generally, the most sophisticated clients access EAs via Application Programming Interfaces (APIs) that allow connections to different data feeds or trading tools, while voice/chats provide relatively quick access for clients that do not want to set up systems or deal directly with the EA software. By volume of transactions, EAs are most frequently accessed via multi-dealer platforms, which allow users a single point of access to their various providers' EAs. These include platforms provided by third parties that "host" the EA providers' algorithms.

Beyond the channels outlined above, independent "technology players" often offer applications that can be positioned within the client's workflow with the incorporated EA tailored to suit the user's very specific needs. Buying such products can often be an intermediate solution between the cost of developing an algorithm suite in-house and relying on third-party providers, such as banks.

Provider-User Relationship

How orders are managed and executed depends on the role a liquidity provider assumes when transacting with a client. The FX Global Code states that market participants should understand and clearly communicate their respective roles and capacities when trading with one another. In this context, three kinds of models can be distinguished.

Traditionally, FX transactions between providers and users have been conducted on either an agency or a principal basis. If liquidity providers act as an agent, they do not take on credit, settlement or market risk themselves but execute orders only for the account and on behalf of the client – thereby acting as a conduit for liquidity and charging an agreed fee for doing so. In contrast, if providers act as a principal, they trade on their own account and on their own behalf and thus take on not only credit and settlement risk, but also market risk, which they can either warehouse or pass on via another trade.

In the context of FX EAs, market participants sometimes describe a third, hybrid form of relationship called "riskless principal." In this arrangement, the EA provider is acting as an agent with respect to market risk, but remains a principal in terms of counterparty and settlement risk exposure. This process effectively allows the EA provider to face the client in a principal capacity, except in the case of market risk, to which the EA provider has no exposure and is "riskless." The term "riskless principal" can carry different interpretations, and it is, therefore, important that participants are clear about the way in which it is applied.

From an economic perspective, a key element is how risks are shared. In most cases of EA usage, users seem to take on the market risk, whereas providers often cover credit risk and the operational risk of an error in the algorithm or missing controls. A crucial takeaway from this report is the need for users to seek clarity on the specific risks and liabilities they bear when using an EA. While the FX Global Code states that market participants should understand and clearly communicate their roles and capacities in managing orders or executing transactions, it is not clear that this allocation of role and responsibilities is spelt out clearly in the EA user agreements and disclosures.

Algorithm Safety

This section describes the key risks associated with the use of EAs. While operational risk stems from potential failures of algorithms, IT systems and processes as well as human errors, market risk arises through potential losses from adverse market moves.

These risks are not unique to FX EAs. Regulated securities markets are required to have controls in place to avoid systemic failures. In the FX market, however, due to their unregulated nature, the onus is on each EA provider, user and trading platform to provide its own safeguards against the risks of automated order execution.

In general, controls can be categorised by the phase of order execution in which they are used pre-trade, in-flight and post-trade.

Pre-trade controls serve as a final check on market orders before they are transmitted to the trading venues. They are required by regulation in the major currency jurisdictions. They allow for automatically blocking, halting or cancelling orders as soon as trades occur outside defined price thresholds, surpass a maximum size, or post an excess amount of orders automatically. The most common examples of controls include defining the maximum order size, checks of market data reasonability, price tolerance limits, or restricting the use of algorithms to trading hours where the market is most liquid. Another key control for avoiding erroneous behaviour is to use restrictions on participation ratios, i.e. limit the share of executed volume at any point in time to a certain percentage of total traded volume. These pre-trade controls become particularly important during times of heightened volatility, as has been emphasised by some providers in reflecting on their Covid-19 crisis experience when liquidity conditions worsened.

In-flight controls allow users or providers to adjust execution parameters during an execution, often when market conditions change, or the algorithm behaves in an undesirable or unexpected way. This is important, for example, in instances of particularly low liquidity when algorithms could dominate trading volume or stop trading altogether. Some EA providers have taken to alerting users mid-way during their transactions when market conditions change significantly. This allows users to decide if they should accelerate, pause or abort a trade in view of changing market conditions. EA providers may also use a built-in "kill switch" – a mechanism designed to automatically pause or halt execution instantaneously in case of malfunction, lack of liquidity, unexplained volatility or unusual levels of trading activity. Unlike circuit breakers and pauses applied by exchanges, kill switches for execution algorithms are implemented and triggered by individual institutions.

Post-trade controls involve continued monitoring of intraday market and credit exposures against limits, carrying trades with counterparties and taking mitigating actions when limits are breached. Transaction logs are reviewed to identify errors or potential conduct issues. At the same time, post-trade and event analysis is used by both users and providers to understand algorithm behaviour under particular scenarios and improve execution strategies and risk controls.

Outlook For The Use Of Execution Algorithms In The FX Market

Looking ahead, the outlook for further adoption of FX EAs will depend in large part on their ability to deliver higher execution effectiveness to users. This relies on EA providers' ability to use "best in class" technology to help users compete effectively in the

FX market. The future use and evolution of FX EAs are likely to be shaped by a number of developments:

The design and application of FX execution algorithms: what they are, what they do and how they work

Types of FX execution algorithms and key trade-offs

Typology of execution algorithms

There are a large number of FX EAs in use today. Notwithstanding the wide range of names for FX EAs, they are minor variations or hybrids of six basic archetypes:

- Time-sliced: algorithms that split parent orders into small child orders evenly over time. These algorithms are also known as time-weighted average price (TWAP) algorithms. In the example in Graph 4, an order is placed to sell USD 60 million USD/JPY through a TWAP algorithm with an execution time of 60 minutes. Based on this input, the broad schedule of execution would imply USD 1 million being executed every minute (black line). Current versions of TWAP algorithms typically provide for some randomisation in the timing of execution to reduce the predictability and signalling from orders (red line). The algorithms would also typically have some flexibility to opportunistically diverge from the broad execution schedule, to obtain a better transacted price (lower and upper trajectory bounds).
- Historical volume-sliced: algorithms that split parent orders into small child orders, scheduled according to historical measures of traded volume. Also known as historical volume-weighted average price (VWAP) algorithms.
- Percentage-of-volume (POV): algorithms that target a level of participation by current estimates of market volume in the particular currency pair.

- Pegged/tracker: algorithms that place orders "tracking" the market. The aim of the pegged/tracker algorithms is to execute the orders at levels better than the prevailing mid-price. To that end, the orders can be placed at the prevailing bid (if buying) or ask (if selling) price, or at levels just slightly above or below these. These algorithms are by nature the most passive, since they follow the market and generally do not trade at prices worse than mid-price.
- Implementation shortfall: algorithms that seek to minimize slippage, defined as the difference between the average price achieved by the EA throughout the entire execution and the arrival price, ie the mid-price at the start of the transaction. Transactions is typically completed within a relatively short time frame but is also aimed at reducing market impact through dynamically adapting the aggressiveness of execution to market conditions.
- Limit-based/sweeping: algorithms that aim for immediate or rapid execution by targeting all liquidity at various venues better than a user-specified limit price. In the example in Graph 5, an order is placed to sell USD 60 million USD/JPY through a limit-based algorithm which will generally first take stock of available liquidity at the various trading venues. In case of sufficient liquidity, the algorithm will instantaneously consume all available liquidity up to the order amount. In case of insufficient liquidity, the algorithm will have several options to complete the remaining part of the order, depending in large part on the user's preferences regarding the urgency of execution.

The relatively nascent development of more dynamic execution algorithms (e.g. implementation shortfall, pegged/tracker algorithms, percent-of-volume (POV) and hybrids of such), their use in the FX market is still relatively limited. However, among large tier-one banks that typically do offer such dynamic EAs, these kinds of algorithms account for a large proportion of EA volumes.

Moreover, anecdotal feedback from market participants suggests that more dynamic algorithms have performed quite well even during the Covid-19-related phase of elevated volatility in March 2020, which may imply that both offerings and usage of dynamic EAs are likely to rise further in the future.

Key trade-offs between execution objectives: the execution algorithm trilemma

The overarching goal of EAs is to achieve optimal execution. However, this concept comprises several competing dimensions and will be defined differently for different users depending on their individual objective functions. While, the various types of EAs, can accommodate several preferences with respect to execution, no single execution algorithm can optimise all aspects simultaneously. This is depicted by the execution algorithm trilemma.

Perold (1988) defines optimal execution as the goal of minimizing "implementation shortfall" in terms of (i) market impact and spread costs, (ii) market risk and (iii) opportunity costs or execution uncertainty:

- Market impact is the difference between a fair price benchmark prior to execution and the actual execution price. This difference incorporates both a spread and any market movement between these two moments in time. Market impact arises for two reasons: (i) the liquidity absorption of orders, ie when an order consumes available liquidity in the opposing direction; and (ii) the information content of orders.
- Market risk is the risk arising from fluctuations in market prices over the duration of the execution covering fluctuations in market prices unrelated to the actions of the EA.

- Opportunity cost is a measure of the forgone profit or avoided loss of not being able to transact the entire order within the allocated time period.

When executing, market participants have to determine the appropriate tradeoff between these three aspects of best execution. For instance, an EA that minimises market risk by executing as swiftly and aggressively as possible will not be able to minimize market impact simultaneously, as the latter would require a much more passive and thus slower execution. Similarly, an EA that seeks to respond dynamically to changing market conditions to optimise the trade-off between market risk and market impact may fail to complete if liquidity conditions are thinner than usual.

Importantly, no single EA can optimise all three components of implementation shortfall at the same time but will inevitably need to strike a balance between the three.

Market impact vs market risk. The main trade-off exists between market impact and market risk.

- This trade-off is exemplified by pegged/tracker algorithms (upper left), which minimise market impact by transacting almost exclusively with passive orders, but are exposed to substantial market risk as execution tends to be slow and market prices can drift substantially over the life of the execution. Conversely, limit-based/sweeping algorithms (lower left) minimise market risk by transacting very rapidly, but can have significant impact on market prices up to the limit price. Implementation shortfall algorithms (middle left) seek to internalize the trade-off between market impact and market risk in a single algorithm, by using proprietary market impact and market volatility risk models to determine an optimal approach to the transaction.

- Most algorithms include user-specified settings on the level of aggression or urgency for an execution, reflecting the importance of user choice in the determination of the trade-off between market impact and market risk. This choice might in turn be shaped by the user's view of the market. For instance, a user may prefer lower (higher) market risk if s/he expects prices to shift unfavourably (favourably) against his transaction, and a lower (higher) tolerance for market impact risk if markets are expected to be illiquid (deep).

Trading costs vs opportunity costs. Another important trade-off is between trading costs (comprising market impact and market risk) and opportunity costs.

- The trade-off is exemplified by the TWAP and historical VWAP algorithms, which provide users with with a high degree of execution certainty, but are unable to optimally manage trading costs as they do not respond dynamically to market conditions. For instance, a TWAP could be set to transact gradually, but will suffer from high exposure to market risk. Conversely, the same algorithm may be set to transact quickly to minimize market risk but will result in significant market impact if the availability of liquidity in the market is lower than expected.
- POV algorithms are better able to manage the trade-off between market risk and market impact, as they will dynamically adjust to the availability of liquidity in the market. Still, they risk opportunity costs as they cannot guarantee completion within a fixed period.

Many providers increasingly recognise that users typically have preferences that do not lie on the corner solutions of the trilemma. Users ideally want to reduce market risk, reduce market impact and have a degree of execution certainty. Hybrid algorithms attempt to bridge this gap with logic to switch between two or more types of algorithms in response to changes in market conditions. One example of such a hybrid algorithm can switch between a TWAP and a limit-based/sweeping algorithm when prices shift from one zone to another. The algorithm may start as a TWAP but will transition to a sweeping algorithm when prices move to a more favourable level.

For some users, the way they benchmark the execution performance will determine their choice of algorithm. This is especially evident for users who undertake large-sized transactions that can be spread out over the course of a day. Widely used benchmarks in such circumstances include VWAP or TWAP benchmarks. Other users that may have requirements to complete their orders in a relatively shorter time could use a point-in-time benchmark like the arrival price. Such users may prefer to use implementation shortfall algorithms since such algorithms seek to minimise slippage relative to the arrival price.

Derived data. Execution venues typically use the above market data and combinations thereof to compute statistical measures, including volatility indicators, cross currency/asset correlation and trends to further enrich the basis for execution decision-making.

Smart Order Routing

The FX market comprises a plethora of trading platforms and liquidity pools, which differ in terms of transparency, anonymity, internalisation practices and firmness of liquidity. EAs enable users to navigate this complex market structure by using a technology known as smart order routing (SOR).

SOR constitutes a powerful tool that entails key execution decisions: it governs which liquidity is accessed in which pool, at what time and at which price. It is the gateway to FX liquidity, the last interface between the order and the market. All subsequent actions of execution relate to the actual placement of EA orders in the market, the execution scheduling, which is discussed in the following section.

While the "smart" component of SOR concerns the decision logic related to the choice of trading venue, the degree of sophistication of smart order routers varies. In the more basic variations, order routing logic itself is rather simple, e.g. seeking the best available price. More recent improvements in SOR take into account other factors, including quoted size, queue length, and venue efficacy measures (eg fill ratio and fill probability) to determine the allocation of orders across trading venues. This is enabled by the availability of more real-time data and rising IT capacity/infrastructure investment. Order routing has also been one of the first areas where machine learning techniques have been employed for the development of more flexible EAs, which include self-learning techniques that enhance their ability to respond to market conditions in real time.

Differences in price impact profiles are also important when routing orders to different liquidity pools. Routing rules generally assume a lower price impact for fully internalized orders that is, for client orders that a liquidity provider can offset internally with orders from other clients, without having to resort to an external trading venue, where the trade becomes visible. In contrast, transactions taking place at external trading venues are assumed to result in a larger price impact because of the information leakage associated with a "lit" trade. These assumptions are regularly verified through transaction cost analysis.

Execution Scheduling

Another key function of FX EAs is to slice users' orders into smaller ones in order to limit market impact and to manage the trade-offs outlined in the trilemma above. The decision logic for pricing and scheduling of child orders is an important aspect. Indeed it is typically the design of this decision logic that determines the typology of an FX EA. Further detail on the decision logic and execution profiles of the six archetypes of FX EAs can be found in Annex.

Liquidity Pools Accessed By FX Execution Algorithms

As noted before, EAs help users navigate the fragmented FX market by providing access to different liquidity pools. While primary electronic venues remain important sources of liquidity for price discovery in the FX market, their market share has dwindled in recent years, and many alternative ECNs and liquidity pools have emerged. These various types of liquidity pools can be characterized along two broad dimensions: their degree of anonymity and their use of principal or franchise liquidity.

***Anonymous vs disclosed*:** Anonymous liquidity pools based on a central limit order book (CLOB) do not allow apportioning of liquidity or price discrimination via the use of customised tags or other means to identify a counterparty pre-trade. They typically rely on "firm liquidity," ie trades are matched without the optionality for rejection. In contrast, disclosed liquidity pools or alternative venues allow for liquidity partitioning via the use of customised tags. They typically include "non-firm liquidity," ie the option for counterparties at the venue to reject orders within a specific time frame ("last look").

***Principal vs franchise liquidity*:** In principal liquidity pools, the liquidity provider assumes the risk of the position itself, ie transactions are executed against the market-making desk of the liquidity provider. In franchise liquidity pools, the liquidity provider uses flow from clients to hedge offsetting flows from other clients, ie by internalising rather than hedging on external markets. This would include less lit forms of trading such as dark pools, where there may be relatively little information provided to participants on prices, depth of market, counterparties and other such information which is typically available at other venues on either a pre-trade or a post-trade basis. The main aim of this less lit form of trading is to reduce market impact, with high levels of internalisation expected to improve execution performance. The largest dealers report internalisation ratios of as high as 90%. However, the true market share of internalisation is hard to gauge, as there are multiple interpretations of the term "internalisation." As a result, the reported degree of internalisation can vary from one provider to the other. For instance, internalization at one extreme could include only volumes transacted between users of an EA platform. This would tend to be quite low. At the other extreme, internalization could include the amount of EA volumes routed to a provider's market-making desk, or even include those externalized into mid-matching venues.

Use Of Child Orders And Replenishment Rates

By design, EAs slice the user's transaction or parent order into smaller-sized orders called child orders. The size of these child orders is often close to the minimum transaction size on trading venues, which facilitates the absorption of the order and thereby limits market impact.

In order to achieve the required transaction turnover, passive EAs repeatedly place new individual child orders close to or at the prevailing best bid or offer prices. Hence, in contrast to single block trades that are placed inside the order book in full size at once, EAs constantly "replenish" their quoted liquidity. The rate at which individual orders are being renewed is known as the "replenishment rate."

EAs are also able to place orders quite close to the best market bid and offer as they seek to respond dynamically to price developments. In contrast, manual traders that have slower responses to market developments may tend to place resting orders along various levels in the order book to ensure their orders are transacted.

As a consequence, electronic order books with significant participation by EAs tend to look shallower in terms of visible liquidity at any point in time, as compared with markets in which there is more participation by manual traders. However, this may not imply poorer liquidity if replenishment of consumed liquidity is sufficiently quick and continuous.

The pricing of child orders, i.e. the level of aggression of an algorithm, is mainly determined by the type of algorithm, and to a certain extent by user-defined parameters. While pegged/tracker algorithms give rise almost exclusively to passive orders, a limit-based or sweeping algorithm will rely on almost exclusively on the use of aggressive orders. Most of the other algorithms will use a mix of passive and aggressive orders, and face choices in each time step related to the optimal degree of aggressiveness of the orders.

Such micro-decisions related to execution are usually taken based on internally calibrated static values that determine specific parameters, such as the amount of spread an algorithm is willing to cross to achieve a fill under given conditions. This applies especially to EAs that aim to minimise market impact and spread cost (eg implementation shortfall algorithms), as it is essential for these types of algorithms to consider how their orders affect the market.

In this regard, the modelling of market impact becomes a crucial ingredient for the timing of individual child orders. One approach to market impact modelling assumes that market impact decays very slowly towards zero in a pattern usually referred to as the "mark-out pattern" or "price signature." This means that every child order implies an opportunity cost for later child orders: Because of the lingering price impact of the current order, a less favourable price has to be paid for subsequent orders. Other more recent approaches to market impact modelling may also take into account the implications of individual orders on aggregate order flow and imbalances.

Implications For Market Functioning

This section aims to assess the benefits and risks from the increased use of execution algorithms from a market functioning perspective and, where relevant highlights areas for further research and possible policy recommendations.

Definition Of Market Functioning

Market functioning is a difficult concept to capture in a simple definition. For the purpose of this report, we build on the general definition provided in another recent Markets Committee study and apply it to the analysis of the use of EAs in the FX market. According to that definition, a well functioning market is a market that allows timely and efficient access for participants who wish to trade and that creates price signals that reflect the underlying fundamentals of the relevant currency markets.

Hence, An Effectively Functioning Market Must Fulfil Two Fundamental Functions:

1. **Provide adequate access and matching**: allow participants with diverse trading interests to be brought together in an efficient and cost-effective manner in order to adjust and redistribute their financial exposures.
2. **Allow proper price discovery**: incorporate all relevant publicly available information in an appropriate, prompt and reliable manner, in turn generating meaningful price signals that allow an efficient allocation of resources.

Based on this broad definition, the study group identified three main issues relevant for market functioning that may arise from the increasing use of EAs in the FX market: (i) changes in the microstructure of the FX market; (ii) considerations for the effective use of EAs from a market participants' perspective; and (iii) market-wide implications of the use of EAs.

Market Microstructure Changes And Implications

A key finding of this report is that EAs are both a response and a contributor to the changing microstructure of the FX market. From a market functioning perspective, three drivers that both affect and are affected by the use of EAs are particularly relevant: (i) the increasing fragmentation of the FX market; (ii) price discovery and the role of internalisation; and (iii) the changing patterns of liquidity dynamics.

Market Fragmentation

EAs help market participants overcome hurdles associated with market fragmentation. The FX market is complex, with trading taking place simultaneously on a bilateral basis and at many different trading venues. This reduces the visibility of market transactions, complicates the analysis of market conditions and makes price discovery difficult.

Assessing liquidity in a fragmented market is very challenging. As trading interest may be posted simultaneously across multiple trading venues, this can create a so-called "liquidity mirage," i.e an illusion of deeper liquidity than is actually available for transacting. Once trading interest is matched at one venue, it could be withdrawn immediately from other venues in the market. Alternatively, hidden trading interest can create the perception of lower liquidity than is available. This so-called latent liquidity can emerge when traders opt to hide the actual size of their trading interest. Many providers try to differentiate their EA offering by, among other things, the quality of the various liquidity pools that their EAs can route orders to, and the logic applied in doing so.

In this fragmented environment, an important benefit of EAs is their ability to provide access to liquidity across multiple trading venues. By routing orders to the best available source of liquidity, EAs are an effective tool to help match diverse trading interests. Most providers surveyed indicate that their algorithms access more than 10 liquidity pools. As EAs express trading interests across different venues, market participants are more likely to find a matching interest and execute their trades at the venue that provides the best execution outcome.

Price Discovery And The Role Of Internalisation

EAs contributes to improving the price discovery process. By slicing larger orders into smaller pieces, EAs enable the market to absorb a large order at or close to the best bid or offer available without creating a large implementation shortfall. This allows for smoother price dynamics. By routing orders to a multitude of venues, EAs also help incorporate price signals across the fragmented market. In this way, they support an efficient market-wide price discovery process.

EAs facilitates the internalization of customer flows. As orders are split into smaller pieces and spaced out over time, there is a higher probability that these smaller pieces can be offset internally with trades from other customers (i.e. without having to trade on external trading venues).

Internalisation can be beneficial to both customers and dealers. Dealers benefit from internalisation by avoiding intermediation costs (e.g the costs associated with trading on external venues). Similarly, internalisation can benefit users by reducing the information leakage and hence market impact typically associated with conducting trades on a visible ("lit") trading venue, such as a primary trading venue. This is why many EAs can be configured to route child orders to internal liquidity pools. That said, some market participants point out that certain dealers may try to skew their prices up or downwards, depending on their interest to buy or sell a particular position. This practice may negate some of the market impact reduction initially sought by customers, as skewing prices may reveal information to the broader market.

From a market functioning perspective, a trade-off can emerge between price discovery and internalisation. What is optimal for an individual market participant may not be optimal for broader market functioning. From a market's perspective, "lit trading," e.g. submitting an order to an external trading venue where the order book is displayed is typically preferable, as market prices can more fully reflect available economic information to all market participants. From an individual market participant's perspective, however, "taking trades into the dark" through internalisation may be preferable, as it generally reduces the information leakage and, hence, the market impact of a trade. In other words, the individual incentives for dark trading to limit market impact contrast with the market-wide desirability of lit trading to ensure a smooth price discovery process.

The impact of internalisation on price discovery warrants greater analysis and close monitoring over time. Current levels of internalization or other forms of "dark" trading are not seen as negatively impacting the price discovery process at the moment, or at least not substantially. However, market participants agree that there is likely to be some minimum yet still unknown threshold of necessary trading volume taking place on primary venues to maintain the integrity of the price discovery process. This is because prices from primary trading venues are used as reference prices for other trading venues (lit and dark) as well as for bilateral trading. Thus, understanding how much "lit" vs "dark" trading is needed for primary trading venues to remain reliable sources for reference prices will help better assess the role of EAs in market functioning.

More generally, deepening central banks' understanding of the precise role of primary vs "dark" trading venues will be useful in monitoring the changing nature of price formation dynamics in highly automated and fragmented markets. While the present report focuses on the FX market, this area of analysis could be relevant for other markets facing rapid electronification, such as fixed income markets. Hence, it could become an integral part of the ongoing efforts of central banks to adapt their market monitoring frameworks to increasingly fast and electronic financial markets.

New Liquidity Dynamics

The increasing use of EAs is contributing to the emergence of new liquidity dynamics in the FX market. Several market participants mentioned in interviews conducted by the study group that visible depth in public order books is lower today than it used to be. While this phenomenon is largely driven by the automation of FX trading, there are signs that EAs specifically are contributing to the thinning of the order book as they slice large orders into smaller ones and spread them over time.

However, as long as the order book is replenished fast enough, a thinner order book does not necessarily reduce market functioning. As velocity of trading increases with electronification, some market participants point out that liquidity replenishment, ie the rate at which new top-of-book liquidity is renewed, is what matters for a well functioning market. If market-makers know that liquidity takers demand liquidity in smaller amounts split over time, there is little need to provide a large amount of liquidity at any point in time, provided new liquidity is replenished at an adequate rate. Historically, when trading was done manually, the market relied predominantly on the availability of large limit orders to buffer shocks in periods of stress. Therefore, a thinner order book would mean a lower ability of the market to absorb shocks, such as from unanticipated news or "fat finger" trades. Today, a thinner order book is not necessarily a sign of fragility, as long as the liquidity demanded by EAs can be matched, in small pieces, with liquidity provision at adequate replenishment rates.

Initial observations from the Covid-19 crisis support this conclusion. Most market participants interviewed by the study group stated that EAs were able to continuously execute transactions throughout this period of heightened price volatility, albeit at somewhat higher cost of execution. As market volatility was generally seen as high but not extreme, this recent episode should not be used to draw general conclusions regarding the robustness of order book dynamics and EA performance during shocks.

The use of EAs reinforces the changing pattern of liquidity dynamics. Liquidity providers will always require a premium to buy or sell large amounts instantaneously, because quoting large amounts at tight prices exposes them to adverse market developments and selection risk the risk of being exploited by market participants with superior information or faster technology. The ability of EAs to split large orders into smaller pieces therefore provides an interesting alternative means of execution. Furthermore, the more EAs are being used and the "thinner" the order book becomes the more trades may need to be split into smaller pieces to reduce market impact, reinforcing the importance of EAs.

To adequately assess liquidity conditions in highly fragmented markets such as the FX market, novel liquidity indicators may require to support market monitoring activities in fragmented and fast-paced markets. Immediately available and visible liquidity might be lower and more dispersed. But as long as algorithms can trade in a continuous way, market functioning is not necessarily impaired provided the order book can be replenished quickly. Traditional order book-based indicators may no longer be a good proxy to assess liquidity conditions. Instead, indicators that capture the rate at which liquidity is replenished may be more useful to the use of EAs. Provided the market relevance of EAs continues to grow, central banks could benefit from developing indicators that are specifically designed to account for the changes in the liquidity dynamics. Developing such indicators, however, may be costly and require novel technologies.

Overall, EAs appear to have a net positive impact on the FX market microstructure. In normal market conditions, the ability of EAs to generate quotes that reflect fresh information quickly, and to transmit this information simultaneously across multiple liquidity venues, improves the price discovery process and matching in an otherwise highly fragmented market. Although visible liquidity is likely to be thinner due to the slicing of orders into small pieces, market resilience is not affected as long as the order book is replenished sufficiently fast. Over time, however, by reinforcing the trend towards smaller order sizes and internalisation, EAs could contribute to a reduction in visibility of depth and turnover on primary markets, which could, in the extreme, hamper price discovery and market functioning.

Considerations For The Effective Use Of FX Execution Algorithms

FX EAs endows market participants with more direct control over trade execution and can help them trade more effectively. However, with greater control also comes a greater responsibility for end users to understand, monitor and manage risks appropriately. First, users need to be aware of and actively manage the risks associated with the use of EAs and their inherent trade-offs. Second, they need to evaluate to what extent the superior execution quality compensates for the higher risk they bear. Third, and as a key prerequisite, they need access to relevant information and market data to understand, analyze and make effective use of FX EAs. All three aspects are central to ensuring an efficient redistribution of trading interests.

Managing Execution Risks And Their Trade-Offs

Adequate controls are essential to mitigate operational risks of EAs. EAs allows embedding controls within the execution process. This is an improvement over manual trading, where the applicability and enforcement of controls are far more limited. However, risks may take a new form or a new order of magnitude due to the reliance of EAs on new technology, their higher information-processing speed and greater level of automation.

In contrast to trading at the risk transfer price, users executing via EAs carry market risk for an extended period of time. Furthermore, the use of EAs may alter users' trading habits, as automation enables trading over time zones outside their normal operating hours, which might introduce a new source of risk. In this context, users need to have adequate controls in place to address such risks.

Users need to be aware of the trade-offs inherent in algorithmic execution and need to actively manage them. They face the trade-offs related to execution, as outlined by the Execution Algorithm Trilemma, and need to manage those themselves. Consequently, users' choices related to the style of execution need to weigh market risk against other potential costs such as the market impact or the risk of not fully completing a trade within some allocated period.

Additionally, the resilience of the new distribution of risk is untested so far. The development of EA usage has in large part been concomitant with a global low volatility environment. As a result, there are concerned that, during a stress event, the market might not be able to withstand shocks as efficiently as in the past when banks were the ultimate risk bearers. Encouragingly, the most recent experience during the Covid-19 crisis has been positive in this regard. However, with the most recent bout in volatility being high but far from extreme, an ultimate test in the context of disorderly market conditions remains to be faced.

Evaluating Execution quality

Evaluating the extent to which users are adequately compensated for the additional execution risk they bear is challenging even if one had access to all existing market data. However, given the non-negligible market risk that users carry in the context of EAs, users should scrutinise thoroughly whether a particular EA does in fact deliver on its promise of superior execution quality in comparison with alternative means of execution and adjusted for the additional market risk incurred. In this context, performance analytics come into play.

Ideally, proper performance analytics cover the entire life cycle of an execution. Pre-trade and real-time analytics help inform decisions such as the selection of the execution benchmark, the choice of liquidity provider(s), and the choice of EA itself and its parameterization. Post-trade analytics help evaluate execution performance and can, thereby, serve to validate pre-trade and at-trade decisions. Over time, these performance analytics tools can help improve the execution handling.

When assessing EA performance, it is key to consider both the explicit and the implicit costs of execution. Looking at explicit headline costs e.g bid-ask spreads and fees alone would be incomplete and potentially misleading. Rather, implicit trading costs such as market impact and opportunity costs also need to be taken into account. In addition, the soundness of performance analytics crucially depends on the ability to access independent, external sources of data rather than relying on potentially subjective data and metrics offered by liquidity providers. Such data also comes at a high cost, which needs to be included in the overall performance analysis.

Testing the performance and impact of EAs is technologically challenging. Because many factors can influence the impact of the algorithm, many executions in similar market conditions are necessary to obtain a statistically robust metric that disentangles the performance of the algorithm itself from the underlying market dynamics. The fact that EAs both react to and affect the market constitutes a simultaneous causality problem that further complicates inference. Meaningful analysis may only be possible in a dedicated test environment or through pooling of execution data across many market participants. While the industry is testing the latter, it may face practical obstacles such as confidentiality concerns. Central banks could explore the benefits of pooling expertise and resources to conduct relevant analyses on a dedicated and technologically fit-for-purpose platform to reduce costs while expanding knowledge.

Access To Data And Information

As outlined above, the effective use of FX EAs requires expertise as well as adequate information and data. However, access to market data varies and can be costly. High- quality data on the FX market are not accessible to all end users and can depend on users' ability to pay, their business model and their degree of sophistication. Some market participants are able to pay for access to faster and more granular data thereby further widening information gaps in the market. Some market data, however, may not be available to certain market participants, because they are restricted, e.g. dealers that act as a price-maker for a certain minimum amount of volume per day. Finally, access to data is also dependent on the number of liquidity providers a user has access to with the most sophisticated user groups typically enjoying the broadest menu of data available. Even for this study group, collecting robust metadata in the context of EAs constituted an unsurmountable challenge. As a result, some empirical analysis could not be conducted, as the study group was unable to obtain sufficiently broad, independent trade data where EA-induced transactions were identifiable.

Transparency of trading activity in the FX market is limited by virtue of the market remaining primarily bilateral and OTC in nature, fostering a relatively high degree of opaqueness. In particular, the absence of a common master record of data ("central tape") on transactional prices and volumes makes any objective evaluation of reference prices, benchmark prices or execution performance a difficult task.

CHAPTER 4

Mindset Of An Investor

Speculator Vs Trader Vs Investor

Depending on how you would like to participate in the market, you can choose to speculate, trade or invest. All the three types of participation are different from one another. One has to take a stance on the type of market participant he would like to be. Having clarity on this can have a huge impact on his Profit & Loss account.

To help you get this clarity, let us consider a market scenario and identify how each one of the market participants (speculator, trader, and investor) would react to it.

RBI in the next two days is expected to convene to announce their latest stance on the monetary policy. Owing to the high and sticky inflation, RBI has hiked the interest rates during the monetary policy reviews. Increase in interest rates, as we, know means tougher growth prospects for Corporate India–hence corporate earnings would take a hit.

Assume there are three market participants –Sunil, Tarun, and Girish. Each of them view the above scenario differently, and hence would take different actions in the market. Let us go through their thought process.

Sunil: He thinks through the situation and his thought process is as follows:

He feels the interest rate are at an unsustainably high level

- High interest rates hampers the growth of corporate India.
- He also believes that RBI has hiked the interest rates to a record high level and it would be tough for RBI to hike the rate again
- He looks at what the popular analysts on TV are opinionating about the situation, and he is happy to note that his thoughts and the analyst thoughts are similar
- He concludes that RBI is likely to cut the rates if, not for keeping the interest rates flat
- As an outcome, he expects the market to go up

To put his thoughts into action, he buys call options of State Bank of India.

Tarun: He has a slightly different opinion about the situation. His thought process is as below:

- He feels expecting RBI to cut the rates is wishful thinking. In fact, he is of the opinion that nobody can clearly predict what RBI is likely to do
- He also identifies that the volatility in the markets is high, hence he believes that option contracts are trading at very high premiums
- He knows from his previous experience (via back testing) that the volatility is likely to drop drastically just after RBI makes its announcement.

To put his thoughts into action, he sells 5 lots of Nifty Call options and expects to square off the position around the announcement time.

Girish: He has a portfolio of 12 stocks which he has been holding for over 2 years. Though he is a keen observer of the economy, he has no view on what RBI is likely to do. He is also, not worried about the outcome of the policy as he anyway plans to hold on to his shares for a long period of time. Hence with this perspective he feels the monetary policy is yet another short term passing tide in the market and will not have a major impact on his portfolio. Even if it does, he has both the time and patience to hold on to his shares.

However, Girish plans to buy more of his portfolio shares if the market overreacts to the RBI news and his portfolio stocks falls steeply after the announcement is made.

Now, what RBI will eventually decide and who makes money is not our concern. The point is to identify who is a speculator, a trader, and an investor based on their thought process. All the three men seem to have logic based on which they have taken a market action. Please note, Girish's decision to do nothing itself is a market action.

Sunil seems to be highly certain on what RBI is likely to do and therefore his market actions are oriented towards a rate cut. In reality, it is impossible to call a shot on what RBI (or for that matter any regulator) will do. These are complex matters and not straightforward to analyze. Betting on blind faith, without a rational reasoning backing ones decision is speculation. Sunil seems to have done just that.

Tarun has arrived at what needs to be done based on a plan. If you are familiar with options, he is simply setting up a trade to take advantage of the high options premium. He is clearly not speculating on what RBI is likely to do as it does not matter to him. His view is simple volatility is high; hence the premiums are attractive for an options seller. He is expecting the volatility to drop just prior to RBI decision.

Is he speculating on the fact that the volatility will drop? Not really, because he seems to have back tested his strategy for similar scenarios in the past. A trader designs all his trades and not just speculates on an outcome.

Girish, the investor on the other hand seems to be least bit worked up on what RBI is expected to do. He sees this as a short term market noise which may not have any major impact on his portfolio. Even if it did have an impact, he is of the opinion that his portfolio will eventually recover from it. Time is the only luxury markets offer, and Girish is keen on leveraging this luxury to the maximum. In fact, he is even prepared to buy more of his portfolio stocks in case the market overreacts. His idea is to hold on to his positions for a long period of time and not get swayed by short term market movements.

All the three of them have different mindsets which leads them to react differently to the same situation. The focus of this chapter is to understand why Girish, the investor, has a long term perspective and not really bothered about short term movements in the market.

The Compounding Effect

To appreciate why Girish decided to stay invested and not really react to short term market movement, one has to understand how money compounds. Compounding in simple terms is the ability of money to grow when the gains of year 1 is reinvested for year

For example consider you invest Rs.100 which is expected to grow at 20% year on year (recall this is also called the CAGR). At the end of the first year, the money is expected to grow to Rs.120. At the end of year 1 you have two options:

1. Let Rs.20 in profits remain invested along with the original principal of Rs.100 or
2. Withdraw the profits of Rs.20.

You decide not withdraw Rs.20 profit; instead you decide to reinvest the money for the 2nd year. At the end of 2nd year, Rs.120 grows to Rs.144. At the end of 3rd year Rs.144 grows to Rs.173. So on and so forth.

Compare this with withdrawing Rs.20 profits every year. Had you opted to withdraw Rs.20 every year then at the end of 3rd year the profits would have been just Rs. 60.

However since you decided to stay invested, the profits at the end of 3 years is Rs.173. A good Rs.13 or 21.7% over Rs.60 is generated just because you opted to do nothing and decided to stay invested. This is called the compounding effect. Let us take this analysis a little further, have a look at the chart below:

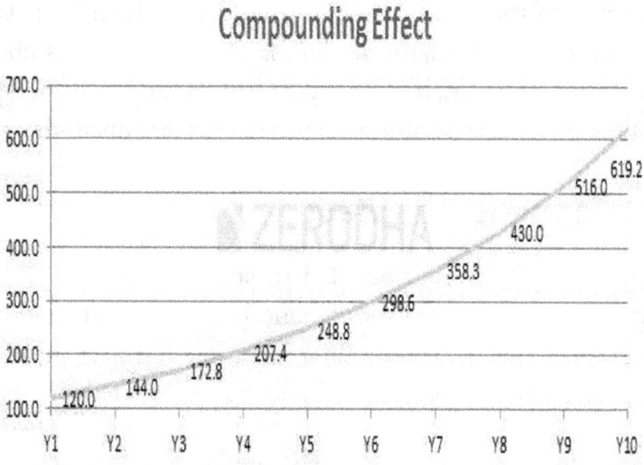

The chart above shows how Rs.100 invested at 20% grows over a 10 year period. If you notice, it took almost 6 years for the money to grow from Rs.100 to Rs.300. However, the next Rs.300, was generated in only 4 years, i.e., from the 6th to 10th year.

This is in fact the most interesting property of the compounding effect. The longer you stay invested, the harder (and faster) the money works for you. This is exactly why Girish decided to stay invested – to exploit luxury of time that market offers.

All investments made based on fundamental analysis require the investors to stay committed for the long term. The investor has to develop this mindset while he chooses to invest.

Does Investing Work?

Think about a sapling – if you give it the right amount of water, manure, and care would it not grow? Of course it will. Likewise, think about a good business with healthy sales, great margins, innovative products, and an ethical management. Is it not obvious that the share price of such companies would appreciate? In some situations, the price appreciation may delay, but it certainly will always appreciate. This has happened over and over again across markets in the world, including India.

An investment in a good company defined by investable grade attributes will always yield results. However, one has to develop the appetite to digest short term market volatility.

Investible Grade Attributes? What Does That Mean?

Like we discussed briefly in the previous chapter, an investible grade company has a few distinguishable characteristics. These characteristics can be classified under two heads namely the 'Qualitative aspect' and the 'Quantitative aspects.' The process of evaluating a fundamentally strong company includes a study of both these aspects. In fact in my personal investment practice, I give the qualitative aspects a little more importance over the quantitative aspects.

The Qualitative aspect mainly involves understanding the non numeric aspects of the business. This includes many factors such as:

1. **Management's Background** – Who are they, their background, experience, education, do they have the merit to run the business, any criminal cases against the promoters etc
2. **Business Ethics** – is the management involved in scams, bribery, unfair business practices
3. **Corporate Governance** – Appointment of directors, organization structure, transparency etc
4. **Minority Shareholders** – How does the management treat minority shareholders, do they consider their interest while taking corporate actions
5. **Share Transactions** – Is the management buying/selling shares of the company through clandestine promoter groups
6. **Related Party Transactions** – Is the company tendering financial favors to known entities such as promoter's relatives, friends, vendors, etc. at the cost of the shareholders' funds?
7. **Salaries Paid To Promoters** – Is the management paying themselves a hefty salary, usually a percentage of profits
8. **Operator Activity In Stocks** – Does the stock price display unusual price behavior especially at a time when the promoter is transacting in the shares
9. **Shareholders** – Who is the significant shareholders in the firm, who are the people with above 1% of the outstanding shares of the company
10. **Political Affiliation** – Is the company or its promoters too close to a political party? Does the business require constant political support?
11. **Promoter Lifestyle** – Are the promoters too flamboyant and loud about their lifestyle? Do they like to display their wealth? A red flag is raised when any of the factors

mentioned above do not fall in the right place. For example, if a company undertakes too many related party transactions, then it would send a signal of favoritism and malpractice by the company. This is not good in the long run. So even if the company has great profit margins, malpractice is not acceptable. It would only be a matter of time before the market discovers matters pertaining to 'related party transactions' and punishes the company by bringing the stock price lower. Hence an investor would be better off not investing in companies with great margins if such a company scores low on corporate governance.

Qualitative aspects are not easy to uncover because these are very subtle matters. However a diligent investor can easily figure this out by paying attention to annual report, management interviews, news reports etc. As we proceed through this module we will highlight various qualitative aspects.

The quantitative aspects are matters related to financial numbers. Some of the quantitative aspects is straightforward, while some of them are not. For example cash held in inventory is straight forward however 'inventory number of days' is not. This is a metric that needs to be calculated. The stock markets pay a lot of attention to quantitative aspects.

Quantitative Aspects Include Many Things, To Name Few:

1. Profitability and its growth
2. Margins and its growth
3. Earnings and its growth
4. Matters related to expenses
5. Operating efficiency
6. Pricing power
7. Matters related to taxes
8. Dividends payout

9. Cash flow from various activities
10. Debt – both short term and long term
11. Working capital management
12. Asset growth
13. Investments
14. Financial Ratios

The list is virtually endless. In fact, each sector has different metrics. **For example:**

For A Retail Industry:

For An Oil And Gas Industry:

- Total number of stores Oil to Natural Gas revenue ratio
- Average sales per store Exploration costs
- Total sales per square foot Opening oil balance (inventory)
- Merchandise margins Developed reserves
- Owned store to franchisee ratio Total production growth

1. The mindset of a trader and an investor is different
2. The investor has to develop an investment mindset if he is serious about investing
3. The investor should stay invested for a long period of time for the returns to compound
4. The speed at which the money doubles increases the more time drastically you stay invested. This is one of the properties of compounding
5. Every investment has to be evaluated on two aspects – qualitative & quantitative
6. Qualitative aspects revolve around the non numeric information related to the company
7. The quantitative aspects involve analyzing numeric data. The financial statements are the important source of finding the quantitative data.

How to Read the Annual Report of a Company

What is an Annual Report?

The annual report (AR) is a yearly publication by the company and is sent to the shareholders and other interested parties. The annual report is published by the end of the Financial Year, and all the data made available in the annual report is dated to 31st March. The AR is usually available on the company's website (in the investors section) as a PDF document or one can contact the company to get a hard copy of the same.

Since the annual report is published by the company, whatever is mentioned in the AR is assumed to be official. Hence, any misrepresentation of facts in the annual report can be held against the company. To give you a perspective, AR contains the auditor's certificates (signed, dated, and sealed) certifying the sanctity of the financial data included in the annual report.

Potential investors and the present shareholders are the primary audience for the annual report. Annual reports should provide the most pertinent information to an investor and should also communicate the company's primary message. For an investor, the annual report must be the default option to seek information about a company. Of course, there are many media websites claiming to give the financial information about the company; however, the investors should avoid seeking information from such sources. Remember the information is more reliable if we get it get it directly from the annual report.

Why would the media website misrepresent the company information you may ask? Well, they may not do it deliberately but they may be forced to do it due to other factors. For example, the company may like to include 'depreciation' in the expense side of P&L, but the media website may like to include it under a separate header. While this would not impact the overall numbers, it does interrupt the overall sequencing of data.

What To Look For In An Annual Report?

The annual report has many sections that contain useful information about the company. One has to be careful while going through the annual report as there is a very thin line between the facts presented by the company and the marketing content that the company wants you to read.

Let us briefly go through the various sections of an annual report and understand what the company is trying to communicate in the AR. For the sake of illustration, I have taken the Annual Report of Amara Raja Batteries Limited, belonging to Financial Year 2013-2014. As you may know Amara Raja Batteries Limited manufactures automobile and industrial batteries. Please remember, the objective of this section is to give you a brief orientation on how to read an annual report. Running through each and every page of an AR is not practical; however, I would like to share some insights into how I would personally read through an AR, and also help you understand what kind of information is required and what information we can ignore.

ARBL's annual report contains the following 9 sections:

- Financial Highlights
- The Management Statement
- Management Discussion & Analysis
- 10-year financial highlights
- Corporate Information
- Director's Report
- Report on Corporate governance
- Financial Section, and
- Notice

Note, no two annual reports are the same; they are all made to suite the company's requirement keeping in perspective the industry they operate in. However, some of the sections in the annual report are common across annual reports.

The first section in ARBL's AR is the Financial Highlights. Financial Highlights contains the bird's eye view on how the financials of the company looks for the year gone by... The information in this section can be in the form of a table or a graphical display of data. This section of the annual report generally does a multi-year comparison of the operating and business metrics.

Here Is The Snapshot Of The Same:

The details that you see in the Financial Highlights section are basically an extract from the company's financial statement. Along with the extracts, the company, can also include a few financial ratios, which are calculated by the company itself. I briefly look through this section to get an overall idea, but I wouldn't say I like to spend too much time on it. The reason for looking at this section briefly is that, I would anyway calculate these and many other ratios myself and while I do so, I would gain greater clarity on the company and its numbers. Needless to say, over the next few chapters we will understand how to read and understand the financial statements of the company and also how to calculate the financial ratios.

The next two sections i.e the 'Management Statement' and 'Management Discussion & Analysis' are quite important. I spend time going through these sections. Both these sections gives you a sense on what the management of the company has to say about their business and the industry in general, as an investor or as a potential investor in the company, every word mentioned in these sections is important. In fact, some of the details related to the 'Qualitative aspects can be found in these two sections of the AR.

In the 'Management Statement' (sometimes called the Chairman's Message), the investor gets a perspective of how the man sitting right on top is thinking about his business. The content here is usually broad based and gives a sense on how the business is positioned. When I read through this section, I look at how realistic the management is. I am very keen to see if the company's management has its feet on the ground. I also observe if they are fine on discussing details on what went right and what went wrong for the business.

One example that I explicitly remember was reading through the chairman's message of a well-established tea manufacturing company. In his message, the chairman was talking about a revenue growth of nearly 10%. However, the historical revenue numbers suggested that the company's revenue was growing at a rate of 4-5%. Clearly, in this context, the growth rate of 10% seem like a celestial move. This also indicated to me that the man on top may not really be in sync with ground reality and hence I decided not to invest in the company. Retrospectively when I look back at my decision not to invest, it was probably the right decision.

Here is the snapshot of Amara Raja Batteries Limited; I have highlighted a small part that I think is interesting. I would encourage you to read through the entire message in the Annual Report.

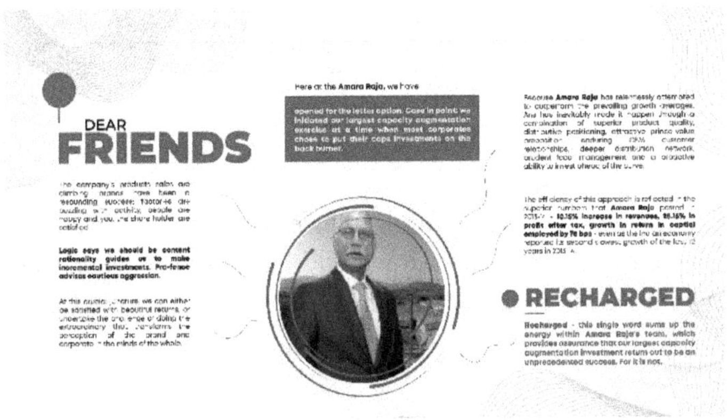

Moving ahead, the next section is the 'Management Discussion & Analysis' or 'MD&A.' This according to me is perhaps one of the most important sections in the whole of AR. The most standard way for any company to start this section is by talking about the macro trends in the economy. They discuss the overall economic activity of the country and the business sentiment across the corporate world. If the company has high exposure to exports, they even talk about global economic and business sentiment.

The Behavior Of Individual Investors

In research published through the late 1990s, the study of investor performance had focused almost exclusively on the performance of institutional investors, in general, and, more specifically, equity mutual funds. This was partially a result of data availability (there was relatively abundant data on mutual fund returns and no data on individual investors). In addition, researchers were searching for evidence of superior investors to test the central prediction of the efficient markets hypothesis: investors are unable to earn superior returns (at least after a reasonable accounting for opportunity and transaction costs).

While the study of institutional investor performance remains an active research area, several studies provide intriguing evidence that some institutions are able to earn superior returns, Grinblatt and Titman in 1989 and Daniel, Grinblatt, Titman, and Wermers study the quarterly holdings of mutual funds. Grinblatt and Titman conclude, "superior performance may in fact exist" for some mutual funds. DGTW use a much larger sample and time period and document "as a group, the funds showed some selection ability." In these studies, the stock selection ability of fund managers generates strong before-fee returns, but is insufficient to cover the fees funds charge.

In financial markets, there is an adding up constraint. For every buy, there is a sell. If one investor beats the market, someone else must underperform. Collectively, we must earn the market return before costs. The presence of exceptional investors dictates the need for subpar investors. With some notable exceptions, which we describe at the end of this section, the evidence indicates that individual investors are subpar investors.

To preview our conclusions, the aggregate (or average) performance of individual investors is poor. A big part of the performance penalty borne by individual investors can be traced to transaction costs (e.g., commissions and bid-ask spread). However, transaction costs are not the whole story. Individual investors also seem to lose money on their trades before costs.

The one caveat to this general finding is the intriguing evidence that stocks heavily bought by individuals over short horizons in the U.S. (e.g., a day or week) go on to earn strong returns in the subsequent week, while stocks heavily sold earn poor returns. It should be noted that the short-run return predictability and the poor performance of individual investors are easily reconciled, as the average holding period for individual investors is much longer than a few weeks. For example, Barber and Odean (2000) document that the annual turnover rate at a U.S. discount brokerage is about 75% annually, which translates into an average holding period of 16 months. (The average holding period for the stocks in a portfolio is equal to the reciprocal of the portfolios' turnover rate.) Thus, short-term gains easily could be offset by long-term losses, which is consistent with much of the evidence we summarize in this section (e.g., Barber, Odean, and Zhu (2009a)).

It should be noted that all of the evidence we discuss in this section focuses on pre-tax returns. To our knowledge, there is no detailed evidence on the after-tax returns earned by individual investors because no existing dataset contains the account-level tax liabilities incurred on dividends and realized capital gains. Nonetheless, we observe that trading generally hurts performance. With some exceptions (e.g., trading to harvest capital losses), it is safe to assume that ceteris paribus investors who trade actively in taxable accounts will earn lower after-tax returns than buy-and-hold investors. Thus, when trading shortfalls can be traced to high turnover rates, it is likely that taxes will only exacerbate the performance penalty from trading.

Long-Horizon Results

Odean in 1999 analyzes the trading records of 10,000 investors at a large discount broker over the period 1987-1993. Using a calendar-time approach, he finds that the stocks bought by individuals underperform the stocks sold by 23 basis points per month in the 12 months after the transaction (with p-values of approximately 0.07) and that this result persists even when trades more likely to have been made for liquidity, rebalancing, or tax purposes are excluded from the analysis. These results are provocative on two dimensions. First, this is the first evidence that there is a group of investors who systematically earn subpar returns before costs. These investors have perverse security selection ability. Second, individual investors seem to trade frequently in the face of poor performance.

Barber and Odean in 2000 analyze the now widely used dataset of 78,000 investors at the same large discount brokerage firm (henceforth referred to as the LDB dataset). Unlike the earlier dataset, which contained only trading records, this dataset was augmented with positions and demographic data on the investors, and the analysis here focuses on positions rather than trades. The analysis of positions, from a larger sample of investors (78,000 v. 10,000) and a different time period (1991-1996 v. 1987-1993), provides compelling evidence that individual investors self-managed stock portfolios underperform the market largely because of trading costs.

Barber and Odean in 2000 sort households into quintiles based on their monthly turnover from 1991-1996. The total sample consists of about 65,000 investors, so each quintile represents about 13,000 households. The 20 % of investors who trade most actively earn an annual return net of trading costs of 11.4 %. Buy-and-hold investors (i.e., the 20 % who trade least actively) earn 18.5 % net of costs. The spread in returns is an economically large 7 percentage points per year.

These raw return results are confirmed with typical asset-pricing tests. Consider results based on the Fama-French three-factor model. After costs, the stock portfolio of the average individual investors earns a three-factor alpha of -31.1 basis points (bps) per month (-3.7 percentage points (pps) annually). Individuals who trade more perform even worse. The quintile of investors who trade most actively averages annual turnover of 258 %; these active investors churn their portfolios more than twice per year! They earn monthly three-factor alphas of -86.4 bps (-10.4 pps annually) after costs.

Grinblatt and Keloharju in 2000 analyzes two years of trading in Finland and provide supportive evidence regarding the poor gross returns earned by individual investors. The focus of their investigation is whether certain investors follow momentum or contrarian behavior with respect to past returns. In addition, they examine the performance of different categories of investors.

Hampered by a short time-series of returns, they do not calculate the returns on portfolios that mimic the buying and selling behavior of investors. Instead, they calculate the buy ratio for a particular stock and investor category on day t, conditional on its future performance from day t+1 to day t+120. They test the null hypothesis that the buy ratio is equal for the top and bottom quartile of future performers. For households, the buy ratio for the top quartile is greater than the buy ratio for the bottom quartile on only 44.8% of days in the two-year sample period. For Finnish financial firms and foreigners, the difference in the ratios is positive on more than 55% of days. Individual investors are net buyers of stocks with weak future performance, while financial firms and foreigners are net buyers of stocks with strong future performance.

Further confirmation regarding the perverse trading ability of individual investors comes from Taiwan. Barber, Lee, Liu, and Odean in 2009 analyze the trading records of Taiwanese investors over the period 1995 to 1999. They construct portfolios that mimic the trading of individuals and institutions, respectively. When portfolios are constructed assuming holding periods that range from one day to six months, the stocks bought by institutions (sold by individuals) earn strong returns, while stocks bought by individuals (sold by institutions) perform poorly. A long-short strategy that mimics the buying and selling of individual investors and assumes a holding period of 140 trading days earns a negative abnormal return of 75 basis points per month before accounting for transaction costs.

The trading losses of individual investors in Taiwan are material. When one considers commissions and the transaction tax on sales, the aggregate trading losses of individuals are equal to 2.8% of total personal income in Taiwan and 2.2% of Taiwan's total GDP. Back-of-the-envelope calculations indicate the net returns earned by individual investors in aggregate are 3.8 percentage points below market returns. Three factors contribute (roughly) equally to the shortfall: perverse stock selection ability, commissions, and the transaction tax, with a somewhat smaller role relegated to poor market timing choices.

The detailed trading information that we have on Finnish and Taiwanese investors is not available in the U.S. However, Hvidkjaer and Barber, Odean, and Zhu use signed small trades from the TAQ database to infer the trading of individual investors in the U.S. The signing algorithm is a modified version of that proposed by Lee and Ready in 1991, which identifies trades as buyer or seller-initiated by comparing transaction prices to spreads. For each stock, both papers calculate a measure of order imbalance based on signed small trades (trades less than $5,000). BOZ verify that this is a reasonable measure of individual investor trading activity. Using the LDB dataset and a second dataset from a full-service broker (1997 to 1999) (hereafter the FSB dataset), BOZ document order imbalance calculated from signed small trades is highly correlated with order imbalance from retail trades at this two brokers. Specifically, the correlation between order imbalance based on small trades in TAQ and order imbalance from the broker trading records is about 50%. In contrast, the correlation between order imbalance based on large trades (trades over $50,000) and broker trading records is reliably negative. This evidence indicates that small trades are a good proxy for the behavior of individual investors during this period.

Using small trades as a proxy for trading of individual investors, both Hvidkjaer and BOZ document that stocks heavily bought by individuals over horizons ranging from one month to one year go on to underperform stocks heavily sold by individuals. For example, Hvidkjaer sorts stocks into deciles based on signed small trade turnover (i.e., buys less sells divided by shares outstanding). At a formation period of six months, the top decile (stocks heavily bought) underperforms the bottom decile (stocks heavily sold) by 89 bases points per month.

Short-Horizon Results

Contrary to the long-run evidence discussed above, the returns earned by individual investors over short horizons (up to a week) appear to be quite strong. Kaniel, Saar, and Titman document individual investor trading positively predicts short run returns. KST identify individual investor trades using the 2000 to 2003 NYSE's Consolidated Audit Trail Data (CAUD) files, which contains detailed information on all orders that execute on the exchange, including a field that identifies whether the order comes from an individual investor. Measuring order imbalance over a nine-week horizon, they document the top decile of stocks heavily bought by individuals earn market- adjusted returns of 16 bps over the next 20 trading days (about a month). In contrast, the bottom decile (i.e., stocks heavily sold) earn -33 bps. KST argue that their results are largely consistent with individual investors acting as "…liquidity providers to institutions that require immediacy". Analyzing the same data, Kaniel, Liu, Saar, and Titman in 2011 find evidence consistent with informed trading by individual investors around earnings announcements. They document that the stocks bought in aggregate by individuals in the 10 days prior to an earnings announcement outperform those sold in aggregate by about 1.5% in the two days around the earnings announcement. They argue liquidity provision and private information contribute equally to the strong returns earned by individuals around earnings announcements.

Similarly, BOZ in 2009 document that small trade order imbalance from TAQ positively predicts returns over short horizons. Specifically, when order imbalance is measured at a weekly horizon, stocks heavily bought outperform for the subsequent two weeks before going on to underperform for the remainder of the year. It is difficult to attribute these patterns to liquidity provision as the order imbalance in BOZ is based on signed rather than all trades. If a stock is bought at a price above the quoted spread, it is categorized as a buy, while if the stock is sold at a price below the quoted spread.

It is categorized as a sell. This signing yields order imbalance measures that are based only on liquidity demanders rather than on liquidity suppliers, presenting a challenge for the KST liquidity provision story. Indeed the contemporaneous relation between returns and order imbalance is positive in BOZ (what one would expect when order imbalance is based on liquidity demanders), but negative in KST (what one would expect when order imbalance is based on liquidity providers). BOZ argue that the combination of a positive relation between small trade order imbalance and short-horizon returns, followed by return reversals at long horizons, can be explained by the correlated sentiment-based trading of individual investors. In the short run, sentiment temporarily pushes prices above fundamental value, leading to predictable long-run return reversals.

Kelley and Tetlock use data routed by retail brokers to two market centers over the period 2003 to 2007 to analyze the trading of individual investors. Brokerage firms route a significant fraction of their order flow (roughly 40%) to these market centers, and the data contain a code that classifies the order submitter as an individual or institution. Using a daily Fama-Macbeth regression approach, KT document that daily order imbalance of retail traders positively predicts returns at horizons up to 20 days. KT argue the strong returns over short horizons is evident in both market and limit orders. They conclude "…retail market orders aggregate private information about firms' future cash flows, whereas retail limit orders provide liquidity to traders demanding immediate execution."

These four papers use somewhat different approaches, datasets, and time periods. All four present intriguing evidence that individual investors' trades positively predict returns at short horizons in the U.S. There is an ongoing debate in the literature regarding the origins of this short-run predictability in the U.S.

In contrast to the consistent finding of short-run predictability in the U.S., the non-U.S. evidence is mixed. Barber, Lee, Liu, and Odean (2009) document that individual investors in Taiwan incur losses over short horizons. Long-short portfolios that mimic the buy-sell trades of individual investors earn reliably negative monthly alphas of -11.0%, -3.3%, and -1.9% over horizons of 1, 10, and 25 days respectively. Andrade, Chang, and Seasholes document a similar result using changes in stocks held in margin accounts by individual investors in Taiwan over the period 1994 to 2002. In Andrade, stocks are sorted into quintiles based on their order imbalance in week; stocks heavily bought go on to earn poor returns in the following week, while those heavily sold earn strong returns. Kaniel, Saar, and Titman speculate that their liquidity provision story does not apply to the Taiwan market, where individual investors dominate trading; roughly 90% of total trading volume can be traced to retail investors in Taiwan.

Market V. Limit Orders

The evidence on the profitability of market v. limit orders of individual investors also yields conflicting results. Kelley and Tetlock, which we discussed in the prior section, document short-term profits on retail trades emanating from both market and limit orders in the U.S. Linnainmaa in 2010 documents losses on limit orders and gains on market orders in Finland. Barber, Lee, Liu, and Odean find the opposite result in Taiwanashort-term gains on passive orders and short-term losses on aggressive (quasi-market) orders.

Linnainmaa in 2010 argues that individual investors perform poorly on their trades because informed traders pick off their limit orders. Assume sleepy individual investors have unmonitored limit orders to sell a stock. A savvy investor learns of a good earnings announcement that will drive the stock's price higher. Armed with this earnings news, the savvy investor places market orders to buy the stock and profits in the short-term by picking off the unmonitored limit orders of individual investors. Linnainmaa in 2010 uses data from the Finnish Stock Exchange over the period 1998 to 2001 that allows him to identify whether an investor has placed a limit or market order. Consistent with the hypothesis that individual investors are picked off, he documents that the returns on individual investor trades that emanate from limit orders lose 51 bps on the day following trade and 3.3% over 63 days. In contrast, the returns on trades that emanate from market orders gain 44 bps on the day following trade and 3.5% over 63 days. In Finland, individual investors lose money on executed limit orders, but make money on executed market orders. When combined, the gains and losses leave individual investors in his sample with profits that are indistinguishable from zero.

The evidence from Taiwan is not consistent with that from Finland. Taiwan is an electronic limit order market. Barber, Lee, Liu, and Odean in 2009 categorize the limit orders as passive or aggressive. Orders to buy with prices in excess of the most recent unfilled sell limit order are categorized as aggressive; those with an order price below the most recent unfilled buy limit order is categorized as passive. (Sell orders are categorized as passive or aggressive in a similar way.) One can view aggressive limit orders as roughly equivalent to market orders since the only way to demand execution in an electronic limit order market is to place an order with an aggressive price (e.g., be willing to buy at a high price or sell at a low price). At short horizons (of one to 10 days following the trade), individual investors make money on their passive trades, though the six-month returns are indistinguishable from zero. Individual investors lose money on their aggressive trades at both short and long horizons. This is in striking contrast to the results in Finland, where individuals lose money on limit orders and make money on market orders.

Cross-Sectional Variation In Performance

The performance of the average individual obscures tremendous variation in outcomes across individuals. Importantly, the cross-sectional variation in performance is predictable and can be traced to investment skill, cognitive abilities, investment style, location, and gender.

There is strong evidence of performance persistence among individual investors. Coval, Hirshleifer, and Shumway use the LDB dataset to analyze performance persistence: Do investors with strong past returns go on to earn strong returns? They sort investors into deciles based on the performance of their buys during the first half of the sample period (1991 to 1993) and analyze the subsequent performance of their purchases in the second half of the sample period (1994 to 1996). Using buys during the latter period, CHS construct a calendar-time portfolio that mimics the buying of investors in each performance decile. The return spread between the top and bottom performance deciles is about 5 bps per day in the week following trade. This return spread does not account for transaction costs; round-trip spreads and commissions would easily wipe out a 25 bps trading advantage. Nonetheless, the evidence of variation in investor skill is intriguing.

Barber, Lee, Liu, and Odean analyze the performance of day traders in Taiwan over the period 1992 to 2006. Day trading in Taiwan is quite common. Over 300,000 individual investors engage in day trading in the typical year, and their combined trading accounts for 17% of total trading volume. This is an ideal setting to analyze the performance of speculators, as day traders are certainly not trading for liquidity, rebalancing, or tax-related reasons (all reasonable motivations for trading). Furthermore, the large population of day traders allows for a more powerful identification of potentially skilled traders. To identify skilled (and unskilled) traders, BLLO in 2011 rank investors based on their day trading performance in year y and analyze their performance in the subsequent year (y+1). The top 500 traders earn intraday returns on day trading that outperform the thousands of traders who perform poorly by over 60 basis points. As in CHS, there is strong evidence of cross-sectional differences in speculative ability though the magnitudes are much larger. The best traders, though a rare breed, earn gross abnormal returns of about 50 bps per day, which is sufficient to cover a reasonable accounting for transaction costs.

Recent papers suggest cognitive abilities play an important role in investor outcomes. Korniotis and Kumar predict cognitive ability using a host of demographic variables (e.g., age, education, and social networks). Using the LDB dataset, they show that smarter investors outperform others by about 30 bps per month (or 3.6% annually) both before and after accounting for transaction costs. Smarter investors earn returns net of trading costs that are on par with appropriate benchmark returns; they make good stock picks, but only good enough to cover their trading costs. Other investors underperform appropriate benchmarks by a bit more than 30 bases points per month (or 3.6% annually) after costs, with about half of the shortfall being traced to trading costs and half to bad stock selection.

In a closely related paper, Korniotis and Kumar use the LDB dataset to analyze the relation between age and performance. Motivated by the observation that cognitive abilities decline with age, the authors predict and find evidence to support the notion that investment performance declines with age.

Using data from Finland, Grinblatt, Keloharju, and Linnainmaa analyze the relation between IQ and stock selection ability. The Finnish Armed Forces administers an intelligence test (120 questions covering verbal, math, and logical reasoning) to recruits around the time of induction into mandatory military duty (generally at the age of 19 or 20). The scores range from 1 to 9, and GKL define a low IQ investor as one with a FAF score from 1 to 4 and a high IQ investor as one with a FAF score of 9. Based on these definitions, 24% of their sample are low IQ investors, while 8% are high IQ investors. The spread in portfolio returns earned by low- versus high-IQ investors is 2.2% per year and is marginally significant. However, an analysis of the returns following purchases provides convincing statistical evidence that high-IQ investors make better trades than low-IQ investors. GKL also document high-IQ investors have better trade execution, though they do not measure the net portfolio returns of high-IQ investors, so it is difficult to know whether high-IQ investors would beat an appropriate benchmark after a reasonable accounting for transaction costs.

Ivkovic, Sialm, and Wiesbenner argue that informed individual investors would tend to concentrate their portfolios in the stocks for which they hold an informational advantage. Using the LDB dataset, they document that investors with concentrated portfolios (with only one or two stocks) outperform diversified portfolios (with three or more stocks) by 16 bps per month. This "concentration" effect is more pronounced for local stock and non-S&P 500 stocks.

Finally, Barber and Odean compare the performance of men and women using data from the LDB dataset. Unlike the studies on cross-sectional performance discussed above, this study focuses on the net returns (i.e., returns net of spreads and commissions) of men and women. The study is motivated by the two observations: (1) men tend to be more prone to overconfidence than women in areas culturally perceived to be in the male domain (Deaux and Farris, 1977), and (2) models that assume investors are overconfident tend to predict investors will trade excessively and to their detriment. When combined, these observations predict that men will trade more than women and that excessive trading will hurt their performance. Consistent with these predictions, Barber and Odean (2001) document that men trade more than women; the annual turnover rates of men are about 80%, while those of women are 50%. The excessive trading of men leads to poor returns. While both men and women earn poor returns, men perform worse. Virtually, all gender-based difference in performance can be traced to the fact that men tend to trade more aggressively than women. Neither men nor women appear to have stock selection ability (i.e., the gross returns earned on their trades are similar), so men's tendency to trade aggressively and the resulting trading costs drag down men's returns. Dorn and Huberman find that men with accounts at a German online brokerage trade more actively than women, but gender effects are reduced if one accounts for differences in self-reported risk-aversion. Choi, Laibson, and Metrick, Agnew, Balduzzi, and Sundén, and Mitchell, Mottola, Utkus, and Yamaguchi, all report that while trading levels are low in 401(k) plans, men trade more actively than women. In contrast to the U.S. and German and 401(k) plan evidence, Feng and Seasholes (2008) find no significant turnover or performance differences in the accounts of men and women in China.

A careful reading of the research on cross-sectional variation in performance yields three general conclusions. First, there is strong evidence of cross-sectional variation in trading skill. Second, security selection skill among individuals is rare (i.e, confined to a relatively small group of stocks or individuals). Third, even the best stock pickers have trouble covering transaction costs.

CHAPTER 5

Why Do Individual Investors Underperform?

The majority of the empirical evidence indicates that individual investors, in aggregate, earn poor long-run returns and would be better off had they invested in a low- cost index fund. This evidence of poor performance is particularly compelling when we include transaction costs (e.g., commissions, bid-ask spreads, market impact, and transaction taxes). While transaction costs are an important component of the shortfall, a second component is the poor security selection ability of individual investors documented in many studies that we reviewed in the prior section. These observations lead one to wonder why investors trade so much and to their detriment.

1. Asymmetric Information

One possibility is that individual investors realize that they are at an informational disadvantage when trading and only do so for non-speculative reasons including liquidity needs, rebalancing, and taxes. Investors may need to purchase stocks to save or sell stocks to consume. At times, investors may need to rebalance their portfolios to manage risk-return tradeoffs. Occasionally, investors will want to harvest tax losses to minimize their tax bill. When faced with this liquidity, rebalancing, or tax management needs, retail investors are forced to trade with others who might be better informed. It is, however, difficult to reconcile non-speculative trading needs with the annual turnover rates of 250 % for the 20 % most active investors in the LDB dataset, annual turnover of 300 % in Taiwan, or annual turnover of 500 % in China. Furthermore, investors who do have unusual non-speculative needs to trade could dramatically lower their asymmetric information and transaction costs by investing in low cost, no load mutual funds.

Why do so many investors self-manage portfolios when they could earn better returns with lower risk in low-cost mutual funds, such as index funds? And why do investors with portfolios of individual equities trade actively when doing so lowers their expected returns? We turn to possible behavioral explanations.

2. Overconfidence

Overconfidence can explain the relatively high turnover rates and poor performance of individual investors. A rich literature in psychology documents that people generally are overconfident. One variety of overconfidence is a belief that one knows more than one does, which is sometimes labeled "miscalibration" or "overprecision." In a classic illustration of this type of overconfidence, subjects are presented a series of 10 difficult questions (e.g., "What is the length of the Nile river?"). They are then asked to provide a low and high guess such that the correct answer is between the low and high guess with a probability of 90 %. The well-calibrated subject would, on average, provide intervals that contain the correct answer nine out of 10 times. Typically, subjects provide intervals that contain far fewer correct answers. A second variety of overconfidence is a belief that one is better than the median person, which has been (mis)labeled the "better-than-average" effect. For example, when asked about their own driving ability relative to the population of drivers, most people rank themselves above the driver of median ability. Related to, but distinct from, the better-than-average effect is the tendency to overestimate one's actual ability. For example, a student might think his score on a test is 80% when he actually scored 65% (and the average score was 90%).

Several papers have developed theoretical models based on the observation that investors are overconfident (Benos (1998), Caballe and Sakovics (2003), Daniel, Hirshleifer, and Subrahmanyam (1998), Gervais and Odean (2001), Hong, Scheinkman, and Xiong (2006), Kyle and Wang (1997), Odean (1998), Peng and Xiong (2006), Scheinkman and Xiong (2003), and Wang (2001)). Generally, these models assume investors suffer from the miscalibration type of overconfidence. For example, one can extend the classic models of Kyle (1985), Grossman and Stiglitz (1980), or Diamond and Varecchia (1981) by assuming some investors are miscalibrated (or overconfident) about the precision of their information (see Odean (1999)). In these three settings, the overconfidence models generally predict that investors will trade too much and to their detriment.

A number of empirical facts line up reasonably well with the predictions of these theoretical models. Investors who trade the most perform the worst (Barber and Odean (2000)). Men, who are more prone to be overconfident than women, trade more and perform worse than women (Barber and Odean (2001)).

Empirical work has attempted to tease out the type of overconfidence, miscalibration or better-than-average, that is linked to excessive trading. Combining survey evidence with trades and positions for 1,345 German investors, Dorn and Huberman (2005) document that investors who think themselves more knowledgeable than average churn their portfolios more. Similarly, Glaser and Weber (2007) use survey evidence and trading records for 215 German investors to document a link between the "better-than-average" type of overconfidence and trading activity. Using, a five-question version of the calibration experiment, described earlier, Glaser and Weber find no reliable link between the miscalibration type of overconfidence and trading activity. (While this is a provocative nonresult, using a five- or 10-question survey to measure miscalibration strikes us as a very noisy measure that would yield low power to reject the null hypothesis that miscalibration and trading activity are unrelated.) Finally, Grinblatt and Keloharju find that Finnish investors with an inflated sense of their own abilities tend to trade more; we elaborate on this finding in more detail in the next section.

Closely related to the notion of overconfidence are self-assessments of competence, Graham, Harvey, and Huang study which. They argue that "people are more willing to bet on their own judgments when they feel skillful or knowledgeable." To test this conjecture, they use survey responses from 475 U.S. investors to study the impact of self-assessed competence on trading. Competence is based on the answer to the following question "How comfortable do you feel about your ability to understand investment products, alternatives, and opportunities?" Subjects responded on a five-point scale ranging from "1-very uncomfortable" to "5-very comfortable." Graham et al. document a strong link between self-assessed competence and the propensity to trade. They measure the better-than-average effect by taking the difference between the answers to questions about an investor's expected return on their own portfolio and the expected return on the market. They find weak evidence that this measure of overconfidence is linked to trading activity.

In summary, a fair amount of evidence indicates that the better-than-average and overestimation varieties of overconfidence are correlated with higher levels of trading by investors. While the evidence that miscalibration is linked to trading is weaker, we suspect this weak link might be partially explained by the current inability to measure miscalibration well.

3. Sensation Seeking

A noncompeting explanation for the excessive trading of individual investors is the simple observation that trading is entertainment and appeals to people who enjoy sensation-seeking activities such as gambling. Using the Finnish dataset, Grinblatt and Keloharju analyze both sensation-seeking and overconfidence as mechanisms that lead to trading. They use traffic tickets as a proxy for sensation-seeking and argue that those who speed are more likely to be sensation seekers. To measure overconfidence, GK uses data from tests administered to men entering the Finnish Armed Forces that measure the candidates' actual ability (i.e., test outcomes) and perceived ability (i.e., self- assessments). GK use the measure of perceived ability that is orthogonal to actual ability as a measure of overconfidence. Using these instruments, GK documents that both sensation-seeking and overconfidence affect trading, though the tenor of their results, depend a bit on whether one focuses on the decision to trade, the number of trades, or portfolio turnover as the dependent variable of interest.

Dorn and Sengmueller in 2009 marry survey responses and trading records for 1,000 investors at a German discount broker. Investors are asked whether they agree or disagree (on a five-point scale) with the following four statements: (1) I enjoy investing, (2) I enjoy risky propositions, (3) Games are only fun when money is involved, and (4) In gambling, the fascination increases with the size of the bet. Investors who agree with this statements tend to trade more. Investors who report enjoying investing (question 1) or gambling (questions 2-4) trade at twice the rate of other investors.

Trading competes with other activities for the attention of sensation-seeking investors. Thus, we would expect trading to wane when there is a number of thrilling activities at their disposal. There is some suggestive evidence that this is the case. Dorn, Dorn, and Sengmueller analyze the trading response of individual investors to multi-state lottery jackpots in the U.S. Using small trades in the TAQ dataset to identify individual investors during the period 1998 to 2004, they document that an one standard deviation increase in multistate lottery jackpots (i.e., Powerball and Mega-Millions) is associated with a 1% reduction in small trader participation (the fraction of trading volume contributed by trades of less than $5,000); this effect is most pronounced for lottery-like stocks (e.g., low-prices stocks with high past volatility and skewness). Similarly, Barber, Lee, Liu, and Odean (2009) find that trading in Taiwan drops by about 25% when a legal lottery was introduced on the island in April 2002. As in Dorn, Dorn, and Sengmueller, Gao and Lin further explore this substitution effect by analyzing the volume of individual investor trading in Taiwan around lotteries with unusually large jackpots. They document trading by individual investors declines during periods with unusually large lottery jackpots; moreover, the effects are greatest in stocks with high levels of individual investors participation and skewed returns.

In related papers, Kumar and Mitton and Vorkink hypothesize that retail investors have a taste for stocks with lottery-like payoffs. Note that this is distinct from the sensation-seeking (or entertainment) hypothesis discussed above. Sensation- seeking investors will trade to entertain themselves but might hold well-diversified portfolios and eschew lottery-like stocks. Investors with a preference for skewness will hold lottery-like stocks but might refrain from trading. Thus, preferences for skewness may lead to underdiversification but has no immediate implications for trading. We elaborate on these findings later when we discuss the literature on diversification.

4. Familiarity

There are debate about whether individual investors possess an informational advantage about companies that are close to where they live or in their industry of employment. Some scholars argue that individual investors are better informed about the prospects of companies close to where they live or in their industry of employment and that this information advantage leads to superior investment performance. Others argue individuals overinvest in these stocks because they are familiar to them, leading to under diversification and average or even below-par returns. In this section, we discuss the evidence on performance. In section VI, we discuss the implications for diversification.

Massa and Simonov in 2006 analyze portfolio holdings of Swedish investors and document that investors tilt their portfolio towards stocks that are most closely related to them, either professionally (e.g., a financial professional investing in a finance stock) or geographically (e.g., a Seattle investor investing in a Seattle stock). They argue that this familiarity-based investing allows investors to earn higher returns because of the information advantage conferred by familiarity. Similarly, Ivkovic and Weisbenner use the LDB dataset to document individual investors tend to overweight local stocks and argue the returns on local stocks are strong. Seasholes and Zhu argue that this result is not robust and leans on faulty statistical methodologies. After considering a battery of tests using the same dataset as Ivkovic and Weisbenner, they conclude that individual investors do not earn superior returns on local stocks. Døskeland and Hvide document that, after excluding own-company stock holdings, individual investors in Norway overweight stocks in the industry in which they are employed despite the diversification disadvantages of doing so and earn negative abnormal returns on the stocks they buy in their industry of employment.

In summary, the performance implication of investing in geographically or occupationally familiar stocks is the subject of ongoing debate. However, investors overweight these stocks in their equity portfolios, which has potentially important implications for diversification, a subject we return to later in this review.

The Disposition Effect: Selling Winners And Holding Losers

Individual investors have a strong preference for selling stocks that have increased in value since bought (winners) relative to stocks that have decreased in value since bought (losers). Shefrin and Statman labeled this behavior the "disposition effect" investors are disposed to sell winners and hold losers.

A number of studies both experimental and empirical confirm the presence of the disposition effect. Weber and Camerer provide early experimental support for the disposition effect. In their experiment, subjects observe price changes on six stocks (stocks A to G) over 14 periods. The probability that a stock will increase in value varies across stocks, but not rounds. Subjects know the distribution of these probabilities, but do not know which stock has the highest probability of increasing in price. A rational Bayesian would conclude that the stock with the most price increases has the greatest chance of being the stock with a high probability of further increasing in value, so the disposition effect (selling winners, holding losers) is clearly counterproductive in this setting. Nonetheless, subjects sell winners at 50% higher rate than losers; 60% of sales are winners, while 40% of sales are losers.

Odean examines trading records for 10,000 accounts at a large U.S. discount brokerage for the period 1987 through 1993. In brief, Odean compares the rate at which investors sell winners (realized gains) and losers (realized losses) and compares the realization of gains and losses to the opportunities to sell winners and losers. He finds that, relative to opportunities, investors realize their gains at about a 50% higher rate than their losses and that this difference is not explained by informed trading, a rational belief in mean-reversion, transactions costs, or rebalancing.

Grinblatt and Keloharju examine the disposition effect using the trading records for virtually all Finnish investors during 1995 and 1996. Controlling for a wide variety of factors, they find that investors have a tendency to hold onto losers. Relative to a stock with a capital gain, a stock with a capital loss of up to 30% is 21% less likely to be sold; a stock with a capital loss in excess of 30% is 32% less likely to be sold. Furthermore, stocks with high past returns or trading near their monthly high are more likely to be sold.

Heath, Huddart, and Lang find that employee stock options are more likely to be exercised when the stock is trading above its previous year's high and that exercise is positively related to stock returns during the previous month and negatively related to returns over longer horizons.

Kaustia tracks trading volume following IPOs and finds that IPOs that opened below their offer price experience significantly more trading volume when they trade above rather than below the offer price. Brown, Chappel, da Silva Rosa, and Walter analyze records for Australian investors who subscribed to IPOs between 1995 and 2000 and find that the disposition effect "... is pervasive across investor classes."

The disposition effect has been documented for individual investors in several countries, for some groups of professional investors, and for different types of assets. Shapira and Venezia analyze the trading of 4,330 investors with accounts at an Israeli brokerage in 1994. About 60% of these accounts are professionally managed, while for other accounts, investors make independent decisions. They measure the duration of round-trip trades conditional on whether the stock was sold for a gain or loss. A tendency to sell winners and hold losers would, ceteris paribus, yield shorter holding periods for winners v. losers. Both professionally managed accounts and independent accounts exhibit the disposition effect (the holding periods for winners is roughly half that of losers), though the effect is somewhat stronger for independent accounts.

Feng and Seasholes use hazard rate models to estimate the magnitude of the disposition effect for 1,511 Chinese investors using trades data from a Chinese broker in 2000. These Chinese investors are 32% less likely to realize a loss. Chen, Kim, Nofsinger, and Rui analyze almost 50,000 Chinese investors using data from a Chinese brokerage firm over the period 1998 to 2002. Using methods similar to those in Odean, Chen et al. document that Chinese investors are 67% more likely to sell a winner than a loser. For a small subsample of 212 institutional investors who trade through this broker, Chen et al. document a much weaker disposition effect as institutions are only 15% more likely to see a winner. Choe and Eom find a disposition effect for investors in Korean stock index futures; the effect is strongest for individual investors.

Compelling evidence beyond Chen et al. and Choe and Eom suggest that institutions suffer from the disposition effect, albeit to a lesser extent than individual investors. Frazzini estimates, from 1980 through 2002, the rates at which U.S. mutual funds realize gains and losses in their equity holdings relative to how many positions they hold for a gain or a loss. For all funds, gains are realized at a rate of 21% higher than losses; for funds in the previous year's bottom performance quintile, gains are realized at a rate 72% higher than losses. Barber, Lee, Liu, and Odean analyze trading records for all investors at the Taiwan Stock Exchange from 1995 to 1999 to compare the disposition effect of individual and various categories of institutional investors. They find a strong disposition effect for individual investors, who are nearly four times as likely to sell a winner rather than a loser. Corporate investors and dealers also are disposed to selling winners (though the effect is much weaker than that observed for individuals), but neither Taiwan mutual funds nor foreign investors in Taiwan are disposed to selling winners.

Consistent with this investment behavior being a mistake that has its origins in cognitive ability or financial literacy, the disposition effect is most pronounced for financially unsophisticated investors. For example, the disposition effect tends to be stronger for individual rather than institutional investors. Dhar and Zhu use the LDB dataset to document that wealthier and professionally-occupied investors are less likely to sell winners and more likely to sell losers. Calvet, Campbell, and Sodini document a similar result among Swedish investors. Finally, in the LDB data, investors who place more trades on the same day are less likely to exhibit the disposition effect (Kumar and Lim and the disposition effect is greatest for hard-to-value stocks.

There is also intriguing evidence that investors learn to avoid the disposition effect over time. Among the Chinese individual investors they study, Feng and Seasholes document that the disposition effect dissipates with trading experience (time since first trade) and various measures of financial sophistication measured early in a trader's history. Seru, Shumway, and Stoffman examine trading records for individual investors in Finland from 1995-2003. They find that the disposition effect declines with experience when experience is measured in number of trades. The drop in the disposition effect is much less when trading experience is measured in years.

The research discussed above presents a remarkably clear portrait of a prototypical individual investor who sells his winners and holds his losers. This behavior is broadly categorized as an investment mistake because it is tax inefficient. Thus, while taxes clearly affect the trading of individual investors, they cannot explain the disposition effect. Investors' reluctance to realize losses is at odds with optimal tax-loss selling for taxable investments. For tax purposes, investors should postpone taxable gains by continuing to hold their profitable investments. They should capture tax losses by selling their losing investments, though not necessarily at a constant rate. Constantinides shows that when there are transactions costs, and no distinction is made between the short-term and long-term tax rates, investors, should increase their tax-loss selling gradually from January to December. Australia has a June tax year-end, so the Constantinides model would predict accelerated selling in June for Australia, a prediction confirmed by Brown.

Barber and Odean document the disposition effect for taxable and tax- deferred accounts for the LDB dataset and for a dataset of trading and position records from January 1998 through June 1999 for 418,332 households with accounts at a large U.S. full-service brokerage. They find that at both the discount and full-service brokers, the disposition effect is reversed in December in taxable, but not tax-deferred, accounts. Using a Cox proportional hazard rate model and the U.S. discount brokerage data, Ivkovich, Poterba, and Weisbenner (2005) document that "Investors are more likely to realize losses in taxable accounts than in tax-deferred accounts, not just in December, but throughout the year."

Why Do Investors Prefer To Sell Winners?

While the tendency of investors to sell winners more readily than losers is empirically robust, recent research focuses on why investors behave this way. Shefrin and Statman attribute the disposition effect to a combination of prospect theory, regret aversion, mental accounting, and self-control issues. Prospect theory was developed from a series of experiments in which Kahneman and Tversky ask students to choose between hypothetical outcomes such as: "Which of the following would you prefer? A: 50% chance to win 1,000, 50% chance to win nothing; B: 450 for sure." It is not obvious exactly how such choices translate into the realm of investing. Shefrin and Statman assume that, due to mental accounting, most investors will segregate gambles and thus tend to evaluate performance at the level of individual securities (e.g., stocks) rather portfolios.

What is less clear is what happens when investors apply prospect theory preferences to stock investments. Barberis and Xiong model the trading behavior of an investor with prospect theory preferences. They find that, if performance is evaluated annually, prospect theory preferences do not necessarily lead to a tendency to realize gains more readily than losses and can even have the opposite effect. Hens and Vlcek's model questions whether investors with prospect theory preferences would even buy stocks in the first place. Henderson develops an optimal stopping model based on prospect theory preferences and finds investors are more likely to realize gains than losses. Kaustia finds that prospect theory can lead to holding onto both losers and winners. Yao and Li model a market in which investors with prospect theory preferences interact with investors with constant relative risk aversion (CRRA) and find that this interaction commonly generates a negative-feedback trading tendency, which favors the disposition effect and contrarian behavior, for prospect-theory investors.

Barberis and Xiong argue that investors gain utility from realizing gains and dub this behavior "realization utility." They show that, if gains and losses are evaluated when they are realized, a disposition effect obtains. In ongoing work using brain-imaging (fMRI) while subjects are making buying and selling decisions in an experimental market, Frydman, Bossaerts, Camerer, Barberis, and Rangel present intriguing results that are consistent with the notion that investors get a burst of utility when they sell a winner.

Summers and Duxbury examine the role of emotions in creating the disposition effect. They find no disposition effect in experimental markets when subjects do not actively choose the stocks in their portfolios; if subjects do not feel responsible for decisions leading to gains and losses, they no longer sell winners more readily than losers. This suggests that the emotions of regret and its positive counterpart referred to by some authors as rejoicing and by others as pride contribute to the disposition effect. Muermann and Volkman develop a model of the disposition effect in which investors respond to anticipated regret and pride. Strahilevitz, Odean, and Barber document that individual investors are more likely to repurchase a stock that they have previously sold if the price has dropped since the previous transaction. They attribute this behavior to the emotions of regret when one repurchases at a higher price than one sold at and rejoicing when one repurchases at a lower price. Consistent with this emotional story, Weber and Welfens confirm in experiments that subjects exhibit this behavior only when they were responsible for the original sale, suggesting that investors refrain from repurchasing stocks at a higher price than their previous sale price to avoid regret.

Reinforcement Learning

The simplest form of learning may be to repeat behaviors that previously coincided with pleasure and avoid those that coincided with pain. Several studies suggest that individual investors engage in such simple reinforcement learning. Choi, Laibson, Madrian, and Metrick document that investors overextrapolate from their personal experience when making savings decisions; investors whose 401(k) accounts have experienced greater returns or lower variance increase their saving rates. Strahilevitz, Odean, and Barber find that investors are more likely to repurchase a stock that they previously sold for a profit than one previously sold for a loss. Huang demonstrates that investors, particularly unsophisticated investors, are more likely to buy a stock in an industry if their previous investments in this industry have earned a higher return than the market. De, Gondhi, and Pochiraju show that individual investors trade is more actively when their most recent trades are successful. Kaustia and Knupfer document that investors are more likely to subscribe to initial public offerings (IPOs) if their personal experience with IPO investments has been profitable. Malmendier and Nagel establish that investor age cohorts who have experienced high stock market returns throughout their lives are less risk averse and more likely to invest in stocks.

Attention: Chasing the Action

Individuals have a limited amount of attention that they can devote to investing. Attention can affect the trading behavior of investors in two distinct ways. On one hand, directing too little attention to important information can result in a delayed reaction to important information. On the other hand, devoting too much attention to (perhaps stale or irrelevant) information can lead to an overreaction.

Recent research provides some support for the notion that distracted investors miss important information. Hirshleifer, Lim, and Teoh find that the market reaction to an earnings surprise is smaller and post-earnings announcement drift is greater for firms that announce earnings on days that many other firms announce earnings; they argue that this is because more firms are competing for for investors' attention. Similarly, Dellavigna and Pollet document the market reaction to Friday earnings announcements is muted and the drift is greater; they argue investors are distracted on Fridays and are unable to fully process Friday announcements. However, Hirshleifer, Myers, Myers, and Teoh are unable to link post-earnings announcement drift to the trades of individual investors in the LDB dataset, who tend to be net buyers subsequent to both positive and negative extreme earnings surprises.

Barber and Odean argue that attention greatly influences individual investor purchase decisions. Investors face a huge search problem when choosing stocks to buy. Rather than searching systematically, many investors may consider only stocks that first catch their attention (e.g., stocks that are in the news or stocks with large price moves). This will lead individual investors to buy attention-grabbing stocks heavily. Since most individual investors own only a small number of stocks and only sell stocks that they own, selling poses less of a search problem and is less sensitive to attention effects. Using abnormal trading volume, the previous day's return, and news coverage as proxies for attention, Barber, and Odean find that individual investors in the LDB and FSB datasets execute proportionately more buy orders for more attention-grabbing stocks.

Examining transaction records for 6,459,723 accounts trading on the Shanghai Stock Exchange, Seasholes and Wu document positive buy-sell imbalances for individual investors when stocks hit upper price limits. They argue that hitting an upper price limit is an attention-grabbing event and find that imbalances are most positive when few other stocks hit upper price limits on the same day. Even investors who have never previously owned a stock are more likely to buy when stocks hit these limits. Seasholes and Wu also find that other (rational) investors systematically profit at the expense of the attention driven individual investors.

Engelberg and Parsons find that individual investors are more likely to trade an S&P 500 index stock subsequent to an earnings announcement if that announcement was covered in the investor's local newspaper. Both buying and selling increase, though buying somewhat more than selling. Engelberg, Sasseville, and Williams look at overnight market reaction to buy and sell recommendations on the television show Mad Money. They find that the market reaction is greater following recommendations made when viewership based on Nielson ratings are higher. Furthermore, consistent with Barber and Odean's hypothesis that attention matters more for buying than selling, they find that "While first-time buy recommendations have a large overnight return of 2.4%, first-time sell recommendations have overnight returns that are smaller in magnitude (-0.29%)."

Da, Engelberg, and Gao use Google search frequency as a measure of investor attention to analyze whether investor attention can cause price pressure effects as described in Barber and Odean. Using data from 2004 to 2008, they document that increases in search frequency predict higher returns in the ensuing two weeks and an eventual reversal within the year.

Failure to Diversify

Risk averse investors should hold a diversified portfolio to minimize the impact of idiosyncratic risk on their investment outcomes. A fair bit of evidence suggests that many investors fail to effectively diversify idiosyncratic risk.

Investors who overinvest in the stock of their employer (company stock) are left exposed to the fortunes of their employer (idiosyncratic risk). Famously, Enron employees had 62% of their retirement plan assets invested in company stock at the end of 2000.

By December 2001, the company had declared bankruptcy and its employees had lost both their jobs and a large fraction of their retirement income. Similar stories unfolded at Global Crossing, Lucent, Polaroid, and Kmart. Poterba analyzes the 20 largest defined contribution plans managed by corporations and documents that 44% of plan assets are invested in company stock. Mitchell and Utkus estimate that five million Americans have over 60 % of their plan assets invested in company stock. Benartzi documents that some of the allocation to company stock is discretionary on the part of employees. Moreover, this discretionary allocation is the largest for companies with strong return performance over the prior 10 years, which is consistent with the general stock buying behavior of individual investors.

The proportion invested in company stock has declined over the past 10 years. According to the Employee Benefits Research Institute, in 1998 60% of recently hired employees invested in company stock. That figure dropped to 36% in 2009. Nonetheless, as of 2009, about 5% of participants had more than 80% of their account balances invested in company stock.

Barber and Odean document that, on average, investors in the LDB dataset hold only four stocks. Goetzmann and Kumar analyze the underdiversification of these investors in detail. They document that investors tend to hold portfolios that are highly volatile and consist of stocks that are more highly correlated than one would expect if stocks were chosen randomly. Mitton and Vorkink argue that this a preference might drive preference for small portfolios for skewness. In support of this hypothesis, they document that investors with small portfolios tend to have more highly skewed outcomes. Moreover, investors with small portfolios tend to pick stocks with above-average skewness (especially idiosyncratic skewness). In a related paper, Kumar shows that individuals prefer stocks with high idiosyncratic volatility, high idiosyncratic skewness, or low stocks prices. He further shows that the same demographic characteristics that predict lottery participation (e.g., education, income, and religious affiliation) also predict the strength of lottery-like preferences in stocks. Grinblatt, Keloharju, and Linnainmaa document that high-IQ Finnish investors are more likely to hold mutual funds and larger numbers of stocks.

Investors prefer local and familiar stocks. They avoid investment in foreign stocks, which arguably provides strong diversification benefits (French and Poterba (1991), Cooper and Kaplanis (1994), Tesar and Werner (1995), Lewis (1999)). The reticence to invest abroad is changing, but still persists. For example, French documents the fraction of the aggregate U.S. investor portfolio allocated to foreign stocks grew from 2% in 1980 to 8.5% in 1990 and 27.2% in 2007. Despite these trends, the home bias remains a strong phenomenon around the globe.

Investors also prefer local stocks within their domestic portfolio. Huberman documents that investors are more likely to invest in a local rather than a distant phone company and attributes the preference to familiarity. Similarly, Finnish investors prefer to hold stocks close to where they live, that communicate in their native language, and that have a CEO of the same cultural background. Investors in the LDB dataset hold about 30% of their portfolio in stocks headquartered within a 240 mile radius of their home, while only 12% of firms are located within the same radius (Ivkovich and Weisbenner, Seasholes and Zhu. Similar results are found for China. Investing in stocks close to home is not a good diversification move for the same reasons that investing in company stock is problematic. Though arguably less severe than overinvesting in company stock, overinvesting in local stocks exposes investors to idiosyncratic local risk that also is likely correlated with their job prospects (i.e., the value of their human capital).

To obtain an accurate picture of an investor's portfolio diversification, one needs to observe the total balance sheet of an investor. Most datasets do not afford this opportunity. A notable exception is the comprehensive dataset of asset holdings by Swedish households. The median household in Sweden holds a well-diversified portfolio with a Sharpe ratio equal to that of a global equity index. Calvet. define an investor's return loss as the difference between her mean return and the maximum achievable consistent with the standard deviation of her portfolio. This return loss is zero for the median household, but a sizable minority of households has economically large return losses. For example, 5% of investors have return losses on their portfolios of 5% per year or more. Matching Swedish online investors to individual tax records, Anderson finds that lower income, poorer, younger, and less well-educated investors invest a greater proportion of their wealth in individual stocks, hold more highly concentrated portfolios, trade more, and have worse trading performance.

In summary, some investors fail to take advantage of the full benefits of diversification. Underdiversified investors might overinvest in company stock, local stocks, familiar stocks, and domestic companies. Doing so may make them feel safe, but it leaves them exposed to increased volatility in their investment returns.

Are Individual Investors Contrarians?

Are individual investors contrarians? Webster defines a contrarian as "a person who buys shares of stock when most other investors are selling and sells when they are buying." By this definition, it is institutions, not individuals, who almost certainly are contrarians since when institutions in aggregate are trading against individuals in aggregate, there will usually be a greater number of investors on individual investors' side of the trade. The Oxford English Dictionary defines a contrarian as "A person who (habitually) opposes or rejects prevailing opinion … an investor who goes against the current consensus when trading, e.g. by buying shares in a company when their price is falling." This definition suggests that it is one's beliefs that make one a contrarian. Suppose investors' beliefs can be inferred from their purchases. In that case, individual investors are not contrarians since they are far more likely to buy a stock when the price has been rising than when it has been falling.

Nevertheless, several authors characterize the trading behavior of individual investors as contrarian. Kaniel, Saar, and Titman argue that dthere is widespread agreement in the literature that individuals tend to be contrarian …" Choe, Kho, and Stulz use data from the Korean stock exchange to examine the positive feedback trading of institutions during the Asian financial crisis and document that during this crisis individuals tend to be contrarian investors. Grinblatt and Kelharju report similar contrarian behavior in Finland.

All of these papers label individual investors as contrarian based on the net buying (i.e., purchases minus sales) of individual investors in response to recent price changes. While the authors are accurate in their empirical observations, in our opinion, labeling individual investors contrarians mischaracterizes their beliefs. Barber, Odean, and Zhu separately analyze the buying and selling of individual investors using the LDB and FSB datasets. They document that positive relation between the aggregate buying of individual investors and returns lagged up to 12 quarters for both datasets. However, a positive relation also exists between aggregate selling of individual investors and returns lagged up to 12 quarters (though these effects are somewhat weaker for the full-service broker).

We provide a simple graphic representation of the prior returns of stocks bought and stocks sold using a standard event-time analysis. Specifically, we calculate the mean market-adjusted return on all purchases in event time, where day 0 is the day of the purchase. These means are cumulated beginning two years (504 trading days) prior to the purchase. There is an analogous calculation for sales. Panel A contains results for the LDB data, while Panel B contains results for the FSB data. It is clear from these graphs that investors both buy and sell stocks with strong past returns. For both the datasets, stocks bought, on average, outperform the market by 40 percentage points over two years prior to purchase. Stocks sold also outperform the market, but not by such a large margin. Over the previous four months at the discount and previous one month at the full-service brokerage, the stocks sold by investors outperform the market by more than stocks bought. This is consistent with the observation that individual investors are net sellers of stocks with strong performance over recent periods but net buyers of stocks with strong performance over longer periods. The tendency of investors both to buy and sell stocks with strong recent performance indicates that they use different thought processes when deciding what to buy versus what to sell.

We believe that buying is forward-looking and selling backward-looking. Investors buy stocks because of what they hope will happen and sell stocks because of what has already happened. When investors buy a stock (that they have not recently owned), they look to the past only to divine the future. Many investors employ the simple heuristic of assuming that the recent past is indicative of what is to come. Selling is different. When selling, investors are concerned about what a stock has done prior to the sale (and since being purchased). In most cases, this leads investors to sell winners and hold losers (i.e., the disposition effect), though, late in the tax year, investors tend to sell losers. It is unlikely that investors sell winners because they believe past winners are future losers; rather investors find it emotionally unpalatable to sell for a loss.

Investment Environment And Investment Management Process

Investing versus financing

The term 'investing" could be associated with the different activities, but the common target in this activities is to "employ" the money (funds) during the time period seeking to enhance the investor's wealth. Funds to be invested come from assets already owned, borrowed money and savings. By foregoing consumption today and investing their savings, investors expect to enhance their future consumption possibilities by increasing their wealth.

But it is useful to make a distinction between real and financial investments. Real investments generally involve some kind of tangible asset, such as land, machinery, factories, etc. Financial investments involve contracts in paper or electronic form such as stocks, bonds, etc. Following the objective as it presented in the introduction this course deals only with the financial investments because the key theoretical investment concepts and portfolio theory are based on these investments and allow to analyze investment process and investment management decision making in the substantially broader context

Some information presented in some chapters of this material developed for the investments course could be familiar for those who have studied other courses in finance, particularly corporate finance. Corporate finance typically covers such issues as capital structure, short-term and long-term financing, project analysis, current asset management. Capital structure addresses the question of what type of long-term financing is the best for the company under current and forecasted market conditions; project analysis is concerned with the determining whether a project should be undertaken. Current assets and current liabilities management addresses how to manage the day-by-day cash flows of the firm. Corporate finance is also concerned with how to allocate the profit of the firm among shareholders (through the dividend payments), the government (through tax payments) and the firm itself (through retained earnings). But one of the most important questions for the company is financing. Modern firms raise money by issuing stocks and bonds. These securities are traded in the financial markets and the investors have possibility to buy or to sell securities issued by the companies. Thus, the investors and companies, searching for financing, realize their interest in the same place – in financial markets. Corporate finance area of studies and practice involves the interaction between firms and financial markets and Investments area of studies and practice involves the interaction between investors and financial markets. Investments field also differ from the corporate finance in using the relevant methods for research and decision making. Investment problems in many cases allow for a quantitative analysis and modeling approach and the qualitative methods together with quantitative methods are more often used analyzing corporate finance problems. The other very important difference is, that investment analysis for decision making can be based on the large data sets available form the financial markets, such as stock returns, thus, the mathematical statistics methods can be used.

But at the same time both Corporate Finance and Investments are built upon a common set of financial principles, such as the present value, the future value, the cost of capital). And very often investment and financing analysis for decision making use the same tools, but the interpretation of the results from this analysis for the investor and for the financier would be different. For example, when issuing the securities and selling them in the market the company perform valuation looking for the higher price and for the lower cost of capital, but the investor using valuation search for attractive securities with the lower price and the higher possible required rate of return on his/ her investments.

Together with the investment the term speculation is frequently used. Speculation can be described as investment too, but it is related with the short-term investment horizons and usually involves purchasing the salable securities with the hope that its price will increase rapidly, providing a quick profit. Speculators try to buy low and to sell high, their primary concern is with anticipating and profiting from market fluctuations. But as the fluctuations in the financial markets are and become more and more unpredictable speculations are treated as the investments of highest risk. In contrast, investment is based upon the analysis, and its main goal is to promise safety of principle sum invested and to earn the satisfactory risk.

There are two types of investors:

- individual investors;
- Institutional investors.

Individual investors are individuals who are investing in their own. Sometimes individual investors are called retail investors. Institutional investors are entities such as investment companies, commercial banks, insurance companies, pension funds, and other financial institutions. In recent years, the process of institutionalization of investors can be observed. As the main reasons for this can be mentioned the fact, that institutional investors can achieve economies of scale, demographic pressure on social security, the changing role of banks.

One of important preconditions for successful investing both for individual and institutional investors is the favorable investment environment.

Our focus in developing this course is on the management of individual investors' portfolios. But the basic principles of investment management are applicable both for individual and institutional investors.

Direct versus indirect investing

Investors can use direct or indirect type of investing. Direct investing is realized using financial markets and indirect investing involves financial intermediaries.

The primary difference between these two types of investing is that applying direct investing investors buy and sell financial assets and manage individual investment portfolio themselves. Consequently, investing directly through financial markets investors take all the risk and their successful investing depends on their understanding of financial markets, its fluctuations and on their abilities to analyze and to evaluate the investments and to manage their investment portfolio.

Contrary, using indirect type of investing investors are buying or selling financial instruments of financial intermediaries (financial institutions) which invest large pools of funds in the financial markets and hold portfolios. Indirect investing relieves investors from making decisions about their portfolio. As shareholders with the ownership interest in the portfolios managed by financial institutions (investment companies, pension funds, insurance companies, commercial banks) the investors are entitled to their share of dividends, interest and capital gains generated and pay their share of the institution's expenses and portfolio management fee. The risk for investor using indirect investing is related more with the credibility of chosen institution and the professionalism of portfolio managers. In general, indirect investing is more related with the financial institutions which are primarily in the business of investing in and managing a portfolio of securities (various types of investment funds or investment companies, private pension funds). By pooling the funds of thousands of investors, those companies can offer them a variety of services, in addition to diversification, including professional management of their financial assets and liquidity.

Investors can "employ" their funds by performing direct transactions, bypassing both financial institutions and financial markets (for example, direct lending). But such transactions are very risky, if a large amount of money is transferred only to one's hands, following the well known American proverb "don't put all your eggs in one basket." That turns to the necessity to diversify your investments. From the other side, direct transactions in the businesses are strictly limited by laws avoiding possibility of money laundering.

Companies can obtain necessary funds directly from the general public (those who have excess money to invest) by the use of the financial market, issuing and selling their securities. Alternatively, they can obtain funds indirectly from the general public by using financial intermediaries. And the intermediaries acquire funds by allowing the general public to maintain such investments as savings accounts, Certificates of deposit accounts and other similar vehicles.

Investment Environment

Investment environment can be defined as the existing investment vehicles in the market available for investor and the places for transactions with these investment vehicles. Thus, further in this subchapter the main types of investment vehicles and the types of financial markets will be described.

Investment Vehicles

In this course we are focused to the financial investments that mean the object will be financial assets and the marketable securities in particular. But even if further in this course only the investments in financial assets are discussed, for deeper understanding the specifics of financial assets comparison of some important characteristics of investment in this type of assets with the investment in physical assets is presented.

Investment in financial assets differs from investment in physical assets in those important aspects:

- Financial assets are divisible, whereas most physical assets are not. An asset is divisible if investor can buy or sell small portion of it. In case of financial assets it means, that investor, for example, can buy or sell a small fraction of the whole company as investment object buying or selling a number of common stocks.
- Marketability (or Liquidity) is a characteristic of financial assets that is, not shared by physical assets, which usually

have low liquidity. Marketability (or liquidity) reflects the feasibility of converting of the asset into cash quickly and without affecting its price significantly. Most of the financial assets are easy to buy or to sell in the financial markets.

- The planned holding period of financial assets can be much shorter than the holding period of most physical assets. The holding period for investments is defined as the time between signing a purchasing order for asset and selling the asset. Investors acquiring physical assets usually plan to hold it for a long period, but investing in financial assets, such as securities, even for some months or a year can be reasonable. Holding period for investing in financial assets vary in very wide interval and depends on the investor's goals and investment strategy.
- Information about financial assets is often more abundant and less costly to obtain, than information about physical assets. Information availability shows the real possibility of the investors to receive the necessary information which could influence their investment decisions and investment results. Since a big portion of information important for investors in such financial assets as stocks, bonds is publicly available, the impact of many disclosed factors having influence on value of these securities can be included in the analysis, and the decisions made by investors.

Even if we analyze only financial investment, there is a big variety of financial investment vehicles. The on going processes of globalization and integration open wider possibilities for the investors to invest into new investment vehicles which were unavailable for them some time ago because of the weak domestic financial systems and limited technologies for investment in the global investment environment.

Financial innovations suggest for the investors the new choices of investment but at the same time make the investment process and investment decisions more complicated, because even if the investors have a wide range of alternatives to invest they can't forgot the key rule in investments: invest only in what you really understand. Thus, the investor must understand how investment vehicles differ from each other and only then to pick those which best match his/her expectations.

The most important characteristics of investment vehicles on which bases the overall variety of investment vehicles can be assorted are the return on investment and the risk which is defined as the uncertainty about the actual return that will be earned on an investment. Each type of investment vehicles could be characterized by certain level of profitability and risk because of the specifics of these financial instruments. Though, all different types of investment vehicles, can be compared using characteristics of risk and return and the most risky as well as less risky investment vehicles can be defined. However the risk and return on investment are close related and only using both important characteristics we can really understand the differences in investment vehicles.

The main types of financial investment vehicles are:

- Short term investment vehicles;
- Fixed-income securities;
- Common stock;
- Speculative investment vehicles;
- Other investment tools.

Short - term investment vehicles are all those which have a maturity of one year or less. Short term investment vehicles often are defined as money-market instruments because they are traded in the money market which presents the financial market for short term (up to one year of maturity) marketable financial assets. The risk as well as the return on investments of short-term investment vehicles usually is lower than for other types of investments. The main short term investment vehicles are:

- Certificates of deposit;
- Treasury bills;
- Commercial paper;
- Bankers' acceptances;
- Repurchase agreements.

Certificate of deposit is debt instrument issued by bank that indicates a specified sum of money has been deposited at the issuing depository institution. Certificate of deposit bears a maturity date and specified interest rate and can be issued in any denomination. Most certificates of deposit cannot be traded and they incur penalties for early withdrawal. For large money-market investors financial institutions allow their large-denomination certificates of deposits to be traded as negotiable certificates of deposits.

Treasury bills (also called T-bills) are securities representing financial obligations of the government. Treasury bills have maturities of less than one year. They have the unique feature of being issued at a discount from their nominal value and the difference between nominal value and discount price is the only sum which is paid at the maturity for these short term securities because the interest is not paid in cash, only accrued. The other important feature of T-bills is that they are treated as risk-free securities ignoring inflation and default of a government, which was rare in developed countries, the T-bill will pay the fixed stated yield with certainty. But, of course, the yield on T-bills changes over time influenced by changes in overall macroeconomic situation. T-bills are issued on an auction basis. The issuer accepts competitive bids and allocates bills to those offering the highest prices. Non-competitive bid is an offer to purchase the bills at a price that equals the average of the competitive bids. Bills can be traded before the maturity, while their market price is subject to change with changes in the rate of interest. But because of the early maturity dates of T-bills large interest changes are needed to move T-bills prices very far. Bills are thus regarded as high liquid assets.

Commercial paper is a name for short-term unsecured promissory notes issued by corporation. Commercial paper is a means of short-term borrowing by large corporations. Large, well-established corporations have found that borrowing directly from investors through commercial paper is cheaper than relying solely on bank loans. Commercial paper is issued either directly from the firm to the investor or through an intermediary. Commercial paper, like T-bills is issued at a discount. The most common maturity range of commercial paper is 30 to 60 days or less. Commercial paper is riskier than T-bills, because there is a larger risk that a corporation will default. Also, commercial paper is not easily bought and sold after it is issued because the issues are relatively small compared with T-bills and hence their market is not liquid.

Banker‘s acceptances are the vehicles created to facilitate commercial trade transactions. These vehicles are called bankers acceptances because a bank accepts the responsibility to repay a loan to the holder of the vehicle in case the debtor fails to perform. Banker‘s acceptances are short-term fixed-income securities that are created by non-financial firm whose payment is guaranteed by a bank. This short-term loan contract typically has a higher interest rate than similar short –term securities to compensate for the default risk. Since bankers' acceptances are not standardized, there is no active trading of these securities.

Repurchase agreement (often referred to as a repo) is the sale of security with a commitment by the seller to buy the security back from the purchaser at a specified price at a designated future date. Basically, a repo is a collectivized short-term loan, where collateral is security. The collateral in a repo may be a Treasury security, other money-market security. The difference between the purchase price and the sale price is the interest cost of the loan, from which repo rate can be calculated. Because of concern about default risk, the length of maturity of repo is usually very short. If the agreement is for a loan of funds for one day, it is called overnight repo; if the term of the agreement is for more than one day, it is called a term repo. A reverse repo is the opposite of a repo. In this transaction, a corporation buys the securities with an agreement to sell them at a specified price and time. Using Repos helps to increase the liquidity in the money market.

Our focus in this course further will be not investment in short-term vehicles. Still, it is useful for an investor to know that short term investment vehicles provide the possibility for temporary investing of money/ funds, and investors use these instruments managing their investment portfolio.

Fixed-income securities are those which return is fixed, up to some redemption date or indefinitely. The fixed amounts may be stated in money terms or indexed to some measure of the price level. This type of financial investments is presented by two different groups of securities:

- Long-term debt securities
- Preferred stocks.

Long-term debt securities can be described as long-term debt instruments representing the issuer's contractual obligation. Long term securities have maturity longer than 1 year. The buyer (investor) of these securities is landing money to the issuer, who undertake obligation periodically to pay interest on this loan and repay the principal at a stated maturity date. Long-term debt securities are traded in the capital markets. From, the investor's point of view these securities, can be treated as a "safe" asset. But in reality, the safety of investment in fixed –income securities is strongly related with the default risk of an issuer. The major representatives of long-term debt securities are bonds, but today there are a big variety of different kinds of bonds, which differ not only by the different issuers (governments, municipals, companies, agencies, etc.), but by different schemes of interest payments which is a result of bringing financial innovations to the long-term debt securities market. As demand for borrowing the funds from the capital markets is growing the long-term debt securities today are prevailing in the global markets. And it is really become the challenge for the investor to pick long-term debt securities relevant to his/ her investment expectations, including the safety of investment. We examine the different kinds of long-term debt securities and their features important to understand for the investor, together with the other aspects in decision making investing in bonds.

Preferred stocks are equity security, which has infinitive life and pay dividends. But preferred stock is attributed to the type of fixed-income securities, because the dividend for preferred stock is fixed in amount and known in advance.

Though, this security provides for the investor the flow of income very similar to that of the bond. The main difference between preferred stocks and bonds is that for preferred stock the flows are for ever if the stock is not callable. The preferred stockholders are paid after the debt securities holders but before the common stock holders in terms of priorities in payments of income and in case of liquidation of the company. If the issuer fails to pay the dividend in any year, the unpaid dividends will have to be paid if the issue is cumulative. If preferred stock is issued as noncumulative, dividends for, the years with losses do not have to be paid. Usually, same rights to vote in general meetings for preferred stockholders are suspended. Because of having the features attributed for both equity and fixed-income securities preferred stocks is known as hybrid security. A most preferred stock is issued as noncumulative and callable. In recent years the preferred stocks with option of convertibility to common stock are proliferating.

The common stock is the other type of investment vehicles, which is one of most popular among investors with long-term horizon of their investments. Common stock represents the ownership interest of corporations or the equity of the stock holders. Holders of common stock are entitled to attend and vote at a general meeting of shareholders, to receive declared dividends and receive their share of the residual assets, if any if the corporation is bankrupt. The issuers of the common stock are the companies which seek to receive funds in the market and though are "going public." The issuing common stocks and selling them in the market enables the company to raise additional equity capital more easily when using other alternative sources. Thus many companies are issuing their common stocks which are traded in financial markets and investors have wide possibilities for choosing this type of securities for the investment. The questions important for investors for investment in common stock decision making will be discussed later in the chapter.

Speculative investment vehicles following the term "speculation" could be defined as investments with a high risk and high investment return. Using these investment vehicles speculators try to buy low and to sell high, their primary concern is with anticipating and profiting from the expected market fluctuations. The only gain from such investments are the positive difference between selling and purchasing prices. Of course, using short-term investment strategies investors can use for speculations other investment vehicles, such as common stock, but here we try to accentuate the specific types of investments which are riskier than other investment vehicles because of their nature related with more uncertainty about the changes influencing the their price in the future.

Speculative investment vehicles could be presented by these different vehicles:

- Options;
- Futures;
- Commodities, traded on the exchange (coffee, grain metals, other commodities);

Options are the derivative financial instruments. An option contract gives the owner of the contract the right, but not the obligation, to buy or to sell a financial asset at a specified price from or to another party. The buyer of the contract must pay a fee (option price) for the seller. There is a big uncertainty about if the buyer of the option will take the advantage of it and what option price would be relevant, as it depends on not only demand and supply in the options market, but on the changes in the other market where the financial asset included in the option contract are traded. Though, the option is a risky financial instrument for those investors who use it for speculations instead of hedging.

Futures are the other type of derivatives. A future contract is an agreement between two parties than they agree tom transact with the respect to some financial asset at a predetermined price at a specified future date. One party agree to buy the financial asset, the other agrees to sell the financial asset. It is very important that in futures contract case both parties are obligated to perform and neither party charges the fee.

There are two types of people who deal with options (and futures) contracts: speculators and hedgers. Speculators buy and sell futures for the sole purpose of making a profit by closing out their positions at a price that is better than the initial price. Such people neither produce nor use the asset in the ordinary course of business. In contrary, hedgers buy and sell futures, to offset an otherwise risky position in the market.

Transactions using derivatives instruments are not limited to financial assets. There are derivatives involving different commodities (coffee, grain, precious metals, and other commodities). But in this course the target is on derivatives where underlying asset is a financial asset.

Other investment tools:

- Various types of investment funds;
- Investment life insurance;
- Pension funds;
- Hedge funds.

Investment companies/ investment funds. They receive money from investors with the common objective of pooling the funds and then investing them in securities according to a stated set of investment objectives. ***Two types of funds:***

- open-end funds (mutual funds) ,
- closed-end funds (trusts).

Open-end funds have no pre-determined amount of stocks outstanding and they can buy back or issue new shares at any point. Price of the share is not determined by demand, but by an estimate of the current market value of the fund's net assets per share (NAV) and a commission.

Closed-end funds are publicly traded investment companies that have issued a specified number of shares and can only issue additional shares through a new public issue. Pricing of closed-end funds is different from the pricing of open-end funds: the market price can differ from the NAV.

Insurance Companies are in the business of assuming the risks of adverse events (such as fires, accidents, etc.) in exchange for a flow of insurance premiums. Insurance companies are investing the accumulated funds in securities (treasury bonds, corporate stocks and bonds), real estate. There are three types of Insurance Companies: life insurance; non-life insurance (also known as property-casualty insurance) and re-insurance. During recent years investment life insurance became very popular investment alternative for individual investors, because this hybrid investment product allows to buy the life insurance policy together with possibility to invest accumulated life insurance payments or lump sum for a long time selecting investment program relevant to investor‘s future expectations.

Pension Funds are an asset pools that accumulates over an employee's working years and pays retirement benefits during the employee's nonworking years. Pension funds are investing the funds according to a stated set of investment objectives in securities (treasury bonds, corporate stocks and bonds), real estate.

Hedge funds are unregulated private investment partnerships, limited to institutions and high-net-worth individuals, which seek to exploit various market opportunities and thereby to earn larger returns than are ordinarily available. They require a substantial initial investment from investors, and usually, have some restrictions on how quickly investor can withdraw their funds. Hedge funds take concentrated speculative positions and can be very risky. It could be noted that originally, the term "hedge" made some sense when applied to these funds. They would by combining different types of investments, including derivatives, try to hedge risk while seeking higher return. But today the word "hedge' is misapplied to these funds because they generally take an aggressive strategies investing in stock, bond and other financial markets around the world and their level of risk is high.

Financial Markets

Financial markets are the other important component of investment environment.

Financial markets are designed to allow corporations and governments to raise new funds and to allow investors to execute their buying and selling orders. In financial markets, funds are channeled from those with the surplus, who buy securities, to those, with shortage, who issue new securities or sell existing securities. A financial market can be seen as a set of arrangements that allows trading among its participants.

The financial market provides three important economic functions:

1. Financial market determines the prices of assets traded through the interactions between buyers and sellers;
2. Financial market provides a liquidity of the financial assets;
3. Financial market reduces the cost of transactions by reducing explicit costs, such as money spent to advertise the desire to buy or to sell a financial asset.

Financial markets could be classified on the bases of those characteristics:

- Sequence of transactions for selling and buying securities;
- Term of circulation of financial assets traded in the market;
- Economic nature of securities, traded in the market;
- From the perspective of a given country.

By sequence of transactions for selling and buying securities:

- Primary market
- Secondary market

All securities are first traded in the primary market, and the secondary market provides liquidity for these securities.

Primary market is where corporate and government entities can raise capital and where the first transactions with the new issued securities are performed. If a company's share is traded in the primary market for the first time this is referred to as an initial public offering (IPO).

Investment banks play an important role in the primary market:

- Usually handle issues in the primary market;
- Among other things, act as underwriter of a new issue, guaranteeing the proceeds to the issuer.

Secondary market - where previously issued securities are traded among investors. Generally, individual investors do not have access to secondary markets. They use security brokers to act as intermediaries for them. The broker delivers an orders received form investors in securities to a market place, where these orders are executed. Finally, clearing and settlement processes ensure that both sides to these transactions honor their commitment. ***Types of brokers:***

- Discount broker, who executes only trades in the secondary market;
- Full service broker, who provides a wide range of additional services to clients (ex., advice to buy or sell);
- Online broker is a brokerage firm that allows investors to execute trades electronically using Internet.

Types of secondary market places:

- Organized security exchanges;
- Over-the-counter markets;
- Alternative trading system.

An organized security exchange provides the facility for the members to trade securities, and only exchange members may trade there. The members include brokerage firms, which offer their services to individual investors, charging commissions for executing trades on their behalf. Other exchange members by or sell for their own account, functioning as dealers or market makers who set prices at which they are willing to buy and sell for their own account. ***Exchanges play very important role in the modern economies by performing the following tasks:***

- Supervision of trading to ensure fairness and efficiency;
- The authorization and regulation of market participants such as brokers and market makers;
- Creation of an environment in which securities' prices are formed efficiently and without distortion. This requires not only regulation of orders and transaction costs but also a liquid market in which there are many buyers and sellers, allowing investors to buy or to sell their securities quickly;
- Organization of the clearing and settlement of transactions;
- The regulation of he admission of companies to be listed on the exchange and the regulation of companies who are listed on the exchange;
- The dissemination of information (trading data, prices and announcements of companies listed on the exchange). Investors are more willing to trade if prompt and complete information about trades and prices in the market is available.

The over-the-counter (OTC) market is not a formal exchange. It is organized network of brokers and dealers who negotiate sales of securities. There are no membership requirements and many brokers register as dealers on the OTC. At the same time, there are no listing requirements and thousands of securities are traded in the OTC market. OTC stocks are usually considered as very risky because they are the stocks that are not considered large or stable enough to trade on the major exchange.

An alternative trading system (ATS) is an electronic trading mechanism developed independently from the established market places – security exchanges – and designed to match buyers and sellers of securities on an agency basis. The brokers who use ATS are acting on behalf of their clients and do not trade on their own account. The distinct advantages of ATS in comparison with traditional markets cost savings of transactions, the short time of execution of transactions for liquid securities, extended hours for trading and anonymity, often important for investors, trading large amounts.

By term of circulation of financial assets traded in the market:

- Money market;
- Capital market

Money market - in which only short-term financial instruments are traded.

Capital market - in which only long-term financial instruments are traded.

By economic nature of securities, traded in the market:

- Equity market or stock market;
- Common stock market;
- Fixed-income market;
- Debt market;
- Derivatives market.

From the perspective of a given country financial markets are:

We could see that various financial assets by nature may be more or less risky and in general their ability to earn returns differs from one type to the other. As an example, for the investor with low tolerance of risk common stock, will be not appropriate type of investment.

Analysis and evaluation of investment vehicles. When the investment policy is set up, investor's objectives defined and the potential categories of financial assets for inclusion in the investment portfolio identified, the available investment types can be analyzed. This step involves examining several relevant types of investment vehicles and the individual vehicles inside these groups. For example, if the common stock was identified as investment vehicle relevant for investor, the analysis will be concentrated to the common stock as an investment. The one purpose of such analysis and evaluation is to identify those investment vehicles that currently appear to be mispriced. There are many different approaches how to make such analysis. Most frequently two forms of analysis are used: technical analysis and fundamental analysis. Technical analysis involves the analysis of market prices in an attempt to predict future price movements for the particular financial asset traded on the market.

This analysis examines the trends of historical prices and is based on the assumption that these trends or patterns repeat themselves in the future. Fundamental analysis in its simplest form is focused on the evaluation of intrinsic value of the financial asset. This valuation is based on the assumption that intrinsic value is the present value of future flows from particular investment. By comparison of the intrinsic value and market value of the financial assets those which are under priced or overpriced can be identified.

This step involves identifying those specific financial assets in which to invest and determining the proportions of these financial assets in the investment portfolio.

Formation of diversified investment portfolio is the next step in investment management process. The investment portfolio is the set of investment vehicles, formed by the investor seeking to realize its' defined investment objectives. In the stage of portfolio formation the issues of selectivity, timing and diversification need to be addressed by the investor. Selectivity refers to micro forecasting and focuses on forecasting price movements of individual assets. Timing involves macro forecasting of price movements of particular type of financial asset relative to fixed-income securities in general. Diversification involves forming the investor's portfolio for decreasing or limiting risk of investment. ***2 techniques of diversification:***

- ***random diversification,*** when several available financial assets are put to the portfolio at random;
- ***objective diversification*** when financial assets are selected to the portfolio following investment objectives and using appropriate techniques for analysis and evaluation of each financial asset.

Investment management theory is focused on issues of objective portfolio diversification and professional investors follow settled investment objectives then constructing and managing their portfolios.

Portfolio revision. This step of the investment management process concerns the periodic revision of the three previous stages. This is necessary, because over time investor with long-term investment horizon may change his / her investment objectives and this, in turn means that currently held investor's portfolio may no longer be optimal and even contradict with the new settled investment objectives. Investor should form the new portfolio by selling some assets in his portfolio and buying the others that are not currently held. It could be the other reasons for revising a given portfolio: over time the prices of the assets change, meaning that some assets that were attractive at one time may be no longer be so. Thus investor should sell one asset and buy the other more attractive in this time according to his/ her evaluation. The decisions to perform changes in revising portfolio depend, upon other things, in the transaction costs incurred in making these changes. For institutional investors portfolio revision is continuing and very important part of their activity. But individual investor managing portfolio must perform portfolio revision periodically as well. Periodic re-evaluation of the investment objectives and portfolios based on them is necessary because financial markets change, tax laws and security regulations change, and other events alter stated investment goals.

Measurement and evaluation of portfolio performance. This the last step in investment management process involves determining periodically how the portfolio performed, in terms of not only the return earned, but also the risk of the portfolio. For evaluation of portfolio performance appropriate measures of return and risk and benchmarks are needed. A benchmark is the performance of predetermined set of assets, obtained for comparison purposes. The benchmark may be a popular index of appropriate assets – stock index, bond index. The benchmarks are widely used by institutional investors evaluating the performance of their portfolios.

It is important to point out that investment management process is continuing process influenced by changes in investment environment and changes in investor's attitudes as well. Market globalization offers investors new possibilities but at the same time investment management become more and more complicated with growing uncertainty.

1. The common target of investment activities is to "employ" the money (funds) during the time period seeking to enhance the investor's wealth. By foregoing consumption today and investing their savings, investors expect to enhance their future consumption possibilities by increasing their wealth.

2. Corporate finance area of studies and practice involves the interaction between firms and financial markets and Investments area of studies and practice involves the interaction between investors and financial markets. Both Corporate Finance and Investments are built upon a common set of financial principles, such as the present value, the future value, the cost of capital). And very often investment and financing analysis for decision making use the same tools, but the interpretation of the results from this analysis for the investor and for the financier would be different.
3. Direct investing is realized using financial markets and indirect investing involves financial intermediaries. The primary difference between these two types of investing is that applying direct investing investors buy and sell financial assets and manage individual investment portfolio themselves; contrary, using indirect type of investing investors are buying or selling financial instruments of financial intermediaries (financial institutions) which invest large pools of funds in the financial markets and hold portfolios. Indirect investing relieves investors from making decisions about their portfolio.
4. Investment environment can be defined as the existing investment vehicles in the market available for investor and the places for transactions with these investment vehicles.
5. The most important characteristics of investment vehicles on which bases the overall variety of investment vehicles can be assorted are the return on investment and the risk which is defined as the uncertainty about the actual return that will be earned on an investment. Each type of investment vehicles could be characterized by certain level of profitability and risk because of the specifics of these financial instruments. The main types of financial investment vehicles are: short- term investment vehicles; fixed-income securities; common stock; speculative investment vehicles; other investment tools.

6. Financial markets are designed to allow corporations and governments to raise new funds and to allow investors to execute their buying and selling orders. In financial markets funds are channeled from those with the surplus, who buy securities, to those, with shortage, who issue new securities or sell existing securities.
7. All securities are the first traded in the primary market and the secondary market provides liquidity for these securities. Primary market is where corporate and government entities can raise capital and where the first transactions with the new issued securities are performed. Secondary market - where previously issued securities are traded among investors. Generally, individual investors do not have access to secondary markets. They use security brokers to act as intermediaries for them.
8. Financial market, in which only short-term financial instruments are traded, is Money market, and financial market in which only long-term financial instruments are traded is Capital market.
9. The investment management process describes how an investor should go about making decisions. Investment management process can be disclosed by five-step procedure, which includes following stages: (1) setting of investment policy; (2) analysis and evaluation of investment vehicles; (3) formation of diversified investment portfolio; (4) portfolio revision; (5) measurement and evaluation of portfolio performance.
10. Investment policy includes setting of investment objectives regarding the investment return requirement and risk tolerance of the investor. The other constrains which investment policy should include and which could influence the investment management are any liquidity needs, projected investment horizon and preferences of the investor.
11. Investment portfolio is the set of investment vehicles, formed by the investor seeking to realize it's defined

investment objectives. Selectivity, timing, and diversification are the most important issues in the investment portfolio formation. Selectivity refers to micro forecasting and focuses on forecasting price movements of individual assets. Timing involves macro forecasting of price movements of particular type of financial asset relative to fixed-income securities in general. Diversification involves forming the investor's portfolio for decreasing or limiting risk of investment.

CHAPTER 6

Quantitative Model Of Investment Analysis

3 basic questions for the investor in decision making:

1. How to compare different assets in investment selection process? What are the quantitative characteristics of the assets and how to measure them?
2. How does one asset in the same portfolio influence the other one in the same portfolio? And what could be the influence of this relationship to the investor's portfolio?
3. What is relationship between the returns on an asset and returns in the whole market (market portfolio)?

The answers of these questions need quantitative methods of analysis, based on the statistical concepts and they will be examined in this chapter.

Investment Income And Risk

A return is the ultimate objective for any investor. But a relationship between return and risk is a key concept in finance. As finance and investments areas are built upon a common set of financial principles, the main characteristics of any investment are investment return and risk. However to compare various alternatives of investments the precise quantitative measures for both of these characteristics are needed.

Return On Investment And Expected Rate Of Return

General definition of return is the benefit associated with an investment. In most cases, the investor can estimate his/ her historical return precisely.

Many investments have two components of their measurable return:

- ***a capital gain or loss;***
- ***Some form of income.***

All the investor knows is that there is a beginning of the investment period and an end. The percent calculated using this formula might have been earned over one month or other the year. Investor must be very careful with the interpretation of holding period returns in investment analysis. Investor can‘t compare the alternative investments using holding period returns if their holding periods (investment periods) are different. Statistical data which can be used for the investment analysis and portfolio formation deals with a series of holding period returns.

But both holding period returns and sample mean of returns are calculated using historical data. However what happened in the past for the investor is, not as important as what happens in the future, because all the investors decisions are focused to the future, or to expected results from the investments. Of course, no one investor knows the future, but he/ she can use past information and the historical data as well as to use his knowledge and practical experience to make some estimates about it. Analyzing each particular investment vehicle possibilities to earn income in the future investor must think about several „scenarios“ of probable changes in macro economy, industry and company which could influence asset prices ant rate of return. Theoretically it could be a series of discrete possible rates of return in the future for the same asset with the different probabilities of earning the particular rate of return. But for the same asset the sum of all probabilities of these rates of returns must be equal to 1 or 100%.

In all cases than investor has enough information for modeling of future scenarios of changes in rate of return for investment, the decisions should be based on estimated expected rate of return. But sometimes sample mean of return (arithmetic average return) are a useful proxy for the concept of expected rate of return. Sample mean can give an unbiased estimate of the expected value, but obviously it's not perfectly accurate, because based on the assumption that the returns in the future will be the same as in the past. But this is the only one scenario in estimating expected rate of return. It could be expected, that the accuracy of sample mean will increase, as the size of the sample becomes longer (if n will be increased). However, the assumption, that the underlying probability distribution does not change its shape for the longer period becomes more and more unrealistic. In general, the sample mean of returns should be taken for as long time, as investor is confident there has not been significant change in the shape of historical rate of return probability distribution.

Investment Risk

Risk can be defined as a chance that the actual outcome from an investment will differ from the expected outcome. Obvious, that most investors are concerned that the actual outcome will be less than the expected outcome. The more variable the possible outcomes that can occur, the greater the risk. Risk is associated with the dispersion in the likely outcome. And dispersion refers to variability. So, the total risk of investments can be measured with such common absolute measures used in statistics as

- ***variance;***
- ***standard deviation.***

Variance can be calculated as a potential deviation of each possible investment rate of return from the expected rate of return.

Variance and the standard deviation are similar measures of risk and can be used for the same purposes in investment analysis; however, standard deviation in practice is used more often.

Variance and standard deviation are used when investor is focused on estimating total risk that could be expected in the defined period in the future. Sample variance and sample standard deviation are more often used when investor evaluates total risk of his /her investments during the historical period – this is important in investment portfolio management.

Relationship Between Risk And Return

The expected rate of return and the variance or standard deviation provide investor with information about the nature of the probability distribution associated with a single asset. However all these numbers are only the characteristics of return and risk of the particular asset. But how does one asset having some specific trade-off between return and risk influence the other one with the different characteristics of return and risk in the same portfolio? And what could be the influence of this relationship to the investor's portfolio? The answers to these questions are of great importance for the investor when forming his/ her diversified portfolio. The statistics that can provide the investor with the information to answer these questions are covariance and correlation coefficient. Covariance and correlation are related and they generally measure the same phenomenon – the relationship between two variables. Both concepts are best understood by looking at the math behind them.

Covariance

Two methods of covariance estimation can be used: the sample covariance and the population covariance.

The sample covariance is estimated than the investor hasn't enough information about the underlying probability distributions for the returns of two assets and then the sample of historical returns is used.

Relationship between the returns on stock and market portfolio

When is picking the relevant assets to the investment portfolio on the basis of their risk and return characteristics and the assessment of the relationship of their returns investor must consider to the fact that these assets are traded in the market. How could the changes in the market influence the returns of the assets in the investor's portfolio? What is the relationship between the returns on an asset and returns in the whole market (market portfolio)? This questions need to be answered when investing in any investment environment. The statistics can be explored to answer these questions as well.

The characteristic line and the Beta factor

Before examining the relationship between a specific asset and the market portfolio the concept of "market portfolio" needs to be defined. Theoretical interpretation of the market portfolio is that it involves every single risky asset in the global economic system, and contains each asset in proportion to the total market value of that asset relative to the total value of all other assets (value weighted portfolio). But going from conceptual to practical approach - how to measure the return of the market portfolio in such a broad its understanding - the market index for this purpose can be used. Investors can think of the market portfolio as the ultimate market index. And if the investor following his/her investment policy makes the decision to invest, for example, only in stocks, the market portfolio practically can be presented by one of the available representative indexes in particular stock exchange.

The most often the relationship between the asset return and market portfolio return is demonstrated and examined using the common stocks as assets, but the same concept can be used analyzing bonds, or any other assets. With, the given historical data about the returns, on the particular common stock (rJ) and market index return (rM), in the same periods of time investor, can draw the stock's characteristic line.

Stock's characteristic line:

- describes the relationship between the stock and the market;
- shows the return investor expect the stock to produce, given that a particular rate of return appears for the market;
- helps to assess the risk characteristics of one stock relative to the market.

Points

1. The main characteristics of any investment are investment return and risk. However, to compare various alternatives of investments the precise quantitative measures for both of these characteristics are needed.
2. General definition of return is the benefit associated with an investment. Many investments have two components of their measurable return: (1) a capital gain or loss; (2) some form of income. The holding period return is the percentage increase in returns associated with the holding period.
3. Investor can't compare the alternative investments using holding period returns, if their holding periods (investment periods) are different. In these cases arithmetic, average return or sample mean of the returns can be used.

4. Both holding period returns and sample mean of returns are calculated using historical data. However all the investors' decisions are focused to the future, or to expected results from the investments. The expected rate of return of investment is the statistical measure of return, which is the sum of all possible rates of returns for the same investment weighted by probabilities.
5. Risk can be defined as a chance that the actual outcome from an investment will differ from the expected outcome. The total risk of investments can be measured with such common absolute measures used in statistics as variance and standard deviation. Variance can be calculated as a potential deviation of each possible investment rate of return from the expected rate of return. Standard deviation is calculated as the square root of the variance. The more variable the possible outcomes that can occur, the greater the risk.
6. In the cases than the arithmetic average return or sample mean of the returns is used instead of expected rate of return, sample variance and sample standard deviation is calculated.
7. Covariance and correlation coefficient are used to answer the question, what is the relationship between the returns on different assets. Covariance and correlation coefficient are related and they generally measure the same phenomenon – the relationship between two variables.
8. The sample covariance is estimated than the investor hasn't enough information about the underlying probability distributions for the returns of two assets and then the sample of historical returns is used. The population covariance is estimated when the investor has enough information about the underlying probability distributions for the returns of two assets and can identify the actual probabilities of various pairs of the returns for two assets at the same time.
9. Analyzing relationship between the assets in the same portfolio using covariance for portfolio formation it is

important to identify which of the three possible outcomes exists: positive covariance, negative covariance or zero covariance. If the positive covariance between two assets is identified the common recommendation for the investor would be not to put both of these assets to the same portfolio because their returns move in the same direction and the risk in portfolio will be not diversified; if the negative - the common recommendation for the investor would be to include both of these assets to the portfolio, because their returns move in the contrariwise directions and the risk in portfolio could be diversified; if the zero covariance - it means that there is no relationship between the rates of return of two assets.

10. The correlation coefficient between two assets is closely related to their covariance. But instead of covariance when the calculated number is unbounded, the correlation coefficient can range only from -1,0 to +1,0. The more close the absolute meaning of the correlation coefficient to 1,0, the stronger the relationship between the returns of two assets. Using correlation coefficients instead of covariance investor can immediately asses the degree of relationship between assets returns.
11. The coefficient of determination is calculated as the square of correlation coefficient and shows how much variability in the returns of one asset can be associated with variability in the returns of the other.
12. Theoretical interpretation of the market portfolio is that it involves every single risky asset in the global economic system, and contains each asset in proportion to the total market value of that asset relative to the total value of all other assets (value weighted portfolio). Investors can think of the market portfolio as the ultimate market index.
13. Stock's characteristic line describes the relationship between the stock and the market, shows the return investor expect the stock to produce, given that a particular rate of return

appears for the market and helps to assess the risk characteristics of one stock relative to the market.

14. The slope of the characteristic line is called the Beta factor. The Beta factor of the stock is an indicator of the degree to which the stock reacts to the changes in the returns of the market portfolio.
15. The intercept is the point where characteristic line passes through the vertical axis. The interpretation of the intercept from the investor's point of view is that it shows what would be the rate of return of the stock, if the rate of return in the market is zero.
16. The residual variance describes the deviation of the asset returns from its characteristic line.

Theory For Investment Portfolio Formation

Markowitz portfolio theory

The author of the modern portfolio theory is Harry Markowitz who introduced the analysis of the portfolios of investments in his article "Portfolio Selection" published in the Journal of Finance in 1952. The new approach presented in this article included portfolio formation by considering the expected rate of return and risk of individual stocks and, crucially, their interrelationship as measured by correlation. Prior to this investors would examine investments individually, build up portfolios of attractive stocks, and not consider how they related to each other. Markowitz showed how it might be possible to better of these simplistic portfolios by taking into account the correlation between the returns on these stocks.

The diversification plays a very important role in the modern portfolio theory. Markowitz approach is viewed as a single period approach: at the beginning of the period the investor must make a decision in what particular securities to invest and hold these securities until the end of the period. Because a portfolio is a collection of securities, this decision is equivalent to selecting an optimal portfolio from a set of possible portfolios. Essentiality of the Markowitz portfolio theory is the problem of optimal portfolio selection.

The method that should be used in selecting the most desirable portfolio involves the use of indifference curves. Indifference curves represent an investor's preferences for risk and return. These curves should be drawn, putting the investment return on the vertical axis and the risk on the horizontal axis. Following Markowitz approach, the measure for investment return is expected rate of return and a measure of risk is standard deviation. The exemplified map of indifference curves for the individual risk-averse investor is presented. Each indifference curve here represents the most desirable investment or investment portfolio for an individual investor. That means that any of investments (or portfolios) plotted on the indiference curves (A, B, C, or D) are equally desirable to the investor.

Features of indifference curves:

- All portfolios that lie on a given indifference curve are equally desirable to the investor. An implication of this feature: indifference curves cannot intersect.
- An investor has an infinitive number of indifference curves. Every investor can represent several indifference curves (for different investment tools). Every investor has a map of the indifference curves representing his or her preferences for expected returns and risk (standard deviations) for each potential portfolio.

Two important fundamental assumptions than examining indifference curves and applying them to Markowitz portfolio theory:

1. The investors are assumed to prefer higher levels of return to lower levels of return, because the higher levels of return allow the investor to spend more on consumption at the end of the investment period. Thus, given two portfolios with the same standard deviation, the investor will choose the portfolio with the higher expected return. This is called an assumption of nonsatiation.
2. Investors are risk averse. It means that the investor, when given the choise, will choose the investment or investment portfolio with the smaller risk. This is called the assumption of risk aversion.

In reality there are an infinitive number of portfolios available for the investment. Is it means that the investor needs to evaluate all these portfolios on return and risk basis? Markowitz portfolio theory answers this question using efficient set theorem: an investor will choose his/ her optimal portfolio from the set of the portfolios that (1) offer maximum expected return for varying level of risk, and (2) offer minimum risk for varying levels of expected return.

Efficient set of portfolios involves the portfolios that the investor will find optimal ones. These portfolios are lying on the "northwest boundary" of the feasible set and are called an efficient frontier. The efficient frontier can be described by the curve in the risk-return space with the highest expected rates of return for each level of risk.

Feasible set is opportunity set, from which the efficient set of portfolio can be identified. The feasibility set represents all portfolios that could be formed from the number of securities and lie either or or within the boundary of the feasible set.

Feasible and efficient sets of portfolios are presented. Considering the assumptions of nonsiation and risk aversion discussed earlier in this section, only those portfolios lying between points A and B on the boundary of feasibility set investor will find the optimal ones. All the other portfolios in the feasible set are are inefficient.

Furthermore, if a risk-free investment is introduced into the universe of assets, the efficient frontier becomes the tagental line shown this line is called the Capital Market Line (CML) and the portfolio at the point at which it is tangential (point M) is called the Market Portfolio.

The Expected Rate Of Return And Risk Of Portfolio.

Following Markowitz's efficient set portfolios approach an investor should evaluate alternative portfolios inside feasibility set on the basis of their expected returns and standard deviations using indifference curves. Thus, the methods for calculating expected rate of return and standard deviation of the portfolio must be discussed.

The expected rate of return of the portfolio can be calculated in some alternative ways. The Markowitz focus was on the end-of-period wealth (terminal value) and using these expected end-of-period values for each security in the portfolio the expected end-of-period return for the whole portfolio can be calculated. But the portfolio really is the set of the securities thus the expected rate of return of a portfolio should depend on the expected rates of return of each security included in the portfolio.

Because a portfolio‘s expected return is a weighted average of the expected returns of its securities, the contribution of each security to the portfolio‘s expected rate of return depends on its expected return and its proportional share from the initial portfolio‘s market value (weight). Nothing else is relevant. The conclusion here could be that the investor who simply wants the highest posible expected rate of return must keep only one security in his portfolio which has a highest expected rate of return. But why the majority of investors don‘t do so and keep several different securities in their portfolios? Because they try to diversify their portfolios aiming to reduce the investment portfolio risk.

Risk of the portfolio. The most often used measure for the risk of investment is standard deviation, which shows the volatility of the securities actual return from their expected return. Suppose a portfolio's expected rate of return is a weighted average of the expected rates of return of its securities. In that case, the calculation of standard deviation for the portfolio can't simply use the same approach. The reason is that the relationship between the securities in the same portfolio must be taken into account. The relationship between the assets can be estimated using the covariance and coefficient of correlation. As covariance can range from "–" to "+" infinity, it is more useful for identification of the direction of relationship (positive or negative), coefficients of correlation always lies between -1 and +1 and is the convenient measure of intensity and direction of the relationship between the assets.

Capital Asset Pricing Model (CAPM)

CAPM was developed by W. F. Sharpe. CAPM simplified Markowitz's Modern Portfolio theory made it more practical. Markowitz showed that for a given level of expected return and for a given feasible set of securities, finding the optimal portfolio with the lowest total risk, measured as variance or standard deviation of portfolio returns, requires knowledge of the covariance or correlation between all possible security combinations (see formula 3.3). When forming the diversified portfolios consisting large number of securities investors found the calculation of the portfolio risk using standard deviation technically complicated.

Measuring Risk in CAPM is based on the identification of two key components of total risk (as measured by variance or standard deviation of return):

- Systematic risk
- Unsystematic risk

Systematic risk is that associated with the market (purchasing power risk, interest rate risk, liquidity risk, etc.)

Unsystematic risk is unique to an individual asset (business risk, financial risk, other risks, related to investment into particular asset).

Unsystematic risk can be diversified away by holding many different assets in the portfolio. However, systematic risk can't be diversified. In CAPM investors are compensated for taking only systematic risk. Though, CAPM only links investments via the market as a whole.

The essence of the CAPM: the more systematic risk the investor carry, the greater is his / her expected return.

The CAPM being theoretical model is based on some important assumptions:

- All investors look only one-period expectations about the future;
- Investors are price takers and they cant influence the market individually;
- There is risk free rate at which an investors may either lend (invest) or borrow money.
- Investors are risk-averse,
- Taxes and transaction costs are irrelevant.
- Information is freely and instantly available to all investors.

Several of the assumptions of CAPM seem unrealistic. Investors really are concerned about taxes and are paying the commisions to the broker when buying or selling their securities. And the investors usually do look ahead more than one period. Large institutional investors managing their portfolios sometimes can influence market by buying or selling big ammounts of the securities. All things considered, the assumptions of the CAPM constitute only a modest gap between the thory and reality. But the empirical studies and especially wide use of the CAPM by practitioners show that it is useful instrument for investment analysis and decision making in reality.

Equation in formula 3.4 represents the straight line having an intercept of Rf and slope of (j) * (E(rM) - Rf). This relationship between the expected return and Beta is known as Security Market Line (SML). Each security can be described by its specific security market line, they differ because their Betas are different and reflect different levels of market risk for these securities.

Arbitrage Pricing Theory (APT)

APT was propseded by Stephen S.Rose and presented in his article "The arbitrage theory of Capital Asset Pricing, "published in Journal of Economic Theory in 1976. Still there is a potential for it and it may sometimes displace the CAPM. In the CAPM returns on individual assets are related to returns on the market as a whole. The key point behind APT is the rational statement that a number of different factors determines the market return. These factors can be fundamental factors or statistical. If these factors are essential, there to be no arbitrage opportunities there must be restrictions on the investment process. Here arbitrage we understand as the earning of riskless profit by taking advantage of differential pricing for the same assets or security.

It is important to note that the arbitrage in the APT is only approximate, relating diversified portfolios, on assumption that the asset unsystematic (specific) risks are negligable compared with the factor risks.

There could presumably be an infinitive number of factors, although the empirical research done by S.Ross together with R. Roll identified four factors economic variables, to which assets having even the same CAPM Beta, are differently sensitive:

- inflation;
- industrial production;
- risk premiums;
- slope of the term structure in interst rates.

In practice, an investor can choose the macroeconomic factors which seems important and related with the expected returns of the particular asset. The examples of possible macroeconomic factors which could be included in using APT model:

- GDP growth;
- an interest rate;
- an exchange rate;
- a defaul spread on corporate bonds, etc.

Including more factors in APT model seems logical. The institutional investors and analysts closely watch macroeconomic statistics such as the money supply, inflation, interest rates, unemployment, changes in GDP, political events and many others. Reason for this might be their belief that new information about the changes in these macroeconomic indicators will influence future asset price movements. But it is important to point out that not all investors or analysts are concerned with the same set of economic information and they differently assess the importance of various macroeconomic factors to the assets they have invested already or are going to invest. At the same time the large number of the factors in the APT model would be impractical because the models seldom are 100 percent accurate and the asset prices are a function of both macroeconomic factors and noise. The noise is coming from minor factors, with a little influence to the result expected rate of return.

The APT does not require identification of the market portfolio, but it does require the specification of the relevant macroeconomic factors. Much of the current empirical APT research are focused on identification of these factors and the determination of the factors' Betas. And this problem is still unsolved. Although more than two decades have passed since S. Ross introduced APT model, it has yet to reach the practical application stage.

The CAPM and APT are not really essentially different, because they are developed for determing an expected rate of return based on one factor (market portfolio CAPM) or a number of macroeconomic factors (APT). But both models predict how the return on asset will result from factor sensitivities and this is of great importance to the investor.

Market Efficiency Theory

The concept of market efficiency was proposed by Eugene Fama in 1965, when his article "Random Walks in Stock Prices" was published in Financial Analyst Journal. Market efficiency means that the price which investor is paying for financial asset (stock, bond, other security) fully reflects fair or true information about the intrinsic value of this specific asset or fairly describe the value of the company the issuer of this security. The key term in the concept of the market efficiency is the information available for investors trading in the market. It is stated that the market price of stock reflects:

1. All known information, including:

- Past information, e.g., last year's or last quarter's, month's earnings;
- Current information as well as events, that have been announced but are still forthcoming, e.g. shareholders' meeting.

2. Information that can reasonably be inferred, for example, if many investors believe that ECB will increase interest rate in the nearest

future or the government deficit increases, prices will reflect this belief before the actual event occurs.

Capital market is efficient, if the prices of securities which are traded in the market, react to the changes of situation immediately, fully and credibly reflect all the important information about the security's future income and risk related with generating this income.

What Is The Important Information For The Investor?

From economic point of view, the important information is defined as such information which has direct influence to the investor's decisions seeking for his defined financial goals. For example, the essential events in the joint stock company, published in the newspaper, etc.

Market efficiency requires thet the adjustment to new information occurs very quickly as the information becomes known. Obvious, that Internet has made the markets more efficient in the sense of how widely and quickly information is disseminated.

There are 3 forms of market efficiency under efficient market hypothesis:

- Weak form of efficiency;
- Semi- strong form of efficiency;
- Strong form of the efficiency.

Under the weak form of efficiency stock prices are assumed to reflect any information that may be contained in the history of the stock prices. So, if the market is characterized by weak form of efficiency, no one investor or any group of investors should be able to earn over the defined period of time abnormal rates of return by using information about historical prices available for them and by using technical analysis. Prices will respond to news, but if this news is random, then price changes will also be random.

Under the semi-strong form of efficiency all publicly available information is presumed to be reflected in stocks' prices. This information includes information in the stock price series as well as information in the firm's financial reports, the reports of competing firms, announced information relating to the state of the economy and any other publicly available information, relevant to the valuation of the firm. Note that the market with a semi-strong form of efficiency encompasies the weak form of the hypothesis because the historical market data are part of the larger set of all publicly available information. Suppose the market is characterized by semi-strong form of efficiency. In that case, no one investor or any group of investors should be able to earn over the defined period abnormal rates of return by using information about historical prices and publicly available fundamental information (such as financial statemants) and fundamental analysis.

The strong form of efficiency which asserts that stock prices fully reflect all information, including private or inside information, as well as that which is publicly available. This form takes the notion of market efficiency to the ultimate extreme. Under this form of market efficiency securities' prices quickly adjust to reflect both the inside and public information if the market is characterized by strong form of efficiency, no one investor or any group of investors should be able to earn over the defined time abnormal rates of return by using all information available for them.

The validity of the market efficiency hypothesis whichever form is of great importance to the investors because it determines whether anyone can outperform the market, or whether the successful investing is all about luck. Efficient market hypothesis does not require to behave rationally, only that in response to information there will be a sufficiently large random reaction that an excess profit cannot be made.

The concept of the market efficiency now is criticezed by some market analysts and participants by stating that no one market can be fully efficient as some irrational behavior of investors in the market occurs which is more based on their emotions and other psychological factors than on the information available (the psychological aspects of investment decision making will be disscussed further, in chapter 6). But, at the same time, it can be shown that the efficient market can exist, if in the real markets following events occur:

- ☐ A large number of rational, profit maximizing investors exist who are actively and continuously analyzing valuing and trading securities;
- ☐ Information is widely available to market participants at the same time and without or very small cost;
- ☐ Information is generated in a random walk manner and can be treated as independent;
- ☐ Investors react to the new information quickly and fully, though causing market prices to adjust accordingly.

Points

1. Essentiality of the Markowitz portfolio theory is the problem of optimal portfolio selection. The Markowitz approach included portfolio formation by considering the expected rate of return and risk of individual stocks measured as standard deviation, and their interrelationship as measured by correlation. The diversification plays a key role in the modern portfolio theory.
2. Indifference curves represent an investor's preferences for risk and return. These curves should be drawn, putting the investment return on the vertical axis and the risk on the horizontal axis.
3. Two important fundamental assumptions than applying indifference curves to Markowitz portfolio theory. An

assumption of non satiation assumes that the investors prefer higher levels of return to lower levels of return, because the higher levels of return allow the investor to spend more on consumption at the end of the investment period. An assumption of risk aversion assumes that the investor when given the choice, will choose the investment or investment portfolio with the smaller risk, i.e. the investors are risk averse.

4. Efficient set theorem states that an investor will choose his/her optimal portfolio from the set of the portfolios that (1) offer maximum expected return for varying level of risk, and (2) offer minimum risk for varying levels of expected return.
5. Efficient set of portfolios involves the portfolios that the investor will find optimal ones. These portfolios are lying on the "northwest boundary" of the feasible set and is called an efficient frontier. The efficient frontier can be described by the curve in the risk-return space with the highest expected rates of return for each level of risk. Feasible set is opportunity set, from which the efficient set of portfolio can be identified. The feasibility set represents all portfolios that could be formed from the number of securities and lie either or or within the boundary of the feasible set.
6. Capital Market Line (CML) shows the trade off-between expected rate of return and risk for the efficient portfolios under determined risk free return.
7. The expected rate of return on the portfolio is the weighted average of the expected returns on its component securities.
8. The calculation of standard deviation for the portfolio can't simply use the weighted average approach. The reason is that the relationship between the securities in the same portfolio measured by coefficient of correlation must be taken into account. When forming the diversified portfolios consisting large number of securities investors found the calculation of the portfolio risk using standard deviation technically complicated.

9. Measuring Risk in Capital asset Pricing Model (CAPM) is based on the identification of two key components of total risk: systematic risk and unsystematic risk. Systematic risk is that associated with the market. Unsystematic risk is unique to an individual asset and can be diversified away by holding many different assets in the portfolio. In CAPM investors are compensated for taking only systematic risk.
10. The essence of the CAPM: CAPM predicts what an expected rate of return for the investor should be, given other statistics about the expected rate of return in the market, risk free rate of return and market risk (systematic risk).
11. Each security has it's individual systematic - undiversified risk, measured using coefficient Beta. Coefficient Beta (β) indicates how the price of security/ return on security depends upon the market forces. The Beta of the portfolio is simply a weighted average of the Betas of its component securities, where the proportions invested in the securities are the respective weights.
12. Security Market Line (SML) demonstrates the relationship between the expected return and Beta. Each security can be described by its specific security market line, they differ because their Betas are different and reflect different levels of market risk for these securities.
13. Arbitrage Pricing Theory (APT) states, that the expected rate of return of security is the linear function from the complex economic factors common to all securities. There could presumably be an infinitive number of factors. The examples of possible macroeconomic factors which could be included in using APT model are GDP growth; an interest rate; an exchange rate; a defaul spread on corporate bonds, etc.
14. Market efficiency means that the price that the investor is paying for financial asset (stock, bond, other security) fully reflects fair or true information about the intrinsic value of this specific asset or fairly describe the value of the company – the issuer of this security. The key term in the concept of

the market efficiency is the information available for investors trading in the market.

15. There are 3 forms of market efficiency under efficient market hypothesis: weak form of efficiency; strong semi-form of efficiency; strong form of the efficiency.Under the weak form of efficiency stock prices are assumed to reflect any information that may be contained in the past history of the stock prices. Under the semi-strong form of efficiency all publicly, available information is presumed to be reflected in stocks' prices. The strong form of efficiency, which asserts that stock prices fully reflect all information, including private or inside information, as well as that which is publicly available.

CHAPTER 7

Psychological Aspects In Investment Decision Making

The finance and investment decisions for some decades in the past are based on the assumptions that people make rational decisions and are unbiased in their predictions about the future. The modern portfolio theory as well as other theories, such as CAPM, APT, was developed following these assumptions. But we all know that sometimes people act in obvious irrational way and they do the mistakes in their forecasts for the future. Investors could be the case of irrational acting to. For example, people usually are risk averse, but the investors will take the risk if the expected return is sufficient. Over the past decade, the evidence that psychology and emotions influence both financial and investment decisions became more and more convincing. Today not only psychologists but the economists as well agree that investors can be irrational. And the predictable decision errors can affect the changes in the markets. So it is very important to understand actual investors' behavior and psychological biases that affect their decision making. In this chapter some important psychological aspects and characteristics of investors' behavior are discussed.

Overconfidence

Overconfidence causes people to overestimate their knowledge, risks, and their ability to control events. Interestingly, people are more overconfident when they feel like they have control of the outcome – even when this clearly not the case, just the illusion. This perception occurs in investing as well. Even without information, people believe the stocks they own will perform better than stocks they do not own. However, ownership of a stock only gives the illusion of having control of the performance of the stock. Typically, investors expect to earn an above -average return.

Investing is a difficult process. It involves gathering information, information analysis and decision making based on that information. However, overconfidence causes us to misinterpret the accuracy of the information and overestimate our skills in analyzing it. It occurs after people experience some success. The self-attribution bias leads people to believe that successes are attributed to skill while failure is caused by bad luck. After some success in the market investors may exhibit overconfident behavior.

Overconfidence can lead investors to poor trading decisions which often manifest themselves as excessive trading, risk taking and ultimately portfolio losses. Their overconfidence increases the amount they trade because it causes them to be to certain about their opinions. Investors' opinions derive from their beliefs regarding accuracy of the information they have obtained and their ability to interpret it. Overconfident investors believe more strongly in their own valuation of a stock and concern themselves less about the believes of others.

Consider an investor who receives accurate information and is highly capable of interpreting it. The investor's high frequency of trading should result in high returns due to the individual's skill and the quality of the information. In fact, these returns should be high enough to beat a simple buy-and-hold strategy while covering the costs of trading. On the other hand, if the investor does does not have superior ability but rather is suffering from a dose of overconfidence, then the high frequency of turnover, will not result in portfolio returns large enough to beat the buy-and-hold strategy and cover costs.

Overconfidence–based trading is hazardous when it comes to accumulating wealth. High commission costs are not the only problem caused by excessive trading. It has been observed that overconfidence leads to trading too frequently as well as to purchase the wrong stocks. So, overconfidence can also cause the investor to sell a good –performing stock in order to purchase a poor one.

If many investors suffer from overconfidence at the same time, then signs might be found within the stock market. Specifically, after the overall stock market increase, many investors may attribute their success to their own skill and become overconfident. This will lead to greater trading by a large group of investors and may impact overall trading volume on the stock exchanges. Alternatively, overall trading is lower aftermarket declines. Investors appears to attribute the success of the good period to their own skill and begin trading more. Poor performance makes them less overconfident and is followed by lower trading activity.

Overconfidence also affects investors' risk-taking behavior. Rational investors try to maximize returns while minimizing the amount of risk was taken. However, overconfident investors misinterpret the level of risk they take. After all, if an investor is confident that the stocks picked will gave a high return, then there is risk? The portfolios of overconfident investors will have higher risk for two reasons. First is the tendency to purchase higher risk stocks. Higher risk sticks are generally from smaller, newer companies. The second reason is a tendency to under diversify their portfolio. Prevalent risk can be measured in several ways: portfolio volatility, beta and the size of the firms in the portfolio. Portfolio volatility measures the degree of ups and downs the portfolio experiences. High-volatility portfolios exhibit dramatic swings in price and are indicative of under diversification. A higher beta of the portfolio indicates that the security has higher risk and will exhibit more volatility than the stock market in general.

Overconfidence comes partially from the illusion of knowledge. This refers to the tendency for people to believe that the accuracy of their forecasts increases with more information; that is, more information increases one's knowledge about something and improves one's decisions. Using the Internet, today's investors, have access to huge quantities of information. This information includes historical data, such as past prices, returns, the firms' operational performance as well as current information, such as real-time news, prices, etc. However, most individual investors lack the training and experience of professional investors and therefore are less sure of how to interpret this information. That is, this information does not give them as much knowledge about the situation as they think because they do not have training to interpret it properly. Many individual investors realize they have a limited ability to interpret investment information, so they use the Internet for help. Investors can get analyst recommendations, subscribe to expert services, join news groups, etc. However, online investors need to take what they see on the screen, but not all recommendations really are from experts. However if investors perceive the messages as having increased their knowledge. They might be overconfident about their investment decisions.

Another important for investor psychological factor is the illusion of control. People often believes they have influence over the outcome of uncontrollable events. Early positive results give the investor greater illusion of control than early negative results. When, a greater amount of information is obtained by investor, illusion of control, is greater as well.

Overconfidence could be learned through the past success. The more successes the investors experience, the more they will attribute it to their own ability, even when much luck is involved. As a consequence, overconfident behavior will be more pronounced in bull markets than in bear markets.

Disposition effect

People usually avoid actions that create regret and seek actions that cause pride. Regret is the emotional pain that comes with realizing that a previous decision turned out to be a bad one. Pride is the emotional joy of realizing that a decision turned out well.

Avoiding regret and seeking pride affects person's behavior and this is the true for the investors' decisions too. Shefrin and Statman were the first economists who showed that fearing regret and seeking pride causes the investors to be predisposed to selling winners (potential stocks with growing market prices) to early and riding losers (stocks with the negative tendencies in market prices) too long. They call this the disposition effect.

Do the investors behave in a rational manner by more often selling losers or are investors affected by their psychology and have a tendency to sell their best stocks? Several empirical studies provide evidence that investors behave in a manner more consistent with the disposition effect. Researchers have found the disposition effect to be pervasive. They found that the more recently the stock gains or losses occurred, the stronger the propensity was to sell winners and hold losers—investors usually hold in their portfolios losers remarkably longer than winners.

The disposition effect not only predicts selling of winners but also suggests that the winners are sold too soon and the losers are held too long. How such investor behavior does affect the potential results from his investments? Selling winners to soon suggests that those stocks will continue to perform well after they are sold and holding losers too long suggests that those stocks will continue to perform poorly. The fear of regret and the seeking of pride can affect investors' wealth in two ways: first, investors are paying more in taxes because of the disposition to sell winner instead of losers; second, investors earn a lower return on their portfolio because they sell the winners too early and hold poorly performing stocks that continue with decreasing market results.

Interesting are the results of some other studies in which individual investors' reaction to the news about the economy and about the company was investigated. Good news about the company that increases the stock price induces investors to sell stock (selling winners). And, controversially, bad news about the firm does not induce investors to sell (holding losers). This is consistent with avoiding regret and seeking pride. However, news about the economy does not induce investor trading. Investors are less likely than usual to sell winners after good economic news and these results are not consistent with the disposition effect. How such results could be explained? Investors' actions are consistent with the disposition effect for company news because the feeling with the disposition effect of regret is strong. In the case of economic news, investors have a weaker feeling of regret because the outcome is considered beyond their control. This leads to actions that are not consistent with the predictions of the disposition effect.

Perceptions Of Investment Risk

People's perception of risk appears to vary. One important factor in evaluating a current risky decision is a past outcome: people are willing to take more risk after earning gains and less risk after losses.

After experiencing a gain or profit, people are willing to take more risk. After gaining big sum of money in gambling people don't fully consider the new money as their own. So, when they are taking additional risk, they act as if they gamble with opponent's money (casino money). This is called as "house-money" effect. The "house-money" effect predicts that investors are more likely to purchase higher-risk stocks after locking in gain by selling stocks at a profit.

After experiencing a financial loss, people become less willing to take a risk. This effect is recognized as "snakebite" effect - the people remember this for a long time and become cautious. Likewise, after having their money lost people often feel they will be unsuccessful in the future too and they avoid taking risk in their investment decisions. For example, picking new stocks to the portfolio can give better diversification of investors' portfolio, but if the newly purchased stocks quickly decline in price, the investor might feel snakebite effect, and be afraid of picking stocks in his portfolio in the future.

But we can observe that sometimes losers don't avoid risk. Then losers use the chance to make up their losses. And the need for breaking even becomes to be stronger than the "snakebite" effect.

People without significant gains or losses prefer not to take the risk. Examining the risks of the investor, the endowment effect must be mentioned too. The endowment effect is when people demand much more to sell thing than they would be willing to pay to buy it. A closely related to endowment effect is a status quo bias - behavior of the people when they try to keep what they have been given instead of exchanging. How can endowment or status quo bias affect investors? People have tendency to hold the investments they already have. The status quo bias increases as the number of investment options increases. That means, the more complicated the investment decision that was needed becomes, the more likely the person is to choose to do nothing. In the real world, investors face the choice of investing in thousands of companies stocks, bonds, other investment vehicles. All these possibilities may affect the investors, and as a result they often choose to avoid making a change. This can be a particular problem when the investments have lost money. We can observe such a behavior of the investors during last years.

Memory is discussed as one of the factors which could affect the investors' behavior too. Memory can be understood as a perception of the physical and emotional experience. These experiences for different people could be different. Memory has a feature of adaptively and can determine whether a situation experienced in the past should be desired or avoided in the future. Usually the people feel better about experiences with a positive peak and end. And the memory of the large loss at the end of the period is associated with a higher degree of emotional pain. For example, the investor feels better about those stocks in his portfolio which price increase dramatically at the end of the period and is more skeptical about other stocks which prices were constantly growing during all period. As, a consequence, making decisions about these stocks for the following period the investor might be to optimistic about the stock with good short term results and to pessimistic about constantly growing stock.

Close related with the memory problems affecting the investors behavior is cognitive dissonance. Cognitive dissonance is based on evidence that people are struggling with two opposite ideas in their brains: "I am nice, but I am not nice." To avoid psychological pain people used to ignore or reject any information that contradicts with their positive self-image. The avoidance of cognitive dissonance can affect the investor's decision-making process in two ways. First, an investor can fail to make important decisions because it is too uncomfortable to contemplate the situation. Second, the filtering of new information limits the ability to evaluate and monitor investor's decisions. Investors seek to reduce psychological pain by adjusting their beliefs about the success of past investment decisions. For example, if the investor made a decision to buy N company's stocks and over time information about the results of this company were good and validate the past decision, investor feels as "I am nice," but if the results of the picked-up company were not good ("I am not nice"), the investor tries to reduce the cognitive dissonance. The investor's brain will filter out or reduce the negative information about the company and fixate on the positive information. Investor remembers that he/she has done well regardless of the actual performance. And obviously it is difficult to evaluate the progress seeking for the investment goals objectively when assessment of past performance is biased upward.

Mental Accounting And Investing

People uses financial budgets to control their spending. The brain uses mental budgets to associate the benefits of consumption with the costs in each mental account. Mental budgeting matches the emotional pain to the emotional joy. We can consider pain of the financial losses similar to the costs (pain) associated with the purchase of goods and services. Similarly, the benefits (joy) of financial gains is like the joy (or benefits) of consuming goods and services.

People do not like to make payments on a debt for a purchase that has already been consumed. For example, financing the vacation by debt is undesirable because it causes a long-term cost on a shot-term benefit. People show the preference for matching the length of the payments to the length of time the goods or services are used.

Economic theories predict that people will consider the present and future costs and benefits when determining a course of action. Contrary to these predictions, people usually consider historic costs when making decisions about the future. This behavior is called the "sunk-cost" effect. The sunk cost effect might be defined as an escalation of commitment to continue an endeavor once an investment in money or time has been made. The sunk costs could be characterized by size and timing. The size of sunk costs is very important in decision making: the larger amount of money was invested the stronger tendency for "keep going." The timing in investment decision making is important too: pain of closing a mental account without a benefit decrease with time negative impact of sunk cost depreciates over time.

Decision makers tend to place each investment into separate mental account. Each investment is treated separately, and interactions are overlooked. Mental budgeting compounds the aversion to selling losers. As time passes, the purchase of the stock becomes a sunk cost. It may be less emotionally distressing for the investor to sell the losing stock later as opposed to earlier. When investors decide to sell a losing stock, they have a tendency to bundle more than one sale on the same day. Investors integrate the sale of losing stocks to aggregate the losses and limit the feeling of regret to one time period. Alternatively, investors like to separate the sale of the winning stocks over several trading sessions to prolong the feeling of joy.

Mental accounting also affects investors' perceptions of portfolio risks. The tendency to overlook the interaction between investments causes investors to misperceive the risk of adding a security to an existing portfolio. In fact, people usually don't think in terms of portfolio risk. Investors evaluate each potential investment as if it were the only one investment they will have. However, most investors already have a portfolio and are considering other investments to add to it. Therefore, the most important consideration for the evaluation is how the expected risk and return of the portfolio will change when a new investment is added. Unfortunately, people have trouble evaluating the interactions between their mental accounts. Standard deviation is a good measure of an investment's risk. However, standard deviation measures the riskiness of the investment, but not how the risk of the investment portfolio would change if the investment were added. It is not the level of risk for each investment that is important – the important measure is how each investment interacts with the existing portfolio. Mental accounting sets the bases for segregating different investments in separate accounts and each of them consider as alone, evaluating their gains or losses.

People have different mental accounts for each investment goal, and the investor is willing to take different levels of risk for each goal. Investments are selected for each mental account by finding assets that match the expected risk and return of the mental account. Each mental account has an amount of money designated for that particular goal. As a result, investor portfolio diversification comes from the investment goals diversification rather than from a purposeful asset diversification according to Markowitz portfolio theory. That means that most investors do not have efficient portfolios and investors are taking too much risk for the level of expected return they are getting.

This mental accounting leads to other psychological biases, like the disposition effect.

Emotions And Investments

How important might be the emotions in the investors' decision making? The investment decisions are complex and include risk and uncertainty. In recent years, the psychologists as well as economists have examined the role of emotions in decision making. People who have stronger emotional reactions seem to let them impact their financial decisions. As some researchers conclude the more complex and uncertain a situation is, the more emotions influence a decision. Of course, the background feelings or mood may also influence investment decisions.

The mood affects the predictions of the people about the future. People often misattribute the mood they are in to their investment decisions. This is called misattribution bias. People who are in bad mood is more pessimistic about the future than people who are in a good mood. Translating to the behavior of investors it means that investors who are in good mood give a higher probability of good events/positive changes happening and a lower probability of bad changes happening. So, good mood will increase the likelihood of investing in riskier assets and bad mood will decrease willingness to invest in risky assets. Even those investors who use quantitative methods such as fundamental analysis must use some assumptions estimating fair value of the stock. Given the influence of mood on uncertain decisions, the expected growth rate taken for estimations of value of the stock using DDM (dividend discount models) may become biased and affect the overall result of estimated value of the stock. An investor who is in good mood may overestimate the growth rate and this would cause the investor to believe the stock is worth more than the believe of unbiased investor. As a consequence for the optimistic investor in this case might be his decision to buy the stock which is underestimated based on his calculations, when in reality it is not. Similar, the investor who is in bad mood may underestimate growth rate and stock value based on his calculations shows the stock is overestimated, when it is not in reality. So, the investors making biased and mood-driven decisions might suffer losses.

Investors who are in a good mood can also suffer from too optimistic decisions. Optimism could affect investors in two ways: first, investors tend to be less critical in making analysis for their decisions investing in stocks; second, optimistic investors tend to ignore the negative information about their stocks (even then they receive information about negative results of the company they were invested in they still believe that the company is performing well). This is why the price of the stock is frequently set up by the optimistic investors. Even if there are enough optimistic and pessimistic investors in the market, the optimists drive up the stock price with their buying, because pessimists are passive. For firms with the high degree of uncertainty optimistic investors tend to set the stock price until that uncertainty is resolved. The prospects of large, well established firms have less uncertainty and their stock prices are generally more reflective of actual prospects than of optimistic prospects of investors).

It is obvious that the weather has an influence on the mood of the people. Sunshine usually is associated with good mood and optimistic thinking and without sun people feel bad. Some studies were performed to answer the question how the weather might affect investors' behavior. The researchers found that the daily returns for sunny days are higher than the daily returns for non-sunny days. The results of this research allow to conclude that sunshine affects the investors that they become more optimistic and are used to buy rather than sell the stocks. Then this tendency prevails in the market the stock prices are growing.

The investors' behavior might be influenced by other factors which affect the emotions. Sport is investigated as one of such factors). The research results of Edmans, Garcia, Norli showed that stock market reaction to soccer game loss day after for losing team stock market was negative (decreasing). And the stock market reaction was stronger in countries which have positive historical results in soccer.

However general level of optimism and pessimism or social mood changes over time. as Nofsinger showed in his investigation. Investors tend to bee most optimistic when the market reaches the top and they are most pessimistic when market is at the bottom. This fluctuating social mood is defined as market sentiment. Knowing, the phenomenon of market sentiment might, allow to predict the returns in the market when investors become too optimistic on the top of the market or too pessimistic when marketing reaches its bottom.

A market bubble could be explained by the situation when high prices seem to be generated more by investors (traders in the market) optimism then by economic fundamentals. Extreme prices that seem to be at odds with rational explanations have occurred repeatedly throughout history.

Points

1. Overconfidence causes people to overestimate their knowledge, risks, and their ability to control events. This perception occurs in investing as well. Even without information, people believe the stocks they own will perform

better than stocks they do not own. Typically, investors expect to earn an above -average return.

2. Overconfidence can lead investors to poor trading decisions which often manifest themselves as excessive trading, risk-taking and ultimately portfolio losses. If many investors suffer from overconfidence at the same time, then signs might be found within the stock market.
3. Overconfidence affects investors' risk-taking behavior. Rational investors try to maximize returns while minimizing the amount of risk taken. However, overconfident investors misinterpret the level of risk they take.
4. Avoiding regret and seeking pride affects person's behavior and this is called the disposition effect. Fearing regret and seeking pride causes the investors to be predisposed to selling winners (potential stocks with growing market prices) to early and riding losers (stocks with the negative tendencies in market prices) too long. Selling winners to soon suggests that those stocks will continue to perform well after they are sold and holding losers too long suggest that those stocks will continue to perform poorly.
5. The "house-money" effect predicts that after experiencing a gain or profit, people are willing to take more risk. The investors are more likely to purchase higher-risk stocks after locking in gain by selling stocks at a profit.
6. The "snakebite" effect predicts that after experiencing a financial loss, people avoid to take risk in their investment decisions.
7. The endowment effect is when people demand much more to sell thing than they would be willing to pay to buy it. A closely related to endowment effect is a status quo bias - behavior of the people when they try to keep what they have been given instead of exchanging. The status quo bias increases as the number of investment options increases. That means, the more complicated the investment decision that was needed becomes, the more likely the person is to choose to do nothing.

8. Memory can be understood as a perception of the physical and emotional experience. Memory has a feature of adaptivity and can determine whether a situation experienced in the past should be desired or avoided in the future. Usually, the people, feel better about experiences with a positive peak and end. And the memory of the large loss at the end of the period is associated with a higher degree of emotional pain.
9. Cognitive dissonance is based on evidence that people are struggling with two opposite ideas in their brains: "I am nice, but I am not nice." To avoid psychological pain people used to ignore or reject any information that contradicts with their positive self-image. The avoidance of cognitive dissonance can affect the investor's decision-making process. Investors seek to reduce psychological pain by adjusting their beliefs about the success of past investment decisions.
10. Mental budgeting matches the emotional pain to the emotional joy. The pain of the financial losses could be considered as similar to the costs (pain) associated with the purchase of goods and services. Similarly, the benefits (joy) of financial gains is like the joy (or benefits) of consuming goods and services.
11. People's behavior which more consider historic costs when making decisions about the future is called the "sunk-cost" effect. The sunk cost effect might be defined as an escalation of commitment – to continue an endeavor once an investment in money or time has been made. The size of sunk costs is very important in decision making: the larger amount of money was invested the stronger tendency for "keep going."
12. People have different mental accounts for each investment goal, and the investor is willing to take different levels of risk for each goal. Investments are selected for each mental account by finding assets that match the expected risk and return of the mental account. Each mental account has an amount of money designated for that particular goal. As a

result, investor's portfolio diversification comes from the investment goals diversification rather than from a purposeful asset diversification according to the portfolio theory.

13. The mood affects the predictions of the people about the future. Misattribution bias predicts that people often misattribute the mood they are in to their decisions. People who are in bad mood are more pessimistic about the future than people who are in a good mood. Translating to the behavior of investors it means that investors who are in good mood give a higher probability of good events/ positive changes happening and a lower probability of bad changes happening.
14. General level of optimism and pessimism or social mood changes over time. Investors tend to bee most optimistic when the market reaches the top and they are most pessimistic when marketing is at the bottom. This fluctuating social mood is defined as market sentiment.
15. A market bubble could be explained by the situation when high prices seem to be generated more by investors (traders in the market) optimism then by economic fundamentals.

Basic Concepts Of Trading

Random Walk Theory

Before you decide if you want to be a trader, you have to first decide whether or not it's even reasonable to believe that trading can be a profitable endeavor. In order to make that call, you have to choose which basic market theory you believe.

A "random walk" is a statistical phenomenon where a variable follows no discernible trend and moves seemingly at random. The random walk theory as applied to trading, most clearly laid out by Burton Malkiel, an economics professor at Princeton University, posits that the price of securities moves randomly (hence the name of the theory), and that, therefore, any attempt to predict future price movement, through either fundamental or technical analysis, is futile. The implication for traders is that it is impossible to outperform the overall market average other than by sheer chance. Those who subscribe to the random walk theory recommend using a "buy and hold" strategy, investing in a selection of stocks that represent the overall market – for example, an index mutual fund or ETF.

Basic Assumptions Of The Random Walk Theory

1. The Random Walk Theory assumes the price of each stock follows a random walk.
2. The Random Walk Theory also assumes that the movement in the price of one security is independent of price movement in another security.

One of the main criticisms of the Random Walk Theory is that the stock market consists of a large number of investors and the amount of time each investor spends in the market is different. Thus, it is possible for trends to emerge in the prices of securities in the short run, and a savvy investor can outperform the market by strategically buying stocks when the price is low and selling stocks when the price is high within a short time. Other critics argue that the entire basis of the Random Walk Theory is flawed and that stocks prices do follow patterns or trends even over the long run. They argue that because the price of a security is affected by an extremely large number of factors, it may be impossible to find out the pattern or trend followed by the price of that security, but just because a pattern cannot be found does not mean that a pattern does not exist.

A Non-Random Walk

In contrast to the random walk theory is, the contention of believers in technical analysis, those who think that future price movements can be predicted based on trends, patterns, and historical price action. The implication arising from this point of view is that traders with superior market analysis and trading skills can significantly outperform the overall market average.

Both sides can present evidence to support their position, so it's up to each individual to choose what they believe. However, there is one fact, perhaps a decisive one, which goes against the random walk theory: the fact that there are some individual traders who consistently outperform the market average for long periods of time. According to the random walk theory, a trader should only be able to outperform the overall market by chance, or luck. This would allow for there being some traders who, at any given point in time, would – purely by chance – be outperforming the market average. But what are the odds then that the same traders would be "lucky" year in and year out for decades? Yet there are indeed such traders, people like Paul Tudor Jones, who have managed to generate above average trading returns on a consistent basis over a long span of time.

It's important to note that even the most devout believers in technical analysis – those who think that future price movements in the market can be predicted – don't believe that there's any way to infallibly predict future price action. It is more accurate to say that probable future price movement can be predicted by using technical analysis, and that by trading based on such probabilities it is possible to generate higher returns on investment.

So, who do you believe? If you believe in the random walk theory, then you should invest in a good ETF or mutual fund designed to mirror the performance of the S&P 500 Index, and hope for an overall bull market. If on the other hand, you believe that price movements are not random, then you should be polishing your fundamental or technical analysis skills, confident that doing such work will pay off with superior profits through actively trading the market.

Since you're reading a book on trading, we'll assume that you fall into the latter camp. We wholeheartedly agree with you. So keep reading…

Fundamental And Technical Analysis

I still like the old joke that goes, "How can I end up with a million dollars through trading stocks?" – "Start with two million and trade using technical analysis." Let me put a disclaimer on that by saying that I am, in fact, primarily a technical trader myself and very much an advocate of technical trading. But it's still a good joke.

Fundamental analysis and technical analysis are the two broad, general approaches to market analysis and trading. Each approach has its advocates and its detractors, and there are hugely successful – and unsuccessful – traders in both camps.

The Fundamentals of Fundamental Analysis

Fundamental analysis aims at identifying the real, intrinsic value of a security, based on the belief that the genuine value of something is what will ultimately determine its price. Fundamental market analysts attempt to identify a stock or other security's intrinsic value by looking at factors such as overall economic conditions, industry trends, company management, profit and loss data, and any of a number of financial metrics that are used to determine the financial health and future prospects for a company. Some of the most commonly used financial metrics are the price-to-earnings ratio (P/E), price-to-book ratio (P/B), debt-to-equity ratio(D/E), return on investment (ROI), and return on assets (ROA).

Fundamental stock traders rely heavily on data such as a company's quarterly and annual earnings reports, to see the earnings-per-share which indicates a company's profitability as divided among the total amount of publicly-traded equity in the company. Additional data for analysis by fundamental traders is gleaned from the published financial statements of publicly traded companies, such as a company's income statement and balance sheet.

The exact nature of fundamental analysis varies according to investments. For example, fundamental traders of the foreign exchange – forex – market eye data such as gross domestic product (GDP), manufacturing, import and export data, and the consumer price index (CPI) in order to assess the overall health of a nation's economy. Logically, nations with stronger economies will also likely have relatively stronger currencies.

Advocates of fundamental analysis points out that it is based on solid financial data, and therefore likely to be reliable. However, a drawback of fundamental analysis is that it requires time-consuming research, and doing things like financial modeling and company valuations is not an endeavor well-suited to many investors.

The Fundamentals of Technical Analysis

(Get it?–the FUNDAMENTALS of TECHNICAL analysis? See what I did there?)

Technical analysts ignore all of the factors considered by fundamental analysts, and instead concentrate their evaluation of a security solely on analyzing market price action to identify current and likely future price trends. The basic belief of technical traders is that all relevant factors of supply and demand are reflected in the price movement of a security. Technical traders argue, for example, that there's no need to engage in the practice of fundamental traders attempting to assess whether current economic or marketplace conditions favor increasing demand for a company's products Instead, technical traders would say that if the company's stock price is rising steadily, then that shows that their products are in increasing demand.

The basic tool of technical analysts is the price chart. Technical analysts look at all manner of data that can be plotted on a price chart for security, such as trend lines, trading volume, moving averages, and support and resistance levels. Technical analysts don't bother attempting to identify intrinsic value of s security, instead using chart analysis to identify price action patterns that indicate probable future price direction and movement.

Both the strength and the weakness of technical analysis lie in the fact that there is virtually an endless list of technical indicators to choose from in analyzing a security. That's strength because you have a wealth of price analysis tools at your disposal to help you determine probable future price movements. It's a weakness because of the fact that you can get an endless number of conflicting indications and trading signals from different technical indicators. Among the endless choices of indicators to look at such as moving averages, candlestick patterns, momentum indicators, and pivot points, how do you know what to pay attention to? And the simple answer is: you don't. Technical traders select the indicators they use based on any number of reasons, and then hope that those indicators are the ones giving the most reliable trading signals.

So Which One Should You Use – Fundamental or Technical Analysis?

Use the analytical approach that you're most comfortable using, that you have the most confidence in. Okay, you want something more than that? All right, but in the end your chosen method of market analysis really is going to come down to your personal preference and what is best suited to your personal trading style, financial goals, and risk tolerance.

The practical fact is that while 50 or 100 years ago fundamental analysis held sway, the arrival of computers has made technical analysis both easier and more widely used. These days, most of the largest market players such as investment banks base nearly all of their trading decisions on complex computer algorithms. It's estimated that as much as 70-80% of all the trading volume on exchanges is generated through technical analysis. That doesn't mean that fundamental analysis is a useless dinosaur as a trading approach. Still, it does mean that even fundamental market analysts have to pay attention to technical factors that may be driving market prices.

Many traders use some combination of fundamental and technical analysis. For example, a stock trader might select companies to invest in based on fundamental analysis of market sectors and various companies, but select specific price entry and exit points based on technical analysis.

How to Read Stock Charts

If you're going to actively trade stocks, then you need to know how to read stock charts. Even traders who primarily use fundamental analysis to select stocks still often use technical analysis of stock price movement to determine specific buy, or entry, and sell, or exit, points. Stock charts are freely available on websites such as Google Finance and Yahoo Finance, and stock brokerages always make stock charts available for their clients. In short, you shouldn't have any trouble finding stock charts to examine.

Stock Chart Construction – Lines, Bars, Candlesticks

Stock charts can vary in their construction from bar charts to candlestick charts to line charts to point and figure charts. Nearly all stock charts give you the option to switch between the various types of charts, as well as the ability to overlay various technical indicators on a chart. You can also vary the time frame shown by a chart. While daily charts are probably the most commonly used, intraday, weekly, monthly, year-to-date (YTD), 5-year, 10-year, and complete historical lifetime of stock are also available.

There are relative advantages and disadvantages to using different chart construction styles and to using different time frames for analysis. What style and time frame will work best for you as an individual analyst or trader is something that you can only discover through actually doing stock chart analysis. You can glean valuable indications of probable stock price movement from stock chart analysis. You should choose the chart style that makes it easiest for you to read and analyze the chart, and trade profitably.

Looking At A Stock Chart

Below is a year-to-date daily chart of Apple Inc. (AAPL), courtesy of stockcharts.com. This chart is a candlestick chart, with white candles showing up days for the stock and red candles showing down days. In addition, this chart has several technical indicators added: a 50-period moving average and a 200-period moving average, appearing as blue and red lines on the chart; the relative strength indicator (RSI) which appears in a separate window above the main chart window; the moving average convergence divergence indicator (MACD) which appears in a separate window below the chart.

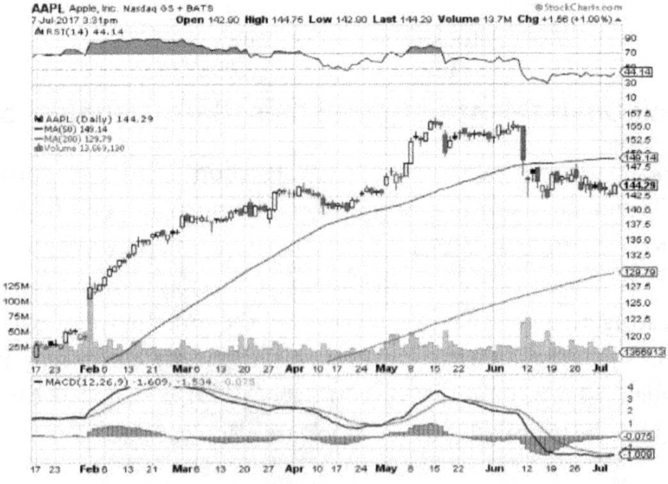

Along the bottom of the main chart window, the daily trading volume is shown. Note the large spike in volume that occurred on February 1st, when the stock gapped higher and began a strong uptrend which lasted until early June. Also, note the high amount of selling volume (indicated by red volume bars which indicate days with a greater amount of selling volume than buying volume) that occurs when the stock moves sharply downward around June 12th.

The Importance of Volume

Volume appears on nearly every stock chart that you'll find. That's because trading volume is considered a critical technical indicator by nearly every stock trader. On the chart above, in addition to showing the total level of trading volume for each day, days with greater buying volume are indicated with blue bars and days with greater selling volume are indicated with red bars.

The reason that volume is considered to be a very important technical indicator is a simple one. The vast majority of stock market buying and selling is done by large institutional traders, such as investment banks, and by fund managers, such as mutual fund or exchange-traded fund (ETF) managers. When those investors make major purchases or sales of a stock, it creates high trading volume, and it is that kind of major buying and selling by large investors that typically move a stock higher or lower.

Therefore, individual or other institutional traders watch volume figures for indications of major buying or selling activity by large institutions. This information can be used either to forecast a future price trend for the stock or to identify key price support and resistance levels. In fact, many individual traders determine their buying and selling decisions almost solely based on following the identified actions of major institutional traders. They buy stocks when volume, and price movement indicates that major institutions are buying, and sell or avoid buying stocks when there are indications of major institutional selling. Such a strategy works best when applied to major stocks that are generally heavily traded. It will likely be less effective when applied to stocks of small companies that are not yet on the radar screens of large institutional investors and that have relatively small trading volumes even on days when the stock is more heavily traded than usual.

Basic Volume Patterns

There are four basic volume patterns that traders typically watch as indicators.

- *High volume trading on Up Days* – This is a bullish indication that a stock's price will continue to rise Low volume trading on Down Days – This is also a bullish indication since it indicates that on days when the stock's price falls back a bit not many investors are involved in the trading. Therefore, such down days occurring in an overall bull market are commonly interpreted as temporary retracements or corrections rather than as significant indicators of future price movement.
- *High Volume Trading on Down Days* – This is considered a bearish indicator for a stock, as it shows that major institutional traders are aggressive selling the stock.
- Low Volume Trading on Up Days – This is another bearish indicator, although not as strong as high volume trading on down days. The low volume tends to peg the trading action on such days as less significant and usually evidence of just a short-term counter-trend retracement upward in an overall, long-term bearish trend.

Using Technical Indicators

In analyzing stock charts for stock market investing, traders use a variety of technical indicators to help them more precisely determine probable price movement, identify trends, and anticipate market reversals from bullish trends to bearish trends and vice-versa. One of the most commonly used technical indicators is a moving average. The moving averages that are most frequently applied to daily stock charts are the 20-day, 50-day, and 200-day moving average. Generally speaking, as long as a shorter period moving average is above a longer period moving average, a stock is considered to be in an overall uptrend. Conversely, if shorter term moving averages are below longer term moving averages, then that indicates an overall downtrend.

Another commonly used indicator is the trendline. A trendline is drawn on a chart connecting the lowest price points in an uptrend or the highest price points in a downtrend. Price breaking substantially below the trendline in an uptrend indicates a possible market reversal to the downside, while price moving substantially above a downtrend line indicates a possible reversal to the upside.

The Importance of the 200-Day Moving Average

The 200-day moving average is considered by most analysts as a critical indicator on a stock chart. Traders who are bullish on a stock want to see the stock's price remain above the 200-day moving average. Bearish traders who are selling short a stock want to see the stock price stay below the 200-day moving average. If a stock's price crosses from below the 200-day moving average to above it, this is usually interpreted as a bullish market reversal. A downside cross of price from above the 200-day moving average is interpreted as a bearish indication for the stock.

The interplay between the 50-day and 200-day moving averages is also considered as a strong indicator for future price movement. When the 50-day moving average crosses from below to above the 200-day moving average this event is referred to by technical analysts as a "golden cross." A golden cross is basically an indication that the stock is "gold," set for substantially higher prices. On the flip side, if the 50-day is moving average crosses from above to below the 200-day moving average, this is referred to by analysts as a "death cross." You can probably figure out on your own that a "death cross" isn't considered to bode well for a stock's future price movement.

Trend and Momentum Indicators

There is virtually an endless list of technical indicators for traders to choose from in analyzing a chart. Experiment with various indicators to discover the ones that work best for your particular style of trading and as applied to the specific stocks that you trade. You'll likely find that some indicators work very well for you in forecasting price movement for some stocks but not for others.

Technical analysts often use indicators of different types in conjunction with each other. Technical indicators are classified into two basic types: trend indicators such as moving averages, and momentum indicators such as the MACD or the average directional index (ADX). Trend indicators are used to identify the overall direction of a stock's price, up or down, while momentum indicators gauge the strength of price movement.

Analyzing Trends

When reviewing a stock chart, in addition to determining the stock's overall trend, up or down, it's also helpful to look to identify aspects of a trend such as the following: How long has a trend been in place? Stocks do not stay in uptrends or downtrends indefinitely. Eventually, there are always trend changes. If a trend has continued for a long period of time without any significant corrective retracement moves in the opposite direction, you want to be especially alert for signs of an impending market reversal.

How does a stock tend to trade? Some stocks move in relatively slow, well-defined trends. Other stocks tend to experience more volatility on a regular basis, with price making sharp moves up or down even in the midst of a general long-term trend. If you are trading a stock that typically evidences high volatility, then you know not to place too much importance on the trading action of any single day. Are there signs of a possible trend reversal? Careful analysis of stock price movement often reveals signs of potential trend reversals. Momentum indicators often indicate a trend running out of steam before the price of a stock actually peaks, giving alert traders the opportunity to get out of a stock at a good price before it reverses to the downside. Various candlesticks or other chart patterns are also often used to identify major market reversals.

Identifying Support and Resistance Levels

Stock charts can be particularly helpful in identifying support and resistance levels for stocks. Support levels are price levels where previously fresh buying has come in to support a stock's price and turn it back to the upside. Conversely, resistance levels represent prices at which a stock has shown a tendency to fail in attempting to move higher, turning back to the downside. Identifying support and resistance levels can be especially helpful in trading a stock that tends to trade within an established trading range over a long period. Some stock traders, having identified such a stock, will look to buy the stock at support levels and sell it at resistance levels over and over again, making more and more money as the stock traverses the same ground multiple times.

For stocks that have well-identified support and resistance levels, price breakouts beyond either of those levels can be important indicators of future price movement. For example, if a stock has previously failed to break above $50 a share, but then finally does so, this may be a sign that the stock will move from there to a substantially higher price level. The chart of General Electric (GE) below shows that the stock traded in a tight range between $29 and $30 a share for several months, but once the stock price broke below the $29 support level, it continued to fall substantially lower.

Using Stock Chart Analysis

Stock chart analysis is not infallible, not even in the hands of the most expert technical analyst. If it were, every stock investor would be a multi-millionaire. However, learning to read, a stock chart will definitely help turn the odds of being a successful stock market trader in your favor.

Stock chart analysis is a skill, and like any other skill, one only becomes an expert at it through practice. The good news is that virtually anyone willing to work diligently at analyzing stock charts can become, if not an outright expert, at least pretty good at it – good enough to improve their overall profitability in stock market trading. Therefore, it's in your best interest as a trader to begin or continue your education in stock chart analysis.

Stock Investing – Value Investing

Since, the publication of "The Intelligent Investor," by Benjamin Graham, what is commonly known as "value investing" has become one of the most widely respected and widely followed methods of stock-picking. Famed investor Warren Buffet, while actually employing a mix of growth investing and value investing principles, has publicly credited much of his unparalleled success in the investment world to following Graham's basic advice in evaluating and selecting stocks for his portfolio.

However, as the markets have changed over more than half a century, so too has value investing. Over the years, Graham's original value investing strategy has been adapted, adjusted, and augmented in a variety of ways by investors and market analysts aiming to improve on how well a value investing approach performs for investors in the 21st century. Even Graham himself devised additional metrics and formulations aimed at more accurately determining the true value of a stock. Keep in mind that whenever you evaluate a company and its stock price, you need to interpret the numbers in light of things such as specific industry and general economic conditions.

In addition, good stock analysis requires that you always review past and current financial metrics with an eye to the future, projecting how well you think a company will fare moving forward, given its current finances, assets, liabilities, marketplace position, and plans for expansion. It's also important to avoid getting lost in a purely numerical analysis to the point where you lose sight of the forest for the trees. Non-numerical "value" factors that investors should not overlook include things such as how effectively a company's management is achieving goals and moving the company forward in a way that is consistent with pursuing its corporate mission statement. A company may be showing impressive profitability for the moment, but in today's excessively competitive marketplace a company that is not carefully mapping, planning out, reviewing (and when needed, re-routing) its progress will nearly always eventually be eclipsed by a company that is doing those things.

Value Investing vs. Growth Investing

Before we move ahead to review traditional value investing and then look at some of the newer, alternative value investing strategies, it's important to note that "value investing" and "growth investing" are not two contradictory or mutually exclusive approaches to picking stocks. The basic idea of value investing – selecting currently undervalued stocks that you expect to increase in value in the future obviously involves assessing probable future growth.

The differences between value investing and growth investing strategies tend to be more just a matter of emphasizing different financial metrics (and to some extent a difference in risk tolerance, with growth investors typically willing to accept higher levels of risk). Ultimately, value investing, growth investing, or any other basic stock evaluation approach has the same end goal: choosing stocks that will provide an investor with the best possible return on investment.

The Basics of Traditional Value Investing

In "The Intelligent Investor" Ben Graham proposed and explained a method for screening stocks that he developed to assist even the most inexperienced investors with their stock portfolio selections. In fact, that's one of the major appeals of Graham's value investing approach – the fact that it's not overly intricate or complicated, and can, therefore, be easily utilized by the average investor.

Graham's value investing strategy involves some basic concepts that underlie or form the foundation or basis, for the strategy. For Graham, a key concept was that of intrinsic value specifically, the intrinsic value of a company or its stock. The essence of value investing is using a stock analysis method to determine the stock's genuine value, with an eye toward buying stocks whose current share price is below the stock's genuine value or worth.

Value investors are essentially applying the same logic as careful shoppers in looking to identify stocks that are "a good buy," that are selling for a price lower than the real value they represent. A value investor searches out and snaps up what they determine are undervalued stocks, with the belief that the market will eventually "correct" the share price to a higher level that more accurately represents the stock's true value.

Graham's Value Investing Approach

Graham's approach to value investing was geared toward developing a simple process for stock screening that the average investor could easily utilize. Overall, he did manage to keep things fairly simple, but on the other hand, classic value investing is a little more involved than just the often-recited refrain of, "Buy stocks with a price-to-book (P/B) ratio of less than 1.0."

The P/B ratio guideline for identifying undervalued stocks is, in fact, only one of a number of criteria Graham used to help him identify undervalued stocks. There's some argument among value investing aficionados as to whether one is supposed to use a 10-point criteria checklist that Graham created, a longer 17-point checklist, a distillation of either of the criteria lists that usually appears in the form of a four- or five-point checklist, or one or the other of a couple of single criterion stock selection methods that Graham also advocated.

In an attempt to avoid as much confusion as possible, we're going to present here the main criteria that Graham himself considered most important in identifying good value stocks, i.e., those with an intrinsic value greater than their current market price.

1. A value stock should have a P/B ratio of 1.0 or lower; the P/B ratio is important because it represents a comparison of the share price to a company's assets. One major limitation of the P/B ratio is that it functions best when used to assess capital- intensive companies, but is less effective when applied to non-capital-intensive firms.

Note: Rather than looking for an absolute P/B ratio lower than 1.0, investors may just look for companies with a P/B ratio that is relatively lower than the average P/B ratio of similar companies in the same industry or market sector.

2. The price-to-earnings (P/E) ratio should be less than 40% of the stock's highest P/E over the previous five years.

3. Look for a share price that is less than 67% (two-thirds) of the tangible per share book value, AND less than 67% of the company's net current asset value (NCAV).

Note: The share-price-to-NCAV criterion is sometimes used as a standalone tool for identifying undervalued stocks. Graham considered a company's NCAV to be one of the most accurate representations of a company's true intrinsic value.

4. A company's total book value should be greater than its total debt.

Note: A related, or perhaps an alternative, financial metric to this is examining the basic debt ratio, the current ratio which should be greater than 2.0.

5. A company's total debt should not exceed twice the NCAV, and total current liabilities and long-term debt should not be greater than the firm's total stockholder equity.

Investors can experiment with using Graham's various criteria and determine for themselves which of the valuation metrics or guidelines they consider to be most essential and most reliable as indicators. There are some investors who still use only an examination of a stock's P/B ratio to determine whether or, not a stock is undervalued. Others rely heavily, if not exclusively, on comparing current share price to the company's NCAV. More cautious, conservative investors may only buy stocks that pass everyone of Graham's suggested screening tests.

We think you'll find that incorporating at least some of Graham's value investing principles into your portfolio selection process will improve your overall stock trading performance.

Alternative Methods of Determining Value

Value investors continue to give Graham and his value investing metrics attention. However, the development of new angles from which to calculate and assess value means that alternative methods for identifying underpriced stocks have arisen as well. One increasing popular value metric is the Discounted Cash Flow (DCF) formula.

DCF and Reverse DCF Valuation

Many accountants and other financial professionals have become ardent fans of DCF analysis. DCF is one of the few financial metrics that take into account the time value of money – the notion that money available now is more valuable than the same amount of money available at some point in the future because whatever money is available now can be invested and thus used to generate more money. DCF analysis uses future free cash flow (FCF) projections and discount rates that are calculated using the Weighted Average Cost of Capital (WACC) to estimate the present value of a company, with the underlying idea being that its intrinsic value is largely dependent on the company's ability to generate cash flow.

The essential calculation of a DCF analysis is as follows:

(Enterprise value is an alternative metric to market capitalization. It represents market capitalization + debt + preferred shares – total cash, including cash equivalents). If the DCF analysis of a company renders a per share value higher than the current market share price, then the stock is considered undervalued. DCF analysis is particularly well-suited for evaluating companies that have stable, relatively predictable cash flows since the primary weakness of DCF analysis is that it depends on accurate estimates of future cash flows.

Some analysts prefer to use reverse DCF analysis in order to overcome the uncertainty of future cash flow projections. Reverse DCF analysis starts with a known quantity the current share price and then calculates the cash flows that would be required to generate that current valuation. Once the required cash flow is determined, then evaluating the company's stock as undervalued or overvalued is as simple as making a judgment about how reasonable (or unreasonable) it is to expect the company to be able to generate the required amount of cash flows necessary to sustain the current share price. An undervalued stock is identified when an analyst determines that a company can easily generate and sustain more than enough cash flow to justify the current share price.

Katsenelson's Absolute P/E Model

Katsenelson's model, developed by Vitally Katsenelson, is another alternative value investing analysis tool that is considered particularly ideal for evaluating companies that have strong, positive, established earnings scores. The Katsenelson model focuses on providing investors with a more reliable P/E ratio, known as "absolute P/E." The model adjusts the traditional P/E ratio in accord with several variables, such as earnings growth, dividend yield, and earnings predictability.

***The formula is as follows*:**

Earnings growth points are determined by starting with a no-growth P/E value of 8, and then adding .65 points for every 100 basis points the projected growth rate increases until you reach 16%. Above 16%, .5 points are added for every 100 basis points in projected growth. The absolute P/E number produced is then compared to the traditional P/E number. If the absolute P/E number is higher than the standard P/E ratio, then that indicates the stock is undervalued. Obviously, the larger the discrepancy between the absolute P/E and the standard P/E, the better bargain the stock is. For example, if a stock's absolute P/E is 20 while the standard P/E ratio is only 11, then the true intrinsic value of the stock is likely much higher than the current share price, as the absolute P/E number indicates that investors are probably willing to pay a lot more for the company's current earnings.

The Ben Graham Number

You don't necessarily have to look away from Ben Graham to find an alternative value investing metric. Graham himself created an alternate value assessment formula that investors may choose to employ – the Ben Graham Number. The formula for calculating the Ben **Graham Number is as follows:**

For example, the Ben Graham Number for a stock with an EPS of $1.50 and a book value of $10 per share calculates out to $18.37. Graham generally felt that a company's P/E ratio shouldn't be higher than 15 and that its price-to-book (P/B) ratio shouldn't exceed 1.5. That's where the 22.5 in the formula is derived from (15 x 1.5 = 22.5). However, with the valuation levels that are commonplace these days, the maximum allowable P/E might be shifted to around 25 and acceptable P/B ratio to 3.0.

Once you've calculated a stock's Ben Graham Number, which is designed to represent the actual per-share intrinsic value of the company – you then compare it to the stock's current share price.

- If the current share price is lower than the Ben Graham Number, this indicates the stock is undervalued and may be considered as a buy.
- If the current share price is higher than the Ben Graham Number, then the stock appears overvalued and is not a promising buy candidate.

Value investors are always looking to buy undervalued stocks selling at a discount to intrinsic value in order to make sizeable profits with minimal risk. There are a variety of tools and approaches that traders can use to try to determine the true value of a stock and whether or not it's a good fit for their investment portfolio.

The best stock evaluation process is never just a mathematical formula that one plugs numbers into and then in return receives a solid, guaranteed determination of a particular stock as a "good" or "bad" investment. While there are important stock valuation formulas and financial metrics to consider, the process of evaluating a stock is ultimately part art and part science – and partly a skill that can only be mastered with time and practice.

Stock Investing – Growth Investing

Traders can take advantage of growth investing strategies in order to more precisely hone in on stocks or other investments offering above-average profit potential. When it comes to trading stocks, there are always a variety of approaches that can be taken. The goal, however, is generally always the same, regardless of the approach grow your investments and increase your profits. Growth investors are continually on the hunt for individual stocks or stock-related investments such as mutual funds or ETFs – that are poised to grow and offer the potential for above average returns on investment. The trades you make should, of course, always fall in line with your short-term and long-term financial goals, risk tolerance, and a number of other factors. Still, there are basic techniques, principles, and strategies that growth investors follow that suit virtually any individual investing plan. In this guide, we want to explain growth investing as a strategy itself, and then break down more specific approaches and strategies that growth investors can employ.

The Basics of Growth Investing

Growth investing is essentially the process of investing in companies, industries, or sectors that are currently growing and are expected to continue growing rapidly over a substantial period of time. In the investment world, growth investing is typically looked at as more of an offensive rather than a defensive investing strategy. This simply means that growth investing is a more active attempt to generate the highest possible returns on the capital that you invest. Defensive investing, in contrast, tends more toward investments that generate passive income and work to protect the capital you've already earned such as bonds or blue-chip stocks that offer steady dividends.

Investing in Hot Sectors

One approach growth investors can take is to invest in stocks, mutual funds, or ETFs in specific sectors and industries. The success of businesses in various sectors changes over time. However, it's fairly easy to identify sectors that are "hot" in the sense of producing above average returns as compared to most publicly traded companies. For example, two sectors that have been particularly hot for a couple of decades or more are healthcare and technology.

Companies that deal with technology, technological advances, or are constantly putting out new hardware, software, and devices are usually good picks for growth investors. The same is true for companies in the healthcare sector. Think about it logically: Everyone, at some point, needs to care for their health and there are companies that are constantly developing new medications, therapies, treatments, and places to go to access superior health care. The healthcare sector is likely to continue enjoying rapid growth as it serves an aging baby-boomer generation. In fact, these two sectors are related, as many recent technology developments have actually been advances in healthcare technology.

Growth investors can simplify sector investing by taking advantage of investment vehicles such as mutual funds and ETFs that contain a basket of stocks linked to specific sectors. As noted previously, ETFs are an increasingly popular investment option due to their superior liquidity and lower trading costs as compared to mutual funds.

Understanding Earnings

For growth investors in stocks, understanding a company's net earnings is essential. This doesn't mean simply knowing their current earnings, but also considering their historical earnings as well, since this enables you to evaluate current earnings relative to a company's past performance. Also, reviewing a company's earnings history provides a clearer indication of the probability of the company generating higher future earnings. A high earnings performance in a given quarter or year may represent a one-time anomaly in a company's performance, a continuing trend, or a certain point in an earnings cycle that the company continues to repeat over time. Even companies with relatively low, or sometimes even negative, earnings may still be a good pick for a growth investor. Remember that earnings are what's left over after subtracting all production, marketing, operating, labor, and tax costs from a company's gross revenue. In many instances, smaller companies attempt to make a breakthrough by funneling more capital toward growing their business, which may negatively impact their earnings in the short run, but in the long run generate higher returns and greater profits for investors. In such a situation, smart traders consider other factors, such as the quality of a company's management, to ascertain clues to a company's true growth potential.

Growth Investing through Value Investing

Growth investors are effectively value investors sometimes, in that they seek out companies whose stock may be currently undervalued due to reasons that may be as simple as the fact that the company is relatively new and has not yet caught the attention of many investment analysts or fund managers.

The goal for such investors is to grab up shares at a low price of a company that is well-positioned to enjoy a sizeable and continued surge in growth. There are a number of possible ways to approach identifying such companies, one of which we've already touched on looking at companies in hot sectors. Investors who can identify a new, well-managed and well-funded company that is part of a hot sector can often reap substantial rewards. Another possible approach is to examine companies that are on the downslope, such as those that have gone through bankruptcy or reorganization, but that are likely to survive and recover.

Using the Price-to-Earnings Ratio

The price/earnings (P/E) ratio is a financial metric that growth investors often favor to help them in choosing stocks. Generally speaking, a higher P/E ratio indicates that investors are willing to take greater risk on buying a stock because of its projected earnings and growth rate.

The P/E ratio is particularly useful for growth investors who are trying to compare companies that operate in the same industry. In established industries and sectors, there tends to be average P/E ratios for that particular industry or sector. Knowing such industry or sector averages makes a company's P/E ratio a much more useful number than simply looking at it in comparison to the market as a whole.

Looking at a company's P/E ratio remains a useful analytical tool for growth investors, but adding consideration of other fundamental financial metrics can help to fine tune your stock picks.

Using the Price-to-Book Ratio

The price-to-book ratio or P/B ratio is often considered more the basic analytical metric of value investors as opposed to growth investors. However, the fact is that the P/B ratio can also be utilized as an effective tool in identifying stocks with high growth potential.

The P/B ratio is calculated by dividing a stock's per share price by the book value per share. In order to determine, the book value of a stock preferred stock that has been issued must be subtracted from the total stockholder equity. The figure calculated from this takeaway must then be divided by all common shares still outstanding. The final number is the company's book value per share of common stock. It is often helpful for investors, especially growth investors, to compare a company's book value to its market value. This comparison can provide a good indication of whether a stock is undervalued or overvalued. Companies with high growth potential are frequently undervalued due to heftier debt loads and capital expenditures.

High-Risk Growth Investments

Growth investing may also extend into investments beyond traditional stock market investing.

Investing in high-risk growth investments also referred to as speculative investments is an approach that is not suited for individuals with a low threshold for risk. This is a strategy best suited for individuals looking for maximum profits within a relatively short time frame and who have sufficient investment capital to sustain them during periods of losses.

CHAPTER 8

Guide To Mutual Fund Investing

Many investors turn to mutual funds to meet their long-term financial goals. They otter the benefits of diversification and professional management and are seen as an easy and efficient way to invest. However, as with all investment choices, investing in mutual funds involves risks. Helping you to understand these risks, and how to choose the funds that are in line with your own personal goals, is one of the many services your Financial Advisor can provide, Helping you reach your financial goals. Millions of investors find mutual funds the right solution for their long-term financial goals. Some reasons include:

PROFESSIONAL MANAGEMENT The fund's portfolio is professionally managed by experienced money managers who research and select investments that are appropriate for the fund's objective, and provide full-time monitoring of the performance of those investments. If changes are necessary, they're able to modify the fund's holdings.

DIVERSIFICATION The concept of diversification is as simple as the time-tested advice, "Don't put all your eggs in one basket." By spreading your investments across a wide range of companies and industry sectors, you can better protect your assets during market fluctuations. Mutual fund ownership makes it easy for an investor to maintain a diversified investment portfolio.

AFFORDABILITY To invest in a diversified portfolio of individual securities would require a large investment. Many mutual funds allow investors to purchase shares for a relatively low dollar amount for initial and subsequent purchases.

LIQUIDITY Investors may redeem their mutual fund shares for any reason at the current net asset value (NAV), plus any fees and charges assessed on redemption.

DIVIDEND PAYMENTS A fund can earn income in the form of dividends and interest on the securities in its portfolio, which is passed on to shareholders in the form of dividends.

DIVIDEND REINVESTMENT You can set up your account for the automatic reinvestment of any dividends generated by your fund, allowing you to accumulate more shares without incurring a sales charge.

CAPITAL GAINS DISTRIBUTION Occurs when the fund sells a security that has increased in value. At the end of each year, most funds will distribute any capital gains (minus any capital losses) to their investors. You may also elect to have these distributions reinvested without incurring a sales charge.

NOTE

Mutual funds are not guaranteed by the Federal Deposit Insurance Corporation (FDIC) or any other government agency. You can lose money investing in mutual funds.

Past performance is not a reliable indicator of future performance. However, past performance can help you assess a fund's volatility over time. All mutual funds have costs that lower your investment returns. The mutual funds and share classes available at J.P. Morgan Securities are limited and will change from time to time. It is important to work with your Financial Advisor to determine which funds and share classes are available for purchase in your account.

Before you invest, be sure to read the fund's prospectus and shareholder reports to learn about the fund you're considering. By clearly understanding the investment you're considering, you'll be better prepared to make a sound investment decision. To obtain a prospectus, please contact your Financial Advisor.

Learning More About Mutual Funds

A mutual fund is an investment company that pools assets from many investors and invests the money in stocks, bonds and other securities or assets in some combination. The holdings of the mutual fund are its "portfolio." Each share of the mutual fund represents an investor's proportionate ownership of the fund's holdings and the income those holdings may generate. ***Mutual funds also have some unique characteristics that investors need to consider before making the decision to invest:***

COSTS DESPITE NEGATIVE RETURNS Sales charges, annual fees and other expenses must be paid by the mutual fund investor regardless of how the fund performs. Investors may also be required to pay taxes on any capital gains distribution they receive, even if the fund declines in value after the shares are purchased, or the shares have been held a relatively short period of time. This is especially important at the end of the year, when many funds distribute capital gains.

KNOWLEDGE OF PORTFOLIO HOLDINGS By relying on the fund managers to manage the fund's holdings, the individual investors usually have little current knowledge of the exact makeup of a fund's portfolio. Additionally, they have no direct influence on the timing or selection of securities the fund manager buys or sells.

DEGREES OF RISK All mutual funds carry some degree of risk. You may lose some or all of the money you invest your principal because the securities held by a fund fluctuates in value on a daily basis. Any dividends or interest payments may also fluctuate due to changing market conditions.

BUYING AND SELLING MUTUAL FUNDS Investors may purchase mutual fund shares in a number of ways. The two most common are from the fund itself or through a Financial Advisor. The price paid for mutual fund shares is the fund's per share net asset value (NAV), plus any shareholder fees that the fund may impose at the time of purchase, such as sales loads. The NAV is calculated at the end of each business day by dividing the total value of the fund's holdings (less expenses) by the number of shares owned by the fund's shareholders. Investors of mutual funds purchase at the NAV next calculated after they place their trade order. Mutual fund shares are "redeemable," meaning that investors can sell their shares back to the fund at any time. The portfolios of mutual funds are managed by separate entities known as "Investment Advisors," which are registered with the U.S. Securities and Exchange Commission (SEC).

Most mutual funds that invest in stocks and bonds are designed for long-term investors, not active traders. Mutual funds are strive to achieve a particular investment objective, such as capital appreciation or current income, over time. Therefore, they are not designed for investors seeking quick profits or for those attempting to "time the market." Instead, mutual funds may be appropriate for those who have made a long-term commitment to investing and realize that it takes time for stocks and bonds to achieve their potential.

MARKET TIMING Most mutual funds implement practices and procedures that protect shareholders from investors who are active traders and seek to practice a market timing strategy. Market timing involves the rapid buying and selling of mutual fund shares in an attempt to realize short-term profits. This excessive trading of mutual fund shares may disrupt a fund's investment strategy. It also may negatively influence performance results by increasing trading costs and/or causing fund managers to hold more cash than they otherwise, would prefer to hold. In order to discourage investors from using their funds to practice market timing, a fund may:

IMPOSE REDEMPTION FEES Some mutual funds charge fees to investors who redeem their shares within a few months of purchasing them. Usually, the fund company returns the redemption fees to the fund's portfolio to ottset the costs associated with short-term trading.

IMPLEMENT TRADING RESTRICTIONS Most funds limit the number of exchanges (selling shares of one fund and using the proceeds to purchase shares of another in the same fund family) and "round-trip" transactions (a purchase followed by a redemption) that shareholders may make within a specific time period. For example, a fund may limit shareholders to two substantive exchanges within a 30-day period.

MODIFY EXCHANGE PRIVILEGES Most mutual fund families let their shareholders exchange shares of one fund they manage for shares of another fund they manage, with some restrictions. If this practice results in excessive trading, the fund may modify the exchange privilege. For example, it may make exchanges into certain funds ettective on a delayed basis in order to disrupt a market timing strategy.

IDENTIFY AND ISOLATE MARKET TIMERS Some funds attempt to identify market timers by monitoring shareholder transactions. Upon identifying market timers, the fund may restrict the timers' trading privileges or expel them from the fund.

Different Types Of Mutual Funds

Investors today have thousands of choices when it comes to investing in mutual funds. Understanding your individual financial goals and risk tolerance either on your own or with the help of your Financial Advisor is the first step in the journey to reaching your long-term financial goals. This will help you to begin narrowing your choices.

Mutual funds fit into three main categories money market funds, bond funds, and stock funds (also called "equity" funds). Each category has unique features, risks, and rewards. In general, the higher the potential return, the higher the potential risk of loss. Mutual funds are not FDIC-insured or guaranteed by any governmental agency.

What's in a name? There are rules requiring a fund to invest at least 80% of its assets in the type of investments suggested by its name. However, funds can invest up to 20% of their holdings in other types of securities. Always read the prospectus carefully before investing.

MONEY MARKET FUNDS Typically less volatile than other types of mutual funds because they invest in high-quality. These short-term money market instruments are issued and payable in U.S. dollars. A money market fund is not designed to otter capital appreciation. Money market funds pay dividends that are usually declared daily, paid monthly, and generally reflect short-term interest rates. "Inflation risk," the risk that the inflation rate will grow faster than the investment's return over time, can be a concern for money market fund investors.

A money market fund that qualifies as a "government money market fund" under applicable regulations must invest 99.5% of its assets in cash, government securities and/or repurchase agreements that are backed by cash and government securities. Other types of money market funds may invest in government securities as well as certificates of deposit, commercial paper of companies, or other highly liquid and low-risk securities. These types of money market funds may include funds that seek to operate as a "retail money market fund" under applicable regulations. A "retail money market fund" is a fund that will maintain policies and procedures reasonably designed to limit all beneficial owners of the fund to natural persons. Effective October 14, 2016, only "government" and "retail" money market funds may maintain a stable $1.00 net asset value per share, and only "government" money market funds can operate without the possible imposition of a liquidity fee and/or redemption gate.

You could lose money by investing in a money market fund. With respect to a money market fund that qualifies as a "retail" or "government" money market fund, although the money market fund seeks to preserve the value of your investment at $1.00 per share, it cannot guarantee it will do so. In the case of a money market fund that does not qualify as a "retail" or "government" money market fund, because the share price of the money market fund will fluctuate, when you sell your shares they may be worth more or less than what you originally paid for them. If a money market fund does not qualify as a "government" money market fund, ettective October 14, 2016, the money market fund may impose a fee upon sale of your shares or may temporarily suspend your ability to sell shares if the moneymarket fund's liquidity falls below required minimums because of market conditions or other factors. An investment in a money market fund is not insured or guaranteed by the FDIC or any other government agency. A money market fund's sponsor has no legal obligation to provide financial support to the fund, and you should not expect that the sponsor will provide financial support to the fund at any time.

BOND (OR INCOME) FUNDS Generally have higher risks than money market funds due to the fact that they typically pursue strategies aimed at producing higher yields. Unlike money market funds, there are no laws to restrict bond funds to high-quality or short-term investments. And because there are many different types of bonds, these funds can vary dramatically in their risks and rewards. One of the major risks associated with bond funds is "credit risk," or the risk that companies or other issuers may fail to pay their debts. The credit quality of the bonds contained in a fund will have a direct impact on their credit risk. Another risk is "interest rate risk," or the risk that the market value of the bonds will go down when interest rates increase. Funds that invest in longer-term bonds tend to have a higher interest rate risk and fluctuate more dramatically in value. Interest earned on a bond fund's portfolio is passed through to investors as dividends, which may be taken in cash or reinvested. This component of a bond fund's earnings (less expenses) is called its yield. The two major factors that attect a bond fund's yield are the quality and maturity of the bonds in the portfolio. In general, lower-quality bonds and those with longer maturities entail greater risk and generally otter higher yields. The share price or NAV of a bond fund may change based on the market value of the bonds in the portfolio. The value of the bonds in the portfolio may change in response to changes in interest rates. To calculate the total return of a bond fund, it is necessary to include the change in share price along with any income earned (dividends and capital gains distributions).

STOCK (OR EQUITY) FUNDS Typically have higher risks and volatility than money market and bond funds. However, over the long term, stocks have historically performed better than any other type of investment. "Market risk" is the greatest potential risk for investors in stock funds. Stock prices can fluctuate dramatically for many reasons, such as the overall strength of the economy or demand for particular products or services. ***Types of stock funds include:***

GROWTH FUNDS Focus on stocks (companies) that may not pay a regular dividend but have the potential for large growth. There are also different types of growth funds, including small, medium and large cap funds, which will invest in the stock of these types of companies.

SECTOR FUNDS May specialize in a particular industry segment, such as technology or consumer products stocks. A sector fund concentrates its investments in one sector and involves more risks than a fund that invests more broadly.

EQUITY INCOME FUNDS Invest in stocks that pay regular dividends.

INDEX FUNDS Seek to achieve the same return as a particular market index, such as the S&P 500 Composite Stock Price Index, by investing in all or many of the companies included in the index. It is not possible to directly invest in an index.

BALANCED FUNDS Provide investors with a combination of both stock and bond holdings in one mutual fund.

UNIT INVESTMENT TRUSTS (UITs) Type of investment company that buys and holds a generally fixed portfolio of stocks, bonds or other securities. "Units" in the trust are sold to investors who receive a share of principal and dividends or interest. UITs have a stated termination date. Like mutual funds, UITs may charge an initial sales charge and a deferred sales charge. The UIT's prospectus contains information about the portfolio of securities within the UIT and the sales charges.

EXCHANGE-TRADED FUNDS (ETFs) Type of investment company that otters investors a proportionate share of a portfolio of stocks, bonds or other securities. Like individual equity securities, ETFs are traded on a stock exchange and can be bought and sold throughout the trading day through a broker-dealer. Many ETFs attempt to track various stock market sectors, international indices and bond indices. Recently, additional types of ETFs, including leveraged ETFs and actively managed ETFs, have been introduced.

Since ETFs trade on an exchange, prices are determined by the prices buyers and sellers are willing to pay and may not represent the NAV of the underlying securities or investments. ETFs may trade at a premium or discount to the NAV.

NON-TRADITIONAL FUNDS Non-traditional funds are mutual funds or ETFs that pursue alternative investment strategies. While traditional funds generally focus their investment strategies on long- term buy-and-hold stock and bond investing, non-traditional funds generally employ more complex trading strategies, such as selling securities short in anticipation of a drop in their price, using leverage, and purchasing options and futures. Some non-traditional funds also focus their investment strategies on investing in gold, commodities (such as copper and oil) or real assets such as real estate. These strategies have generally has been associated with alternative investment products such as hedge funds. Mutual fund fees and expenses information about the portfolio of securities within the UIT and the sales charges.

SALES CHARGE (LOAD) Paid when you initially purchase mutual fund shares. Usually associated with A shares, this charge is also known as a "front-end load." A portion of this is usually paid to the broker selling the shares. Sales charges reduce the amount of your initial investment, as they are deducted from your initial investment purchase.

CONTINGENT DEFERRED SALES CHARGE (LOAD) Paid when you sell mutual fund shares. Usually associated with B or C shares, this charge is also known as a "back-end load." The amount will depend on how long you own the shares, and may decrease to zero if a B share is held as a long-term investment. May also be paid when selling shares purchased without a front-end load because the purchase was more than $1 million.

EXCHANGE FEE Paid when shareholders exchange (transfer) to another fund within the same fund group.

MANAGEMENT/INVESTMENT ADVISORY FEES Paid out of the fund's assets to the fund's Investment Advisor for investment portfolio management and administrative fees that are not included in the "Other Expenses" category.

DISTRIBUTION/SERVICE FEES (12B-1 FEES) Paid by the fund from fund assets to cover the costs of marketing and selling fund shares and/or to cover the costs of providing shareholder services, such as advertising, printing and mailing of prospectuses, phone centers and more.

OTHER EXPENSES Expenses not included under "Management/ Investment Advisory Fees" or "Distribution/Service Fees," such as custodial expenses, legal and accounting expenses, transfer agent and administrative expenses.

TOTAL ANNUAL FUND OPERATING EXPENSES (EXPENSE RATIO) A line on the fee table that provides the total of a fund's annual operating expenses as a percentage of the fund's average net assets. Annual operating expenses include the ongoing costs of running the fund, and the fund company pays these expenses from the fund's assets before it distributes any earnings to shareholders. Included among the annual operating expenses of all mutual funds is the investment advisory fee, which the fund pays to the Investment Advisor for managing the portfolio. In some cases, the Investment Advisor may enter into revenue-sharing arrangements with firms that distribute the fund. The Investment Advisor finances these Buying, selling and exchanging arrangements out of its investment advisory fee and must disclose the details of such arrangements in the prospectus or Statement of Additional Information (SAI).

REVENUE SHARING Paid by some funds, their Investment Advisors, distributors or other entities to brokerage firms, or other distributors of mutual funds, based on the amount of the fund's shares sold by the distributor. In addition, to sales loads and 12b-1 fees described in the prospectus, some mutual fund advisors, distributors or other entities make payments to J.P. Morgan Securities LLC (JPMS) based on the amount of the fund's shares sold by JPMS or owned by JPMS's clients.

The fund prospectus is a valuable tool that will provide you with information on the various fees. Each fund prospectus is required to provide a "fee table" near the front of the prospectus that can help you compare the costs of diflerent funds. Mutual fund shares can be purchased and sold on any business day. Mutual funds are priced once each day at a time specified in the prospectus, usually 4:00 p.m. ET, which is the close of business on the New York Stock Exchange. When your purchase or sale order is received before the established cut-ott time, your transaction will receive the price calculated for that day.

PURCHASING MUTUAL FUND SHARES When you buy shares, you pay the current NAV per share plus any fee the fund may assess at the time of purchase, such as a sales charge or other type of purchase fee.

SELLING MUTUAL FUND SHARES When you sell your shares, the fund will pay you the current NAV minus any fee the fund assesses at the time of redemption, such as a deferred (or back-end) sales charge or redemption fee.

Understanding Share Classes

EXCHANGING SHARES Many mutual funds companies have several ditterent types of funds in which to invest. Most otter exchange privileges within their family of funds, allowing shareholders to transfer their holdings from one fund to another within the family, without incurring an additional sales charge, as their investment objectives or risk tolerance change.

Exchanges may have tax consequences. Even if the fund doesn't charge you for the exchange, and you'll be liable for any gain on the sale of your original shares or, depending on the circumstances, eligible to take a loss.

Different share classes provide you with choices for how you wish to pay for your investment. Many mutual funds make more than one share class available to investors. Each share class invests in the same portfolio of securities and has the same investment objective and policies; however, each share class has ditterent sales charges and expenses. This multi-class structure allows investors to select a fee and expense structure that is most appropriate for their individual investment goals. Here is a brief description and comparison of the share classes commonly available to individual investors.

CLASS A SHARES In general, Class A shares include a front-end sales charge (or load) that's included in the purchase price of the shares and is determined by the amount you invest. The more you invest, the lower your purchase cost as a percentage of your investment. Many mutual fund families otter volume discounts known as "breakpoints," based on the amount of investment. Information regarding a mutual fund's breakpoints may be found in the prospectus. For long-term investors, Class A shares generally represent the least costly method to purchase mutual funds. Class A shares usually have lower 12b-1 fees (annual marketing or distribution fees) than other share classes offered by the fund. Many mutual funds provide that purchases of 1 million or more of Class A shares will not be subject to a front-end sales charge. However, the purchaser will incur a deferred or back- end sales charge if any of the shares are sold within a specified time period, generally 12–18 months. In addition, certain investors may be entitled to a sales charge or load waiver based, for example, on account type or employment affiliation.

CLASS B SHARES Class B shares usually do not contain front-end loads, but rather include back-end sales charges or Contingent Deferred Sales Charges (CDSC). If you sell the shares within a specified number of years, you pay the sales charge, which usually declines over time. The 12b-1 fees associated with Class B shares generally are higher than those imposed on Class A shares. Most fund companies automatically will convert your Class B shares to Class A shares once you've held the Class B shares for a specified number of years. From that point forward, you'll benefit from the lower 12b-1 fees of the Class A shares. Additionally, higher total fund expenses will result in lower dividend distributions than Class A shares.

CLASS C SHARES Class C shares generally do not include front-end sales charges, but they do contain higher 12b-1 fees and may have a sales charge if you sell within the first year. In addition, 12b-1 fees never convert to a lower amount, and higher total fund expenses will result in lower dividend distributions than Class A shares.

MAKING THE MOST OF MUTUAL FUND CLASS A SHARE DISCOUNT OPPORTUNITIES Mutual funds that charge front- end sales charges, also known as sales loads, may otter a reduced sales charge when a larger investment is made or may otter sales charge waivers for certain investors or account types. The investment levels required to obtain a reduced sales charge are commonly referred to as "breakpoints." Each fund company establishes its own formula for how it will calculate whether an investor is entitled to receive a breakpoint and establishes its own rules for sales charge waivers. It's important to read the prospectus and work with your Financial Advisor to learn how a particular fund establishes eligibility.

Your Financial Advisor can help you ensure you're receiving the correct breakpoint discount or sales charge waiver, or answer any questions about the sales charges applied to your transactions.

A mutual fund's breakpoint schedule and waiver eligibility rules can be found in the fund's prospectus or Statement of Additional Information (SAI).

INSTITUTIONAL, RETIREMENT, NO-LOAD, AND OTHER SHARE CLASSES

Institutional, retirement, no-load and certain other fund shares are generally available only through J.P. Morgan Securities' asset-based fee advisory programs. In these programs, you typically pay an annual fee based on a percentage of the value of the assets held in your account, including the value of the fund shares. These programs provide features and benefits that may not be available in a traditional brokerage account that charges transaction fees. The total cost of purchasing and holding mutual fund shares through an asset-based fee advisory program may be more or less than investing in mutual fund shares in a traditional J.P. Morgan Securities brokerage account that is serviced by your Financial Advisor.

Tax consequences

Mutual funds have ditterent tax consequences than many other investments. When you purchase and hold mutual fund shares, you will owe income tax on any ordinary dividends in the year you receive or reinvest them. Additionally, the law requires mutual funds to distribute capital gains to shareholders when they sell securities for a profit that can't be outset by a loss. You may have to pay taxes on the fund's capital gains for that year even if you still own the shares. Then, when you sell your shares, you will owe taxes on any capital gain you received on the sale.

When you invest in a tax-exempt fund, such as a municipal bond fund, some or all of your dividends will be exempt from federal (and sometimes state and local) income tax. You will, however, owe taxes on any capital gains realized by the fund and on the sale of your shares. Anytime you receive a capital gains distribution, you will usually owe taxes even if the fund has had a negative return from the point during the year when you purchased your shares.

Consider contacting the fund to learn when it makes distributions so you won't pay more than your fair share of taxes. Mutual funds are required to disclose after-tax returns in the "Risk/Return Summary" section of their prospectuses. We encourage you to consult your tax advisor for more information on the tax consequences of mutual fund investing.

Sources of fund information

THE PROSPECTUS when you're considering the purchase of mutual fund shares, you should always review the fund's prospectus before you invest. The prospectus is the fund's selling document, and it contains the following information:

- Fund investment objectives/goals
- Strategies for achieving those goals
- Principal risks of investing in the fund
- Fees and expenses
- Past performance

The prospectus also provides information on the fund's managers and investment Advisors and describes how to purchase and sell fund shares. The SEC requires funds to include specific categories of information in their prospectuses and to present key data (such as fees and past performance) in a standard format so that investors can more easily compare ditterent funds.

STATEMENT OF ADDITIONAL INFORMATION (SAI)

The SAI explains a fund's operations in greater detail than the prospectus. It includes the fund's financial statements and details about the history of the fund, fund policies on borrowing and concentration, the identity of officers, directors and persons who control the fund, investment advisory and other services, brokerage commissions, tax matters and performance such as yield and average annual total return information. The mutual fund is typically required to send you an SAI anytime you request one, and the back cover of a fund's prospectus should contain information on how to obtain the SAI.

SHAREHOLDER REPORTS A mutual fund must also provide shareholders with annual and semiannual reports within 60 days after the end of the fund's fiscal year and 60 days after the fund's fiscal mid-year. These reports contain a variety of updated financial information, a list of the fund's portfolio securities and other information.

You may obtain any of these documents by:

- Contacting your Financial Advisor
- Calling or writing to the fund
- Visiting the fund's website

Tips For Avoiding The Top 20 Common Investment Mistakes

1. Expecting too much or using someone else's expectations

Investing for the long term involves creating a well-diversified portfolio designed to provide you with the appropriate levels of risk and return under a variety of market scenarios. But even after designing the right portfolio, no one can predict or control what returns the market will actually provide. It is important not to expect too much and to be careful when figuring out what to expect. Nobody can tell you what a reasonable rate of return is without having an under- standing of you, your goals, and your current asset allocation.

2. Not Having Clear Investment Goals

The adage, "If you don't know where you are going, you will probably end up somewhere else," is as true of investing as anything else. Everything from the investment plan to the strategies used, the portfolio design, and even the individual securities can be configured with your life objectives in mind. Too many investors focus on the latest investment fad or on maximizing short-term investment return instead of designing an investment portfolio that has a high prob- ability of achieving their long-term investment objectives.

3. Failing To Diversify Enough

The only way to create a portfolio that has the potential to provide appropriate levels of risk and return in various market scenarios is adequate diversification. Often investors think they can maximize returns by taking a large investment exposure in one security or sector. But when the market moves against such a concentrated position, it can be disastrous. Too much diversification and too many exposures can also affect performance. The best course of action is to find a balance. Seek the advice of a professional adviser.

4. Focusing On The Wrong Kind Of Performance

There are two timeframes that are important to keep in mind: the short term and everything else. If you are a long-term investor, speculating on performance in the short term can be a recipe for disaster because it can make you second guess your strategy and motivate short-term portfolio modifications. But looking past near-term chatter to the factors that drive long-term performance is a worthy undertaking. If you find yourself looking short term, refocus.

5. Buying High And Selling Low

The fundamental principle of investing is to buy low and sell high, so why do so many investors do the opposite? Instead of rational deci- sion making, many investment decisions are motivated by fear or greed. In many cases, investors buy high in an attempt to maximize short-term returns instead of trying to achieve long-term investment goals. A focus on near-term returns leads to investing in the latest investment craze or fad or investing in the assets or investment strategies that were effective in the near past. Either way, once an investment has become popular and gained the public's attention, it becomes more difficult to have an edge in determining its value.

6. Trading Too Much And Too Often

When investing, patience is a virtue. Often it takes time to gain the ultimate benefits of an investment and asset allocation strategy. Continued modification of investment tactics and portfolio composition can not only reduce returns through greater transaction fees, it can also result in taking unanticipated and uncompensated risks. You should always be sure you are on track. Use the impulse to reconfigure your investment portfolio as a prompt to learn more about the assets you hold instead of as a push to trade.

7. Paying Too Much In Fees And Commissions

Investing in a high-cost fund or paying too much in advisory fees is a common mistake because even a small increase in fees can have a significant effect on wealth over the long term. Before opening an account, be aware of the potential cost of every investment decision. Look for funds that have fees that make sense and make sure you are receiving value for the advisory fees you are paying.

8. Focusing Too Much On Taxes

Although making investment decisions on the basis of potential tax consequences is a bit like the tail wagging the dog, it is still a common investor mistake. You should be smart about taxes tax loss harvesting can improve your returns significantly but it is important that the impetus to buy or sell a security is driven by its merits, not its tax consequences.

9. Not Reviewing Investments Regularly

If you are invested in a diversified portfolio, there is an excellent chance that some things will go up while others go down. At the end of a quarter or a year, the portfolio you built with careful planning will start to look quite different. Don't get too far off track! Check in regularly (at a minimum once a year) to make sure that your investments still make sense for your situation and (importantly) that your portfolio doesn't need rebalancing.

10. Taking Too Much, Too Little, Or The Wrong Risk

Investing involves taking some level of risk in exchange for potential reward. Taking too much risk can lead to large variations in investment performance that may be outside your comfort zone. Taking too little risk can result in returns too low to achieve your financial goals. Make sure that you know your financial and emotional ability to take risks and recognize the investment risks you are taking.

11. Not Knowing The True Performance Of Your Investments

It is shocking how many people have no idea how their investments have performed. Even if they know the headline result or how a couple of their stocks have done, they rarely know how they have performed in the context of their portfolio. Even that is not enough. You have to relate the performance of your overall portfolio to your plan to see if you are on track after accounting for costs and inflation. Don't neglect this! How else will you know how you are doing?

12. Reacting To The Media

There are plenty of 24-hour news channels that make money by showing "tradable" information. It would be foolish to try to keep up. The key is to parse valuable information out of all the noise.

Successful and seasoned investors gather information from several independent sources and conduct their own proprietary research and analysis. Using, the news as a sole source of investment analysis is a common investor mistake because by the time the information has become public, it has already been, factored into market pricing.

13. Chasing yield

A high-yielding asset is a very seductive thing. Why wouldn't you try to maximize the amount of money you get back? Simple: Past returns are no indication of future performance and the highest yields carry the highest risks! Focus on the whole picture; don't get distracted while disregarding risk management.

14. Trying To Be A Market Timing Genius

Market timing is possible, but very, very, very hard. For people who are not well trained, trying to make a well-timed call can be their undoing. An investor that was out of the market during the top 10 trading days for the S&P 500 Index from 1993 to 2013 would have achieved a 5.4% annualized return instead of 9.2% by staying invested. This difference suggests that investors are better off contributing consistently to their investment portfolio rather than trying to trade in and out in an attempt to time the market.

15. Not Doing Due Diligence

There are many databases in which you can check whether the people managing your money have the training, experience and ethical standing to merit your trust. Why wouldn't you check them? Ask for references and check their work on the investments that they recommend. The worst case is that you trade an afternoon of effort for sleeping better at night. The best case is that you avoid the next "Madoff" scheme. Any investor should be willing to take that trade.

16. Working With The Wrong Adviser

An investment adviser should be your partner in achieving your investment goals. The ideal financial professional and financial service provider not only has the ability to solve your problems but shares a similar philosophy about investing and even life in general. The benefits of taking extra time to find the right adviser far outweigh the comfort of making a quick decision.

17. Letting emotions get in the way

Investing brings up significant emotional issues that can impede decision making. Do you want to involve your spouse in planning your finances? What do you want to happen with your assets after you die? Don't let the immensity of these questions get in the way. A good adviser will be able to help you construct a plan that works no matter what the answers to these questions are.

18. Forgetting About Inflation

Most investors focus on nominal returns instead of real returns. This focus means looking at and comparing performance after fees and inflation. Even if the economy is not in a massive inflationary period, some costs will still rise! It is important to remember that what you can buy with the assets you have is in many ways more important than their value in dollar terms. Develop a discipline of focusing on what is really important: your returns after adjusting for rising costs.

19. Neglecting To Start Or Continue

Individuals often fail to begin an investment program because they lack basic knowledge of where or how to start. Likewise, periods of inactivity are frequently the result of lethargy or discour- agement over previous investment losses. Investment management is a discipline that is not overly complex, but requires continual effort and analysis in order to be successful.

20. Not Controlling What You Can

People like to say that they can't tell the future, but they neglect to mention that you can take action to shape it. You can't control what the market will bear, but you can save more money! Continually investing capital over time can have as much influence on wealth accumulation as the return on investment. It is the surest way to increase the probability of reaching your financial goals.

CONCLUSION

High-risk investments include such things as futures, options contracts, foreign currency exchange (forex), penny stocks, and real speculative estate, such as land that hasn't been developed. These investments involve greater risk in that they offer no guaranteed return and their value tends to change quickly (in other words, they're subject to greater volatility). However, the draw for many investors is that when such investments do pay off, they often pay off big.

If you're considering any of these investments, remember that research is key to success. More so than the average stock or bond investor, you have to know the market you're investing in very well. Because success is based largely on speculation, we strongly recommend that only experienced investors roll the dice on investment assets such as these.

The reality is that there is a multitude of ways that growth investors can find investments to complement their existing portfolio. In the end, it is always up to each individual to choose the methods that work best for them personally, but it is also always helpful to be aware of different approaches to identifying investments with the greatest potential for providing future profits.

OTHER BOOKS BY THE AUTHOR

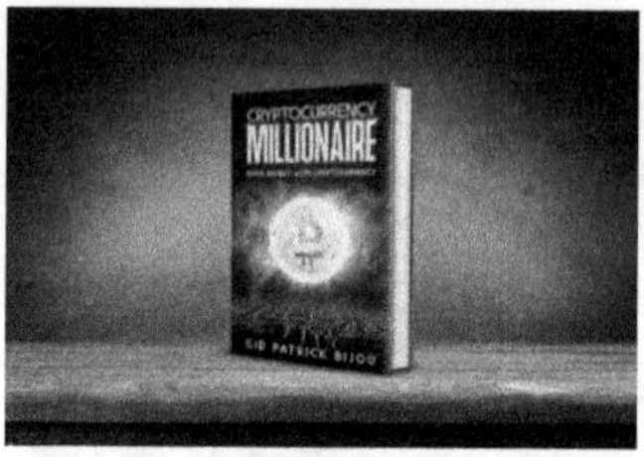

Cryptocurrency Millionaire Make Money With Cryptocurrency

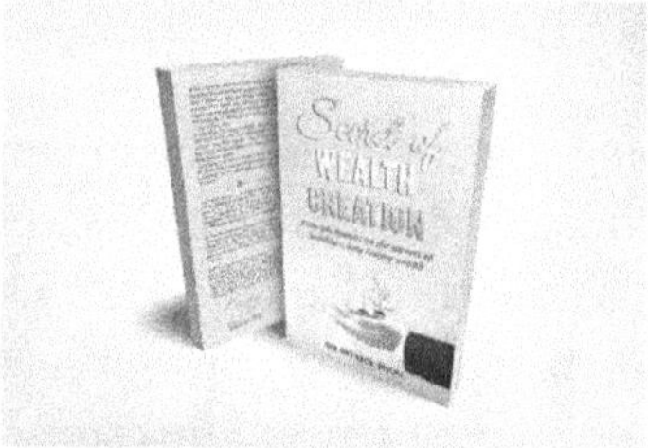

Secret Of Wealth Creation: Principle Lessons On The Secrets Of Building A Long Lasting Wealth

Guide To Private Placement Project Fundingtrade Programs: Understanding High-Level Project Funding Trade Programs

Make Money Doing Nothing

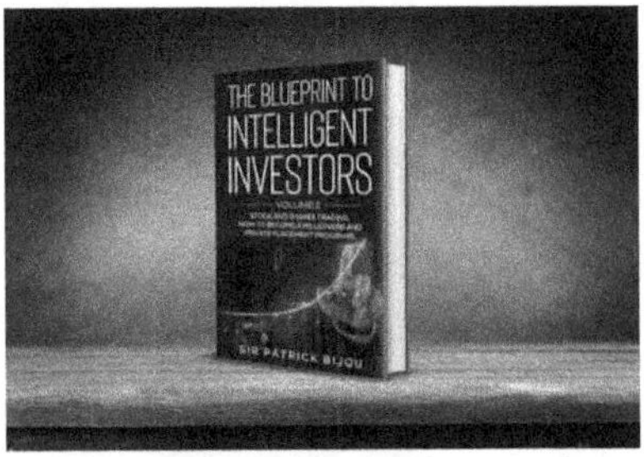

The Blueprint To Intelligent Investors

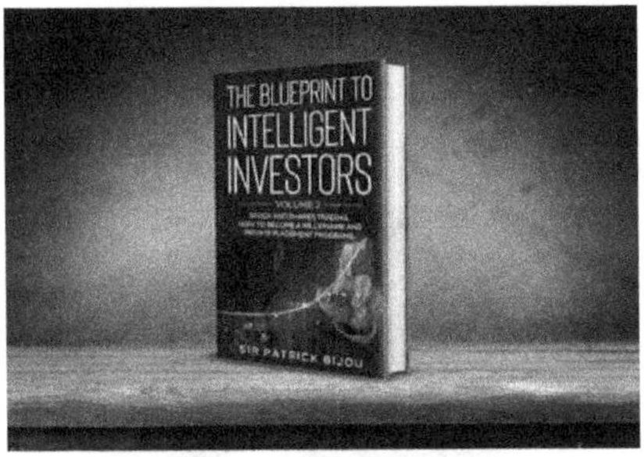

The Blueprint To Intelligent Investors Volume 2

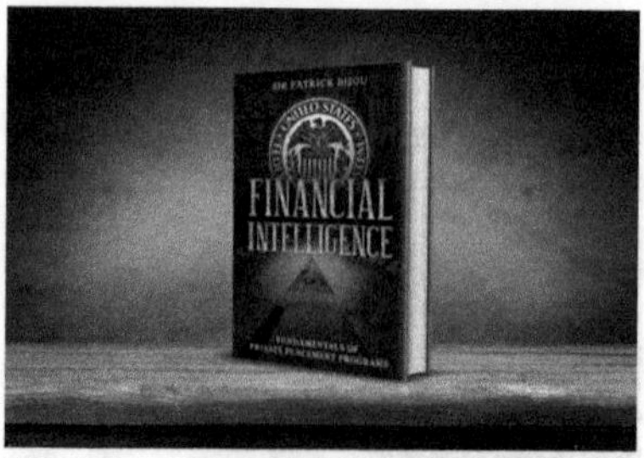

Financial Intelligence: Fundamentals Of Private Placement Programs (PPP)

Private Placement Programs - The Holy Grail

Special Drawing Rights (SDR) And The Federal Reserve

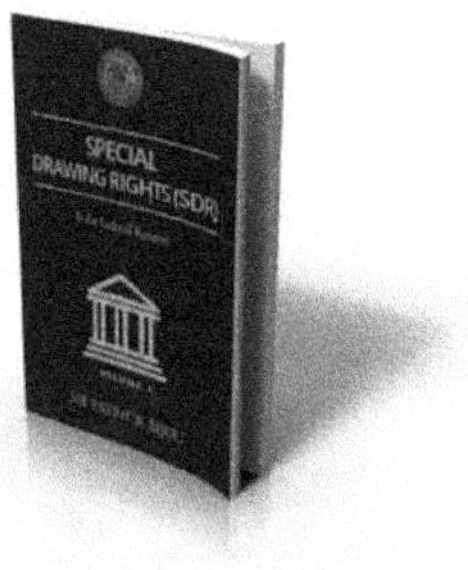

Special Drawing Rights (SDR) And The Federal Reserve
Volume 2.

Cryptocurrency: The Next Level For Banking Reform

www.ingramcontent.com/pod-product-compliance
Lightning Source LLC
Chambersburg PA
CBHW061023220326
41597CB00019BB/3150